WRITERS AND THEIR WORK

ISOBEL ARMSTRONG
General Editor

RUDYARD KIPLING

RUDYARD KIPLING

Jan Montefiore

© Copyright 2007 by Jan Montefiore

First published in 2007 by Northcote House Publishers Ltd, Horndon, Tavistock, Devon, PL19 9NQ, United Kingdom.
Tel: +44 (0) 1822 810066 Fax: +44 (0) 1822 810034.

British Library Cataloguing-in-Publication Data
A catalogue record for this book is available from the British Library

ISBN 978-0-7463-1069-4 hardcover
　　　978-0-7463-0827-1 paperback

Typeset by PDQ Typesetting, Newcastle-under-Lyme
Printed and bound in the United Kingdom

To the memory of my father,
Hugh Montefiore

Contents

Biographical Outline

1865	Joseph Rudyard Kipling born on December 30 in Bombay, India, to Alice and John 'Lockwood' Kipling, teacher of Art and Crafts at the Sir Jamesetjee Jejeeboy School of Art and Industry.
1868	Birth of sister Alice ('Trix').
1871	Rudyard and Alice are taken to England and left in the care of the Holloway family in Lorne Lodge, Southsea ('The House of Desolation'), until 1877.
1875	Lockwood Kipling moves to Lahore as Principal of the Mayo School of Art and as Curator of its Museum.
1878	Rudyard attends the United Services College at Westward Ho!, Devon until 1882.
1881	*Schoolboy Lyrics* privately printed in Lahore, India by Alice Kipling.
	Death of General Gordon at Khartoum.
1882–7	Rudyard leaves school to join his family in Lahore as assistant editor of the *Civil and Military Gazette*.
1883	First Indian National Conference held.
1884	Founding of Indian National Congress. Publication of *Echoes* (with his sister Alice Kipling), privately printed.
1885	*Departmental Ditties* published in Lahore.
1887	Kipling becomes a staff writer on the *Pioneer* newspaper, Allahabad, writing 'Letters of Marque' travel sketches (later collected in *From Sea to Sea*, 1900).
1888	Publication of *Plain Tales from the Hills, Soldiers Three, Wee Willie Winkie, Under the Deodars, The Phantom Rickshaw, In Black and White, The Story of the Gadsbys* by the Indian Railway Library.
1889	Kipling becomes a full-time writer. Travels to China, Japan and USA, as described in 'Letter of Marque'

(collected in *From Sea to Sea*, 1900).

1890   Kipling becomes a freelance writer in London, living near Charing Cross.

Attends music-halls. Meets literary London figures including Andrew Lang, Henry James, W.E.Henley, Wolcott Balestier.

1891   Mental breakdown and recovery. Publication of *Life's Handicap* and *The Light That Failed*. Travels to Australia.

1892   Death of Wolcott Balestier. Returns from Australia to marry Wolcott's sister Caroline Balestier. On their honeymoon journey to USA via Far East, Kipling loses his savings when his bank (New Oriental Banking Co.) goes broke. Publication of *The Naulahka* (with Wolcott Balestier), also of *Barrack Room Ballads* which sells 7,000 copies in its first year.

Birth of daughter Josephine ('Best Beloved').

1893   The Kiplings settle in Brattleboro, Vermont, building their own house 'Naulakha'.

1894   Publication of *The Jungle Book*. 'Jameson Raid' in South Africa

1895   Publication of *The Second Jungle Book*. Dispute between USA and Great Britain over Venezuela. Kipling is offered the post of Poet Laureate, and refuses.

1896   Birth of Elsie, the Kiplings' second daughter. *Captains Courageous* published. Quarrel with Carrie's brother Beatty Balestier leads to the Kiplings leaving Vermont. They take a house in Torquay, Devon.

1897   The Kiplings move to Rottingdean, Sussex. Birth of John Kipling.

Queen Victoria's Diamond Jubilee celebrated; Kipling publishes 'Recessional' in *The Times*.

1898   Kitchener victorious at Omdurman. Publication of *The Day's Work*. The Kipling family visits Cape Town, South Africa; Kipling becomes a friend of Cecil Rhodes and Alfred Milner. He and his family then spend almost every winter in South Africa until 1908. First mental breakdown of his sister 'Trix'.

1899   Disastrously, Kipling and family visit USA in February. Kipling critically ill with pneumonia; his near-death and recovery is worldwide headline news. Death from pneumonia of daughter Josephine.

Stalky & Co. published.
Kipling's poem 'The White Man's Burden' published in *The Times* and *McClure's Journal* in USA, encouraging US annexation of the Philippines. The Boer War begins.
Publication of travel writings in *From Sea to Sea*.

1900   Kipling and family visit South Africa, staying in Cape Town; Kipling visits army to raise morale. Works on *Kim*. His song 'The Absent-minded Beggar' raises £10,000 for dependants of troops in South Africa.

1901   Publication of *Kim*.

1902   Death of Cecil Rhodes. Treaty of Vereening ends the Boer War. Publication in *The Times* of Kipling's poem 'The Islanders', rebuking the British for military unpreparedness.
Kipling purchases his house 'Batemans' in Burwash, Sussex.
Publication of *Just-So Stories*.

1904   *Traffics and Discoveries* published.

1906   *Puck of Pook's Hill* published.

1907   Kipling awarded Hon. D.Litt. by Oxford and Durham Universities, and Nobel Prize for literature (with Mark Twain).

1909   *Actions and Reactions* published

1910   *Rewards and Fairies* published. Death of Edward VII. Death of his mother Alice Kipling. Union of South Africa created, much to Kipling's disgust. (He stops wintering in South Africa after 1908.)

1911   Fletcher's *History of England* published with Kipling's poems. Lockwood Kipling dies. Agitation for women's suffrage; Kipling publishes 'The Female of the Species' in hostile response.

1912   'Marconi scandal' of insider dealing by Liberal cabinet members including Rufus Isaacs.

1913   Isaacs appointed Attorney-General: Kipling writes and privately circulates 'Gehazi' attacking him. Home Rule Bill for Ireland passes Commons (twice), rejected by Lords. Edward Carson foments rebellion in Ulster, supported by Kipling in speeches.

1914   Kipling publishes 'Ulster' supporting Carson's sedition; makes speech in Tunbridge Wells attacking

	Liberals and Home Rule. Britain declares war on Germany. Kipling's son John joins Irish Guards.
1915	Battle of Loos. 2nd Lieutenant John Kipling 'missing believed killed'. Kipling begins to suffer the serious stomach pains that trouble him for the next 20 years.
1916	Easter Rising in Dublin quashed by British Army. Execution of its leaders.
1917	Kipling is asked to write the regimental history of Irish Guards, and agrees. *A Diversity of Creatures* published. Kipling appointed to War Graves Commission. Begins 'Epitaphs of the War'. Russian Revolution.
1918	End of Great War. Election of Sinn Fein in Ireland, leading to unrest and a terror campaign by British army, especially 'Black and Tans'.
1919	General Dyer fires on nationalist crowd at Jallianwallagh, Amritsar. Kipling writes the poem 'Gods of the Copybook Headings'.
1921	Irish Free State established by treaty signed by Lloyd George and leading Irish nationalists.
1923	Kipling ill again with stomach pains, wrongly thought to be cancer. *History of the Irish Guards in the Great War* published. Kipling elected Rector of St Andrews University. *Land and Sea Tales for Scouts and Guides* published.
1924	Daughter Elsie Kipling marries Captain George Bambridge.
1926	*Debits & Credits* published.
1930	*Thy Servant A Dog* published.
1932	*Limits & Renewals* published. Kipling's duodenal ulcer diagnosed. The rising power of the Nazis in Germany moves him to write the poem 'The Storm Cone'. Composes first radio speech for George V, broadcast to the Empire on Christmas Day.
1935	Begins writing his memoir.
1936	Death of Rudyard Kipling
1937	Kipling's memoir *Something of Myself*, published posthumously.

Abbreviations

AR	*Actions and Reactions* (1909)
CC	*Captains Courageous* (1896)
DC	*Debits and Credits* (1926)
D of C	*A Diversity of Creatures* (1917)
DW	*The Day's Work* (1898)
FSS	*From Sea to Sea* (1899)
IG	*History of the Irish Guards in the Great War* (1923)
JB	*The Jungle Book* (1894)
JSS	*The Just-So Stories for Little Children* (1902)
K	*Kim* (1901)
L	*Letters of Rudyard Kipling* (6 vols, 1990–2004)
LH	*Life's Handicap* (1891)
LST	*Land and Sea Tales for Scouts and Guides* (1923)
MI	*Many Inventions* (1893)
PPH	*Puck of Pook's Hill* (1906)
PTH	*Plain Tales from the Hills* (1888)
RW	*Rewards and Fairies* (1910)
S & C	*Stalky & Co.* (1899)
SJB	*The Second Jungle Book* (1895)
SM	*Something of Myself* (1937)
ST	*Soldiers Three* (1888)
TD	*Traffics and Discoveries* (1904)
TSD	*Thy Servant a Dog* (1932)
W	*Poetical Works of Rudyard Kipling* (1994)
WWW	*Wee Willie Winkie* (1888)

Prologue

A DIVIDED WRITER

Rudyard Kipling is a writer whose works have always elicited passionately conflicting responses in his readers, including myself. I cannot agree with those who see him simply as a genius of storytelling – 'But what about Kipling's right-wing politics? His racist stereotyping of Indians, Irish, Jews and those "lesser breeds without the Law" in "Recessional"? His support of General Dyer after the 1919 Amritsar massacre of Indians?'[1] Neither can I side with those who dismiss him as a right-wing racist stereotyper of Indians, Irish, Jews and lesser breeds – 'But what about Kipling's magical storytelling? The fantasy and sheer verbal pleasure of the *Just-So Stories*? The delight taken in cultural differences in the novel *Kim*?' The object of this book is not to reconcile these contradictions, because I don't think this can be done without falsification. I fully agree with the out-and-out admirers that any good criticism of Kipling must start with the many-sided pleasures of his verbal energy, but when Orwell writes that 'Kipling *is* a jingo imperialist, he *is* morally insensitive and aesthetically disgusting. It is better to start by admitting that, and then to try to find out why it is that he survives while the refined people who have sniggered at him wear so badly', or Randall Jarrell that 'Kipling was a great genius; and a great neurotic; and a great professional',[2] their ambivalence seems to me more helpful than unqualified adulation could ever be. This book attempts both to introduce readers to the scope and qualities of Kipling's genius and to clarify its contradictions; not only the contradictions in his writing but in the ways he can be read.

1

This project is complicated by the bewildering diversity of Kipling's *œuvre*. Besides *Kim* (1901), Kipling produced three long prose fictions, *The Light That Failed* (1890), *The Naulahka* (with Wolcott Balestier, 1892), *Captains Courageous* (1896); eleven book-length collections of stories, beginning with *Plain Tales from the Hills*, (1888) and ending with *Limits and Renewals*, (1932); not counting the seven books of children's stories – the two *Jungle Books* (1894, 1895), *The Just-So Stories* (1902), *Stalky & Co.* (1899, followed by four later 'Stalky' stories),[3] the two 'Puck' Books (1906, 1910) and *Land and Sea Tales for Scouts and Guides* (1923). He also wrote a great deal of journalism, propaganda and travel writing including the brilliant early 'Letters of Marque' reporting from independent Indian states in the Punjab, collected in the travel writing volume *From Sea to Sea* (1899), the regimental *History of the Irish Guards in the Great War* (1923), a classic of wartime narrative, a great deal of verse (his *Poetical Works* fill 826 pages), and the reticent yet revealing posthumous autobiography *Something of Myself* (1937). For diversity of writing which escapes conventional classifications, the only English contemporary who can match Kipling is D.H.Lawrence, and as a master of storytelling he has no English rival in the twentieth century.

Yet Kipling, that 'great genius and great neurotic', remains divided and divisive. His poem 'The Two Sided Man', which first appeared in *Kim*, alluding to the hero's double Irish/Indian identity, articulates pride in duality:

> Something I owe to the soil that grew –
> More to the life that fed –
> But most to Allah Who gave me two
> Separate sides to my head.
>
> I would go without shirts or shoes,
> Friends, tobacco or bread
> Sooner than for an instant lose
> Either side of my head.

(K, 186)

One could read these thumping English quatrains invoking 'Allah' as a brilliant intuitive image of the now well-established, neurological difference between the brain's right and left hemispheres, each dominated by a different kind of thinking.

More simply, the poem could also represent Kipling's own writerly capacity for sympathy with opposite or different identities. As the longer (and weaker) revised version has it, he can identify as well with the followers of 'Wesley and Calvin' as with believers in 'Shaman, ju-ju or angekok' (*W*, 587) – that is, both with civilized Protestant Christian *and* with pagan barbarians, or more simply, with colonizers and colonized. Yet this reading makes the verses too easy by a false reconciliation that would redefine contradiction as unproblematic plurality, censoring the oppositions between colonizer and colonized by turning them into interchangeable parallels. The condition of being a 'Two Headed Man' who is also a colonial writer represents a psychological dilemma as well as a creative boast. For those opposing sides represent the daylight, reasonable identity of the imperialist *versus* the night-time dream identity of [being the] colonized. The 'I' could not sustain existence even for an instant without either 'side' because each on its own represents either deadly chaos or equally deadly dryness.

The origins of Kipling's divisions doubtless lie in his childhood experience of dislocation, bitterly described in the early story 'Baa Baa Black Sheep' and the posthumous memoir *Something of Myself*. Born in Bombay, he was, like other children of his class and race, looked after by Indian servants rather than by his loving but busy parents, to whom he spoke, when he saw them, in 'phrases haltingly translated out of the vernacular that one thought and dreamed in' (*SM*, 1-2). His earliest memories were an idyll of 'light and colour and purple and golden fruits', though fear and death existed even then in the 'menacing darkness of tropical eventides' and the vultures gobbling the Parsi corpses on the nearby Towers of Silence. But misery was unknown until the six-year-old Kipling and his four-year-old sister were, like so many other Anglo-Indian children, taken to England – 'a dark land, and a darker room full of cold, in one wall of which a white woman made naked fire'(*SM*, 4). In this strange, unhomely 'Home' (as Anglo-Indians called it) the children were left in the care of a 'Woman' at Southsea, in whose 'House of Desolation' the once loved and spoilt little *baba* was regularly beaten, threatened with hell (the foster mother was a Calvinist Evangelical), bullied by constant inquisition, punished by being made to learn Scripture ('I learned all the

3

Collects that way and a great deal of the Bible': *SM*, 1, 4, 11) and sent to school wearing a placard saying 'Liar'. After six years of bullying and abuse, the boy collapsed into blindness and hallucination, described in 'Baa Baa Black Sheep': 'There was a gray haze upon all his world, and it narrowed month by month until it left him almost alone with the flapping curtains that were so like ghosts, and the nameless terrors of broad daylight that were only coats after all' (*WWW*, 303).

Alerted by a concerned aunt, Kipling's mother came over and rescued him from the 'House of Desolation' , and after a period of convalescence he was sent to the public school which prepared boys for the Army, described (and idealized) in *Stalky & Co.* From its fairly tough regime the sixteen-year-old Kipling returned to India and what he called 'Seven Years Hard' of work as a journalist when 'I never worked less than ten hours and seldom more than fifteen *per diem*'. Reunited with his family, he now appreciated both the rich glamour of India and its harshness. Death was ever-present both for British administrators, 'boys but a few years older than I who lived utterly alone and died from typhoid mostly at the regulation age of twenty-two' and for their native subjects. 'The dead of all times were about us in the vast forgotten Moslem cemeteries where one's horse's hoof of a morning might break through to the corpse below; skulls and bones tumbled out of our mud garden walls and were turned up among the flowers by the Rains' (*SM*, 41–2).

Kipling, as became a literary spokesman of authority, expressed no resentment at these miseries or horrors. On the contrary, he insists that his creativity was stimulated into fantasy games in the 'House of Desolation' in the 'mildewy basement room where I stood my solitary confinements', fenced around by 'a coconut shell strung on a red cord, a tin trunk, and a piece of packing-case which kept off any other world. Thus fenced about, everything inside the fence was quite real, but mixed with the smell of damp cupboards. If the bit of board fell, I had to begin the magic all over again...The magic, you see, lies in the ring or fence that you take refuge in'(*SM*, 9–10). He noted dryly that the bullying regime of the 'House of Desolation' was a good preparation for a freelance writer's career, in that 'it demanded constant wariness, the habit of observation, and attendance on moods and tempers; the noting of discrepancies between speech and action; a certain reserve of demeanour; and automatic suspicion of sudden favours': (*SM*, 15–16). Excellent training for a fiercely independent writer of stories whose elaborately crafted narrative frames would repeat those lonely childhood games with the 'ring or fence that you take refuge in', perhaps even a blessing in disguise? Yet the barely suppressed rage of this self-analysis, not to mention the publication of the bitterly autobiographical 'Baa Baa Black Sheep' in India while his parents were still living there, tell another story. As Randall Jarrell, the subtlest of Kipling's readers, puts it:

> Kipling was someone who spent six years in a concentration camp as a child; he never got over it. As a very young man he spent seven years in an India that confirmed his belief in concentration camps; he never got over this either.... His world had been torn in two and he himself torn in two: for under the part of him that extenuated everything, blamed for nothing, there was certainly a part that extenuated nothing, blamed for everything – a part whose existence he never admitted, most especially not to himself.... His morality is the one-sided, desperately protective, sometimes vindictive morality of someone who has been for some time the occupant of one of God's concentration camps, and has had to spend the rest of his life justifying or explaining out of existence what he cannot forget. Kipling tries so hard to justify and explain true authority, the work and habit and wisdom of the world, because he feels so bitterly the abyss of pain and insanity that they overlie, and can do – even will do – nothing to prevent.[4]

That conflict between identification both with the conquerors and administrators and with the outcast Other which energizes both Kipling's best and worst work was never, outside the charmed worlds of *Kim* and the *Jungle Books*, to be fully resolved.

Not being a biographer, I do not attempt to trace the relation between the inner psychic conflict so acutely and sympathetically described by Jarrell and the divisions within and without Kipling's writing; my point is to show the oppositions that inform and structure it. There is first and most obviously, the opposition between the philistine imperialist who said in a letter home that 'I would swap all the Hindu pantheon for a decent English sanitary engineer' and boasted that 'if we didn't hold the land [i.e.India], in six months it would be one big cock pit of conflicting princelets' (*L* 1, 98), who yet took pains to understand

5

and represent Indian 'vernacular' speech, who wrote with tenderness and humour of Hindu customs and theology in 'The Finances of the Gods' (*LH*) and showed an arrogant English engineer finding the fate of his life's work determined by the Hindu gods in 'The Bridge Builders' (*DW*). More than this, in *Kim* he showed the holy and innocent Teshoo Lama being despised by English racial arrogance in the person of an Anglican chaplain:

> Dignified and unsuspicious, he [the lama] strode into the little tent, saluted the Churches as a Churchman, and sat down by the open charcoal brazier. The yellow lining of the tent reflected in the lamplight made his face red-gold.
>
> Bennett looked at him with the triple-ringed uninterest of the creed that lumps nine-tenths of the world under the title of 'heathen' (*K*, 124)

Kipling's condemnation of the clergyman's 'triple-ringed uninterest' is far more emphatic even than Forster's sharp-eyed satire in *A Passage to India*. Yet though Kipling may see the limitations of English culture and condemn its shallow judgment of other races, it would be naïve to claim him, on the strength of this passage, to be an anti-racist. The point may be clarified by comparing his overt hostility to the Revd. Bennett's incurious ignorance with the meditations of the narrator in the later story 'They' on 'the more than inherited (since it is also carefully taught) brutality of the Christian peoples, beside which the mere heathendom of the West Coast nigger is clean and restrained' (*TD*, 316). This bitter observation that the cruelty of respectable Christians can be worse than heathen barbarism is structured by the value-judgments of a colonial officer class for whom Africans are 'niggers' and whites are supposed to be models of disciplined self-restraint, the comparison with black savages being the strongest imaginable condemnation.

Kipling's attitude to Africans, especially after he moved to the Right during the Boer War (1899–1902), seems, to judge by statements like 'It is pure sentimental bosh to say that Africa belongs to a lot of naked blacks'[5] to have been dismissively racist. Although his own opinions are never directly expressed in his fictions, similar thoughts are echoed by sympathetic characters like the American Laughton O. Zigler in 'The Captive', expressing contempt for 'naked sons of Ham...niggers' and the loyal Sikh in 'A Sahibs' War' who regards *hubshis* [blacks] as 'Kaffirs – filth unspeakable' (*TD*, 8, 85). Racist attitudes occasionally surface even in the nursery playfulness of the *Just-So Stories*. The 'Ethiopian' in 'How the Leopard Got His Spots' cheerfully announces 'Oh, plain black's best for a nigger', and the accompanying illustration by Kipling has a caption explaining that he was 'really a negro, so of course his name was Sambo' (a statement which might surprise real Ethiopians); while Kipling's otherwise charming illustration of King Solomon's feast for the animals in 'The Butterfly That Stamped' includes a box labelled 'SUGAR CANE: Special Slave Grown' (*JSS*, 49, 47, 193): a blithely obnoxious detail.

The difference between the narrator's attitudes to the hypothetical 'West Coast nigger' in 'They' and the description of the lama in *Kim* is that the latter's innocence and dignity and the unselfconscious beauty of his 'red-gold' face in the lamplight, are seen as more important and valuable than the Englishman who despises him. But even here, although Teshoo Lama's universal Buddhist values are represented as superior to Bennett's narrowly racist provincialism, he is represented more as a person to be cherished than as a source of wisdom from whom the English might learn.

A further contradiction exists between Kipling's love of order and his attraction towards chaos. On the one hand he is a famously 'knowing' writer, whose mechanical exactness was acutely characterized by the Edwardian critic Dixon Scott:

> first, a passion for definition ... a hunger for certitude and system ... [secondly] a prodigious mental faculty for enforcing design ... for stamping dream-stuff into shapes as clear and coherent as minted metal discs. And thirdly, a craftsman's cunning and capacity ... for adjusting them like the works of a watch with an exquisite accuracy, achieving miracles of minute mechanical perfection. ...Every [sentence] has its self-contained tune. Prise one of these out of its place and you feel it would fall with a clink. ... Replace it, and it locks up like type in a forme.[6]

Yet this highly self-conscious craftsman who wrote of his art in terms of carefully applied techniques to produce the most concentrated possible writing: 'A tale from which pieces have been raked out is like a fire that has been poked. One does not know that the operation has been performed, but everyone feels the effect', (*SM*, 207), also ascribed his best work to an uncontrollable 'Daemon': 'When your Daemon is in charge, do not try to think consciously. Drift, wait, and obey' (*SM*, 107). And the other side of his controlled 'mechanical perfection' is an ever-present awareness of the chaos that threatens as soon as men become careless. For Kipling has, from the outset of his career, been associated with the daemonic. For all its metallic, type-casting exactness, his writing has something rank, something excitingly uncontrollable about it.

That rank vitality – and the responses it calls up – may be seen in the judgments made by two early critics of Kipling, one approving and one disapproving. Margaret Oliphant, reviewing *Life's Handicap* in 1891, praised Kipling for showing Queen Victoria 'how her Indian Empire ... is ruled and defended and fought for every day against the Powers of Darkness'. Eight years later, Robert Buchanan attacked the populist writer as a moral savage 'on the side of all that is ignorant, selfish, base and brutal in the instincts of humanity', as opposed to an enlightened imperialism that would edify its colonized subjects.[7] Admirer and enemy alike define Kipling's work in terms of a politicized split between an abyss of daemonic destruction and a bulwark of enlightened order; their disagreement is about whether he belongs on the civilized or the daemonic side of the split. It is true, but not enough, to say, as Zohreh Sullivan does, that the liberal Robert Buchanan's condemnation of Kipling and his desire 'to see the empire rationalised and given speech as a single and monolithic structure and the multitudinous mob silenced'[8] were as 'Orientalist' as Margaret Oliphant's praise for his heroic Englishmen struggling against the 'Powers of Darkness'. Of course they were, but these contemporaries were also right in sensing a connection between the political allegiances of Kipling's work and its daemonic energies. This insight is taken further by Sara Suleri and Sullivan herself in their more recent analyses of Kipling's creative ambivalence towards an alluring, threatening colonized Other, perilously subdued by an official power whose rule is never finally guaranteed, which is profoundly though indirectly connected to his 'Daemon' – that is, to the released energy that made certain books come seemingly without being willed. The vitality of that Other energizes his otherwise arid knowingness, even though it appears more often than not as a threat.

The Powers of Darkness are never far away in Kipling's work. Sometimes the perceived threat is military-political, as in 'The Dykes 1902', an allegory of the peril incurred by the British, secure in their tradition of greatness, in neglecting their military defences:

> Look you, our foreshore stretches far, through sea-gate, dyke and groyne,
> Made land all, that our father made, where the flats and the fairway join.
> They forced the sea a sea-league back. They died, and their work stood fast.
> We were born to peace in the lee of the dykes, but the time of our peace is past.
>
> Far off, the full tide clambers and slips, mouthing and testing all,
> Nipping the flanks of the water-edge, baying along the wall,
> Turning the shingle, re-turning the shingle, changing the set of the sand...
> We are too far from the beach, men say, to know how the outworks stand.
>
> (W, 305–6)

Those waves attacking human defences like dogs hunting their prey, are as fascinating as they are sinister, and there is a grim satisfaction in the poem's prophetic conclusion that 'we' shall end up overwhelmed by the disaster we have deserved, 'walking along the wreck of the dykes, watching the work of the seas!' The threat may come even more subversively from within the psyche, as when the narrator of 'The House Surgeon' experiences a waking nightmare in an English country bedroom: 'I moved towards the bed, every nerve aching with foreknowledge of the pain that was to be dealt it, and sat down, while my amazed and angry soul dropped gulf by gulf into that Horror of great darkness which is spoken of on the Bible, and which as the auctioneers say, must be experienced to be appreciated'(AR, 287-8). Such abysses at once threaten to undermine ordinary reality and represent an alluring alternative to it.

DIVIDED READERS

The reception of Kipling's writing has been as contradictory and divided as the work itself. He was an enormously popular writer whose children's books, not to mention their film adaptations, still continue to reach millions. Yet by 1902 he was unpopular with English intellectuals, partly as a result of his public advocacy of the Boer War and, though admired (if often with reservations) by influential critics including George Orwell, Edmund Wilson and more recently Edward Said, has never regained his predominance. In his lifetime this world-famous writer was, in England, popular mainly with middle-class readers, his poems and stories featuring prominently in the petty-bourgeois culture fastidiously evoked by T.S. Eliot as 'short square fingers stuffing pipes, / And evening newspapers, and eyes / Assured of certain certainties'.[9] He was so much despised and ignored by intellectuals that Edmund Wilson could write in 1941 that 'he has in a sense been dropped out of modern literature', and when George Orwell in 1937 described Auden as 'a sort of gutless Kipling', the insult lay quite as much in the name 'Kipling' as in the adjective 'gutless' (which incidentally implies a silently damaging comparison of the modern poet with 'the passion – the power – the – the essential guts' of a Horace ode in Kipling's 'Regulus', D of C, 246.). Yet Orwell himself would invoke Kipling to define his own ideological pilgrimage on 'The road from Mandalay to Wigan', and would later point out how Kipling epigrams like 'The female of the species is more deadly than the male', 'The toad beneath the harrow knows/ Where each tooth of that harrow goes', ' There are nine and sixty ways of constructing tribal lays,/ And every single one of them is right' (W, 367, 26, 342), were constantly quoted by people who didn't know (and often didn't want to know) what author they were citing.[10]

Other twentieth century Kipling admirers include the Indian writer Nirad Chaudhuri and the great Argentinian Jorge Luis Borges; also, nearer to his own times, the French writers Alain Fournier and André Gide (Kipling was much more esteemed in France than Britain). Kipling was highly valued by several of the great European modernists, notably T.S. Eliot who not only parodied him affectionately in Old Possum's Book of Practical Cats

(1937) but drew on the hidden laughing children of the numinous story 'They' in *Burnt Norton*.[11] Bertolt Brecht, for whom according to one biographer 'Kipling...remained to the last among the few twentieth century writers for whom [he] had any deep regard,'[12] admired *Barrack Room Ballads*, translated some and drew on them for the bloodthirsty 'Soldiers' Song' in *Threepenny Opera*, and recycled Kipling's 'The Incarnation of Krishna Mulvaney' (*LH*) into his play *Mann ist Mann*. For Kipling needs to be read not only as a late-Victorian imperialist but as a writer on the cusp of modernism – or rather, as I argue in Chapters seven to nine, as one of the first modernist writers.

The divided reception of Kipling is as much political as literary-critical. Because admiration for his work still often implies political conservatism, it is not surprising that the *Kipling Journal* should have run an editorial in 2002, 'The Last Empress of India', arguing that the late Queen Mother's life was in the best traditions of Kipling's ethic of public service,[13] it was though a nasty shock to this writer to find his poetry cited approvingly on the websites of the extreme right-wing U.S. Heritage Foundation and the white supremacist 'American Patrol.'[14] Yet Kipling's appeal to his political opponents remains strong. His Marxist admirers included not only Brecht but the Communist journalist Claud Cockburn, who would have liked his muck-raking 1930s news-sheet *The Week* to take for its motto his lines 'Who shall doubt the secret hid / Under Cheops' pyramid / Was that the contractor did / Cheops out of several millions?', while Moshe Lewin, the great social historian of Soviet Russia, sums up peasant existence with an unironic Kipling quote: 'This life is a long-drawn out question-mark between a crop and a crop'.[15] Kipling's celebration of work and its values made him popular in the Soviet Union, and after the collapse of communism in 1989, Russian homosexuals used to greet one another with *The Jungle Book* password 'We be of one blood, ye and I' and to wish one another 'Good hunting!' before an evening's cruising.[16] He is also admired by the contemporary Indian writers Salman Rushdie and Arundhati Roy, whose novel *The God of Small Things* begins with two Indian children delightedly quoting *The Jungle Book* to each other in English. His most attentive readers include the socialist George Orwell, the homosexual poet Auden, the Freudian-minded liberal

11

intellectuals Edmund Wilson and Randall Jarrell, and more recently the post-colonials Edward Said, Sara Suleri and Zohreh Sullivan – all of the latter reading him as a divided, haunted writer.

The nature of the divisions that excite such diverse opinions can be clarified by looking in detail at two stories that seem to point towards opposite morals. Kipling is an explicitly ideological writer who constantly addresses the question of the values and customs by which societies live, preoccupations which for Noel Annan made him an essentially 'sociological' writer'.[17] His two-sidedness appears in the contradictory treatment of the claims of Law versus Revenge in two different texts, the early monologue 'Dray Wara Yow Dee' and the children's story 'The Treasure and the Law'(ST and PPH). The first is a Browning-esque prose monologue of obsessive hatred (Randall Jarrell called it 'Kipling's prose equivalent of 'Soliloquy of the Spanish Cloister''[18]), written, or rather 'spoken', in Kipling's archaized English approximation to an Indian vernacular (possibly Urdu, more likely Pushtu) by an Afghan horse-dealer, to an inaudible 'Sahib', a silent equivalent of that 'I' who tells so many Kipling stories and whose responses partly guide the tale.

Although the Afghan turns out to have slaughtered his adulterous wife and, under the pretext of selling horses, to be murderously pursuing her lover through the Punjab, he is nevertheless attractive in his studied courtesy and his lyrical yearning for the mountains of his home: '*Here* is only dust and a great stink. There is a pleasant wind among the mulberry-trees, and the streams are bright with snow-water'(ST, 235). These nostalgic words have an elegance compared to which the English exiles in 'At the End of the Passage' pining in the Indian hot weather for "summer evenings in the country – stained glass window – light going out, and you and she jamming your heads together over one hymnbook" (LH, 194), look coarsely inarticulate. When he rejects a tip, the Afghan's outrage is formidable:

> Fire burn your money ! What do I want with it ? I am rich and I thought you were my friend; but you are like the others – a Sahib. Is a man sad ? Give him money, say the Sahibs. Is he dishonoured? Give him money, say the Sahibs. Hath he a wrong upon his head? Give him money, say the Sahibs. (ST, 233)

12

The 'Sahib' is silenced by this stinging reproach. Does the story then endorse this murderous madman who intends not only to kill his wife's lover but to cripple a girl who he thinks mocked him, and to hell with the Raj and its peaceful rule – 'Your Law! What is your Law to me?' (ST, 238). Officially, the answer must be No; yet Kipling's imaginative sympathy is clearly with the man's murderous hate, desire for beauty, mental torment (like his creator, he suffers from insomnia) and his aristocratic disdain for financial compensation which he regards as a dishonourable bribe.

The other side of the argument is put in the later children's story 'The Treasure and the Law', the final tale of *Puck of Pook's Hill*, where the establishment of money compensation for injury (a modern 'beater' is accidentally injured during a present-day pheasant shoot and paid off by 'Mr. Meyer' with a sovereign), is represented as a triumph of English civic order. As the English spirit Puck explains to the cynical thirteenth-century Jew Kadmiel:

> 'A freeman was a little hurt, by pure mischance, at the hunting.'
> 'I know that mischance! What did his lord do? Laugh and ride over him?' the old man sneered.
> 'It was one of your own people that did the hurt, Kadmiel.' Puck's eyes twinkled maliciously. 'So he gave the freeman a piece of gold, and no more was said.'
> 'A Jew drew blood from a Christian and no more was said?' Kadmiel cried. 'Never! When did they torture him?'
> 'No man may be bound, or fined, or slain till he has been judged by his peers,' Puck insisted. 'There is but one Law in Old England for Jew, or Christian – the Law that was signed at Runnymede.' (PPH, 284–5)

In this exchange Puck, the incarnation of English tradition, represents control, justice and humour: qualities closely linked with the irony and knowingness that characterize the controlling 'I' who frames so many of Kipling's early narratives. Such a narrator would not fit in a children's story, but his characteristic knowing sophistication is present nevertheless in the 'malicious twinkle' of Puck, who knows what the medieval man of the world doesn't – that the offender is a wealthy Jew protected by the civil state.

13

Like all the 'Puck' stories, this one celebrates an everlasting 'Old England' whose continuity is also capable of growth and change. The establishment of financial compensation in place of revenge and violence has been made possible by the establishment of a civil society, beginning with King John's signing of the Magna Carta of English Rights in 1205 – the negotiations for which, we learn, included Kadmiel paying the Barons 'two hundred broad pieces of gold' to write 'To none will we sell, refuse or delay right or justice' instead of '*To no free man*' (*PPH*, 296). The English Law, before which all are now equal, grows directly out of the cruelty and corruption of the past: as Puck tells the children, 'The Sword gave the Treasure, and the Treasure gave the Law. It's as natural as an oak growing' (*PPH*, 303). Violence and lawlessness have in 1906 become such distant memories that Kadmiel's street-wise cynicism looks naïve beside Puck's twinkling irony, born of the knowledge that decency and justice are the essence of England – which, it is implied, makes it right for England to rule her empire to-day. True, even in this 'modern' England, Jews are associated with money and bribery and remain alarmingly 'other', despite Kadmiel's surprise that the children do not fear him:

'Yet surely, surely they are taught to spit upon Jews?'
'Are they?' said Dan, much interested. 'Where at?'(*PPH*, 286)

The comedy of this exchange derives from Dan's innocence; a well-brought-up boy to whom such grossness is unthinkable, he clearly believes that Kadmiel's 'taught' must refer to some peculiar school. (For Kipling himself, such an action was clearly impermissible but not unthinkable; when his writing was refused for *Punch* by 'a non- Aryan – and German' [presumably the Liberal writer R.C.Lehmann], he says he recalled his servant in Lahore spitting 'loudly and openly' when announcing a Jew; though he himself 'swallowed my spittle at once' as a white man should: *SM*, 224.) The schoolboy's innocence here represents an unconscious testimony to the mannerly, law-abiding society that 'Old England' has now become, whose triumph is that it extends its protection *even* to Jews.

These two stories appear to represent a total contradiction between the lawless assassin whose pride is his own honour and who despises money, and the spokesman for the Law for whom the establishment of civil society and money compensation is a matter of enormous though understated pride. The two cannot be equally right. One might try to reconcile the opposition by arguing, like J.M.S.Tompkins, that Kipling's genius for plurality naturally enjoys inventing 'a diversity of creatures' (to quote one of his titles), like Keats' poet who 'has as much delight in conceiving an Iago as an Imogen'.[19] But the difference between these stories is not just between two characters differently conceived, but between the beliefs and customs by which different societies live. The speaker of 'Dray Wara Yow Dee' may be a criminal, but as a Muslim he thinks himself innocent before 'God, the holder of the Scale of the Law' (*ST*, 244). As Noel Annan perceptively wrote: 'Despite the multitude of characters in his stories, [Kipling] is less interested in people than in social realities... The centre of Kipling's world is society itself.'[20] The oppositions of the different societies created in his stories are irreconcilable, and Kipling is not finally well served by attempts to represent him as the resolved, balanced artist that he was not.

I therefore examine the course of Kipling's work in this book, in terms of the contradictions sketched above. Except for the single chapter on *Kim*, my approach is thematic, but it roughly follows the chronology of Kipling's own writings. The opening chapters deal with Kipling's 'Indian' fictions: the anxiety of the colonialist trying to 'know the unknowable' native subject(s), and the literary and ideological implications of Kipling's invented equivalent to the Indian 'vernacular'; I also consider the way his prose and poetry crossed class boundaries by his use of demotic English idiom. Chapters four and five discuss, respectively, the work ethic embodied in poems and stories, and the ideal of imperialist masculinity that informs so much of his writing, contrasting this with the idea of 'Man' as like but unlike the animals of the *Jungle Books*. These chapters set up the critical context for the central chapter on *Kim*, which I agree with most of Kipling's critics in finding his masterpiece; I read it as a colonial fiction which engages with the contradictions explored in the previous fiction and achieves some sort of resolution. The last three chapters read Kipling as a writer on the cusp of modernity, in three aspects: as a Victorian poet whose parodic brilliance and invented 'voices' anticipate the uncertainties and subversions of modernist poetry; as a writer fascinated by and

15

engaged with the revolutionary machineries of communication that transformed the modern world; and as a public writer responding to the First World War with extraordinarily inventive contributions to the literature of mourning that, all in their different ways, undermine their apparently traditionalist modes of representation. The concluding 'Epilogue' briefly surveys Kipling's last years and his highly-wrought late stories.

1

Kipling in India: Knowing the Unknowable

THE KNOWING WRITER

The young Kipling writes, notoriously, as a knowing insider of colonial India hailed by Victorian contemporaries as 'the Revealer of the East'. The early reviewer Charles Whibley wrote approvingly that he knew 'the native of India as he has never been known before'; Margaret Oliphant thought he would 'roll away from us the veil that covers that vast and teeming world.'[1] His narrative statements about India invariably refer to matters of 'common knowledge'. He knows that life is unfair on conscientious officers: 'Good work does not matter, because a man is judged by his worst output, and another man takes all the credit of his best as a rule. Bad work does not matter, because other men do worse, and incompetents hang on longer in India than anywhere else.... Sickness does not matter, because it's all in the day's work, and if you die, another man takes over your place and your office in the eight hours between death and burial.' ('Thrown Away', *PTH*, 17).

He knows about Simla's unpredictable tolerance for illicit liaisons: 'Certain attachments which have set and crystallised through half-a-dozen seasons acquire almost the sanctity of the marriage bond, and are revered as such.' ('At the Pit's Mouth', *WWW*, 35–6). He knows why India must be held by force: 'Asia is not going to be civilised after the methods of the West. There is too much of Asia and she is too old. You cannot reform a lady of many lovers, and Asia has been insatiable in her flirtations aforetime. She will never attend Sunday school or learn to vote save with swords for tickets' ('The Man Who Was', *LH*, 98). With

17

studied ease, he drops little details of the familiar hardships of colonial life: 'Each well-regulated Indian Cemetery keeps half-a-dozen graves permanently open for contingencies and incidental wear and tear. In the Hills these are more usually baby's size, because children who come up weakened and sick from the Plains often succumb to the effects of the Rains in the Hills or get pneumonia from their *ayahs* taking them through damp pinewoods after the sun has set. In Cantonments, of course, the man's size is more in request: these arrangements varying with the climate and population.' (*WWW*, 38). Between the lines of these brittle ironies can be heard a litany of settler complaints, all the louder for not being directly spoken: 'There's no justice or appreciation of our work, the climate kills our children, native servants are lazy and unreliable, our soldiers die like flies'. (Or like natives?). Such dogmatic statements draw on colonial common knowledge in a way that makes it impossible for an uninstructed reader to disentangle facts from received orthodoxies, as in the opening of 'The Phantom Rickshaw':

> One of the few advantages that India has over England is a great Knowability. After five years' service a man is directly acquainted with the two or three hundred Civilians in his Province, all the Messes of ten or twelve Batteries, and some fifteen hundred other people of the non-official caste. In ten years his knowledge should be doubled, and at the end of twenty he knows, or knows something about, every Englishman in the Empire and may travel anywhere and everywhere without paying hotel-bills... ...The men who do not trouble to conceal from you their opinion that you are an incompetent ass, and the women who blacken your character and misunderstand your wife's amusements, will work their fingers to the bone if you fall sick or into serious trouble. ('The Phantom Rickshaw', *WWW*, 123–4)

Yet one should be wary of taking these brassy generalizations too easily as Kipling's real opinions. As Zohreh Sullivan rightly says, 'the problem of representing imperialism as charmed circle and as a family affair opens up the possibility of expulsion from its charms, and consequently loss of power and agency.'[2] For the apparently blithe certainties of the above paean to Anglo-Indian communal solidarity, in which 'India' means a few thousand white officers and administrators, friends in need who might easily pass for 'your' enemies, preface a story about a man

18

whose betrayal of a woman leads him to fall out of that safety net into madness and death. As so often, Kipling's knowledgeably ironic 'frame' narrator is not to be trusted.

It would, however, be naïve to assume that Kipling is always aware of the limitations of his own dogmatism. Both the extent and the limitations of his knowledge of India can be gauged from an early letter to his cousin Margaret Burne-Jones in which he warns her against typing 'natives' by producing an elaborate list of native types:

> When you write of 'the native' who do you mean? The Mahommedan who hates the Hindu: the Hindu who hates the Mahommedan; the Sikh who despises both; or the semi-anglicized product of our Indian colleges who is hated and despised by Sikh, Hindu and Mahommedan? Do you mean the Punjabi who will have nothing to do with the Bengali; the Mahrattha to whom the Punjabi's tongue is as incomprehensible as Russian to me; the Parsee who controls the whole trade of Bombay and ranges himself on all questions as an Englishman; the Sindee who is an outsider; the Bhil or the Gond who is an aborigine; the Rajput who despises everything on God's earth but himself; the Delhi traders who control trade to the value of millions; the Afghan who is only kept from looting these same millions by dread of English interference? Which one of all the thousand conflicting tongues, races, nationalities and peoples between the Khaibar Pass (*sic*) and Ceylon do you mean? There is no such thing as the natives of India, any more than the 'People of India' as our friends the Indian delegates would have you believe. (*L.I*, 97–8)

Craig Raine cites this passage as evidence against Kipling's racism on the grounds that 'Kipling recorded these distinctions. He didn't invent them.'[3] But it would be disingenuous to describe this passage as objective. The early catalogue of different ethnic types prefigures the vision in *Kim* of Indian diversity benignly controlled by British power as its crowds move along the Grand Trunk Road; but though the youthful Kipling's rhetoric begins by questioning the oversimplified 'native', his answer is a proliferation of essentialized racial types whose definition is clearly inflected by self-serving colonial prejudices, most obviously against 'the semi-anglicized product of our Indian colleges who is hated and despised by Sikh, Hindu and Mahommedan' (and certainly by Rudyard

19

Kipling). This reduction of Indians to types whom the writer knows better than they know themselves produces an illusion of mastery and knowledge that justifies English hegemony: 'If we didn't hold the land in six months it would be one big cock pit of conflicting princelets'. He tells his cousin that the 'proper way to handle 'em . . . is as men with a language of their own which it is your business to understand; and proverbs, which it is your business to quote and byewords and allusions which it is your business to master; and feelings which it is your business to enter into and sympathize with. Then they'll believe you and do things for you.'(*L* I, 98, 100–1). Conceding the reality of other men's culture, their language, proverbs, allusions, feelings, is a means of control – for 'you' here evidently doesn't mean Cousin Margaret, Kipling's ostensible addressee. The one whose 'business it is' to understand and control Indians is the Anglo-Indian official – watchful, in control of himself as well as others, endlessly conscientious in his mastering of an alien culture.

It is noticeable that while Kipling's list of different peoples purports to confer an orderly sequence on their potentially chaotic multiplicity, the sheer length of his catalogue threatens to get out of hand, suggesting that no one man, including the writer himself, can understand a reality this complex. Listing is a frequent trope of Kipling's short stories, whose metonymic realism offers particular details to represent a typical way of life, as when Morrowbie Jukes makes his methodical inventory of the pathetically schoolboyish contents of a mummified English-man's pockets: '1. Bowl of a briarwood pipe, serrated at the edge; much worn and blackened; bound with string at the screw. 2. Two patent-lever keys; wards of both broken' etc., etc., (*WWW*, 193). Equally typical is the furniture of an unpretentious minor official living in a bungalow in the Punjab: 'There were the usual blue-and-white striped jail-made rugs on the uneven floor; the usual glass-studded Amritsar *phulkaris* draped into nails driven into the flaking whitewash of the walls; the usual half-dozen chairs that did not match, picked up at sales of dead men's effects' ('William the Conqueror, *DW*, 185), signifying the modest resources and short lives of hard-pressed junior administrators. Conversely, the prized jewellery of an English-man's Indian wife in 'Without Benefit of Clergy' represents an exotic culture in a few ornaments:

Ameera wore all that she valued most. The diamond nose-stud that takes the place of the Western patch in drawing attention to the curve of the nostril, the gold ornament in the centre of the forehead, studded with tallow-drop emeralds and flawed rubies, the heavy circlet of beaten gold that was fastened round her neck by the softness of the pure metal, and the chinking curb-patterned silver anklets hanging low over the rosy ankle-bone. She was dressed in jade-green silk as befits a daughter of the Faith, and from shoulder to elbow and elbow to wrist ran bracelets of silver tied with floss silk, frail glass bangles slipped over the wrist in proof of the slenderness of the hand, and certain heavy gold bracelets that had no part of her country's ornaments, but, since they were Holden's gift and fastened with a cunning European snap, delighted her immensely' ('Without Benefit of Clergy', *LH*, 159).

These lists keep their punch-lines to the end; those second-hand chairs, previously owned by dead men, emphasize once again the hard and dangerous lives of underpaid English officials, while the Indian girl's pleasure in her English lover's gift and the technology of the 'cunning European snap' both emphasizes the story's inter-cultural theme and avoids making the girl, with her slender arms and 'rosy ankle-bone', into just another beautifully exotic possession. Without such rhetorical control, over-extended listing would end up evoking not completeness of understanding but an endless, ultimately incomprehensible multiplication of examples that risks subverting the catalogue's claim to order. Unlike Joyce's *reductio ad absurdum* of naturalist detail in the 'Ithaca' chapter of *Ulysses*, which describes in ever-proliferating detail the water's progress from reservoir through pipe to tap to kettle, Kipling's naturalist details remain at the manageable level of synecdoche, the part standing for a knowable whole.

Such listing of details is an aspect of the numbering and measurement which represent a powerful if, again, ambivalent imagery of knowledge and control in Kipling's fictions of empire. The best known instance of control by numbers is the famous passage in *Kim* where the hero successfully resists the shadow-vision imposed on him by the 'native' hypnotism of Lurgan Sahib:

There was one large piece of the jar where there had been three, and above them the shadowy outline of the entire vessel...thickening and darkening with each pulse...

'Look! It is coming into shape!' said Lurgan Sahib.

So far Kim had been thinking in Hindi, but his mind leaped up from a darkness that was swallowing it and took refuge in – the multiplication-table in English!

'Look! It is coming into shape!' whispered Lurgan Sahib.

The jar had been smashed – yess, smashed – not the native word, he would not think of that – but smashed – into fifty pieces, and twice three was six, and thrice three was nine, and four times three was twelve. He clung desperately to the repetition. The shadow-outline of the jar cleared like a mist after rubbing eyes. There were the broken shards, there was the spilt water drying in the sun, and through the cracks of the veranda showed, all ribbed, the white house-wall below – and thrice three was thirty-six! (K, 126)

Kim's chant of 'twice two is three ' is 'magical art' as defined in R.G. Collingwood's *Principles of Art*: 'a representation where the emotion evoked is valued on account of its function in practical life, and fed by the generative or focusing magical activity into the life that needs it'.[4] Kim's incantation is naturally, so to speak, represented as a victory for daylight English language and reason over shadowy Indian magic. It enables him to see through the 'darkness that was swallowing up' his mind the real sunlight shining through the cracks of the verandah, and is presented as both a victorious spell and a reassuring statement of fact, for he is indeed witnessing a multiplication of fragments: 'smashed – into fifty pieces – and twice three was six'. According to Lurgan Sahib, the master whose respect he earns by resistance, the Irish boy's capacity to see the jar steadily and see it smashed, proves him 'strong enough to make anyone do anything that he wants' (*K*, 245), which would, presumably, gain him the ultimate accolade of the poem 'If' – 'Yours is the Earth and everything that's in it / And – which is more – you'll be a Man, my son!'(*W*, 577)

English empiricist knowledge, represented here by the multiplication-table, works its magic over Indian irrationalism simply, we are asked to believe, because it is true. This does not mean that Kipling's Indians are necessarily shown as ignorant of numeration; an earlier scene shows a Brahmin priest casting a horoscope by means of complex mathematical calculations which enable him to prophesy correctly that Kim's future lies with 'war and armed men – many hundreds' (the 'Maverick' regiment that is shortly to claim Kim as a white boy). These astrological calculations, though, are represented as part of Indian magic, real enough in its own terms, just as Lurgan Sahib's hypnotic powers and Kim's psychic vulnerability are real (if they weren't, Kim's would be a sham victory), but potent only in their own night-time world of dream and intuition. Kim's daytime knowledge, articulated in an Indian-accented English ('yess, smashed – not the native word, he would not think of that') represents a conscious defence against 'native' darkness and irrationalism.

Kim's mathematical abilities not only defend his sanity and earn him an expensive and useless prize at school ('*The Life of Lord Lawrence,* tree-calf, two vols., nine rupees, eight annas', *K,* 233); they prove vital to his work as a Government spy, enabling him to make a map of 'the wild walled city of Bikanir', 'pac[ing] his distances by means of a bead rosary [and using] the compass for bearings' which actually reaches and is used by the Government. We are told in a splendidly plausible off-hand detail that it 'was on hand a few years ago (a careless clerk filed it with the rough note of E.23's second Seistan survey', *K,* 242–3). Both the technique of measurement and example of Bikanir testify to Kipling's participation in imperialist techniques of knowledge and measurement, particularly the illicit surveying carried out by means of paces measured by rosary, that allowed English authority to map and control the Indian sub-continent. For Thomas Richards[5] has shown how the details of Kim's training in taking his illicit surveys replicate General Montgomerie's strategy of secretly mapping Tibet from 1862 by disguising his surveyors as monks, training them to measure the length of their own pace, to count the number of paces they took in a day, and to keep count by using the Buddhist rosary, just as Kim does.

THE UNKNOWABLE ABYSS

But Kim, as usual, is an exception. Earlier attempts by Kipling's Englishmen to master irrational Indian darkness by means of English formulae and knowledge are much less successful. The guilty Jack Pansay of 'The Phantom Rickshaw' story , haunted by the hallucinatory vision of his pleading discarded mistress in her rickshaw pulled by natives in 'magpie' uniforms, tries to ward off his visions by thinking, like Kim, of 'the workaday Anglo-Indian world I knew so well. I even repeated the multiplication-table to myself, to make quite sure that I was not taking leave of my senses. It gave me much comfort' ('The Phantom Rickshaw', WWW, 151). But it has no more power to halt Pansay's disintegration than does his bluff would-be saviour Dr Hetherlegh, who prescribes cold baths and exercise as a cure, 'maintains that overwork slew Pansay' and admits no doubt of Pansay's trouble: 'Write him off to the System that uses one man to do the work of two and a half' (WWW, 125). The whole point of the story is the hopeless inadequacy of this diagnosis to cope with the nightmarish possibility that 'there was a crack in Pansay's head and a little bit of the Dark World came through and pressed him to death' (WWW, 124–5) – a condition strikingly close to Kipling's own much later haunting phrase for his own lifelong insomnia, 'the night got into my head' (SM, 18).

A similar theme of the impotence of medical knowledge when confronted with the inexplicable reappears in the later horror story 'At the End of the Passage' set in the hot-weather Punjab where the lonely engineer Hummil, maddened by heat, loneliness, insomnia and hallucinations of meeting himself, suffers terrible nightmares of 'a blind face that cries and can't wipe its eyes, a blind face that chases him down corridors'(LH, 204).[6] So frightful is this apparition of rage and grief that Hummil puts a spur in his mattress to prevent himself from falling asleep and being caught by it. When he is found dead, staring in 'terror beyond the expression of any pen' (LH, 207), his servant guesses from seeing the spur what has happened: 'This that was my master has descended into the Dark Places, and there has been caught because he was not able to escape with sufficient speed... Thus have I seen men of my own race do with thorns when a spell was laid upon them to overtake them in their sleeping-hours and they dared not sleep.' Dr Spurstow, whose morphia injection had not saved Hummil, brushes this off – 'Chuma, you're a mud-head' – but himself has no better explanation: 'He died from – oh, anything; stoppage of the heart, heat-apoplexy, or some other visitation.' (LH, 208–9). He tries photographing the images in the dead man's eye, but as soon as he develops the film he destroys it, together with the camera. So far from mastering or explaining the unimaginable horror, Western technology can only reproduce it with photographs that must be censored.

Outside the charmed world of *Kim*, then, the ghosts of weakness, – the discarded mistress everlastingly beseeching '*Please* forgive me!' (*WWW*, 138,) or the blind malignant weeping face that torments Hummil – English power and knowledge are impotent. Kipling's stories of Englishmen attempting to use technological power and measuring skills on Indian land are similarly nightmarish. When the hero of 'The Strange Ride of Morrowbie Jukes' falls into a pit (near 'Bikanir, which is in the heart of the Great Indian Desert': *WWW*, 168), he measures its dimensions with the expert eye of a Civil Engineer:

> A horse-shoe shaped crater of sand with steeply-graded sand walls about thirty-five feet high. (The slope, I fancy, must have been about 65 degrees.) This crater enclosed a level piece of ground about fifty yards long by thirty at its broadest part, with a rude well in the centre. Round the bottom of the crater, about three feet from the level of the ground proper, ran a series of eighty-three semicircular, ovoid, square and multilateral holes, all about three feet at the mouth. No sign of life was visible in those tunnels, but a most sickening stench pervaded the entire amphitheatre – a stench fouler than any which my wanderings in Indian villages have introduced me to' (*WWW*, 172).

That sickening 'native' smell indicates that this Crusoe-like technological expertise does Jukes no good in the pit he has fallen into, a stinking prison whose sand-walls can't be climbed and whose one open side is guarded both by trigger-happy sentries and by a deadly quicksand. As Zohreh Sullivan observes of this hell-hole that rapidly transforms the Sahib Jukes into a hysterical weakling, 'A metaphoric and genderized vaginal space has swallowed up and unmanned the colonizer'.[7] Out of the holes numbered with such vain exactitude will creep the half-starved, naked and stinking Indian inhabitants, the dead who have not died resembling 'a band of loathsome fakirs' hooting with mirth at the sight of the Sahib trapped like themselves. Jukes finds a dead version of himself in the 'yellow-brown mummy' of another Englishman who fell in the same trap and died there (*WWW*, 193), and a more hideous parody still in Gunga Dass, a clever English-speaking Bengali and former telegraph-clerk, known to and abused by Jukes in their former lives as public servants. He is recognizable by a 'scar on his right cheek – the result of an accident for which I was responsible' (WWW, 175). Dass becomes his torturer-mentor in the pit, mocking him with superior knowledge, teaching him literally to eat crow, taking his money, and relishing every moment of his superiority over the 'Sahib'. In this paranoid fable of colonial relations, Dass is both a filthy stinking outcast *and* an educated master of the colonizer's own discourse, making horridly witty republican jokes at Jukes' expense by offering him a share of his own dead horse: 'Gunga Dass explained that horse was better than crow, and "greatest good of greatest number is political maxim... If you like, we will pass a vote of thanks. Shall I propose?"' (WWW, 189–90). He shows greater practical intelligence than Jukes when the latter discovers, among the dead Englishman's possessions, a paper with the mysterious words '*Four out from crow-clump; three left; nine out; two right*', (WWW, 195). Much quicker on the uptake than Jukes poring over his inventory of the dead man's oddments, Dass promptly realizes that these are directions for getting past the quicksand at the pit's mouth, measured by '"the length of the gun-barrels without the stock.... Four gun-barrels out from the place where I caught crows"' (WWW, 197).

To post-Freudian, post-colonial readers, the salvation from a hollow pit full of filth by means of measurements taken in gun-barrels reads as a cartoonishly crude colonial fantasy of phallocratic conquest. The gun, at once an obvious metonym of European political hegemony and military-technological power (outside of the 'native states', Indian men didn't carry guns unless they were soldiers in the service of the occupying power), and an equally obvious phallic metaphor, offers a chance of escape from the soft stinking Indian earth that imprisons the white man by giving way beneath him. Naturally the treacherous Gunga Dass tries to monopolize this chance by knocking Jukes senseless, and the latter is eventually pulled to safety out of the nightmare pit by his faithful Indian dog-boy Dunnoo – a convenient *deus ex machina* from the much cosier fantasy world of colonial daydream.

The use of gun-barrels to measure and evade the hostility of an alien land is the theme of the much shorter and less well-known sketch, innocuously entitled 'Bubbling Well Road'. Hunting wild pig, the narrator and his dog 'Mr. Wardle' unwisely enter a 'patch of the plumed jungle-grass, that turns over in silver when the wind blows, from ten to twenty feet high and from three to four miles square' (*LH*, 365). Looked down on from a distance, the 'patch' is a beautiful landscape; entered, it becomes a suffocating labyrinth whose single track leads inwards to a dead end haunted by strangely echoing laughter. Pushing his gun-barrels through the grass into chuckling emptiness, the narrator finds 'a black well so deep I could scarcely see the water in it', containing the corpses of unwary travellers. 'The laughing sound came from the noise of a little spring, spouting halfway down the well' (*LH*, 368). Crawling backwards through the grass and probing with his gun-barrels, he finds a sinister scarred native priest, and with the help of his gun and his dog ('Mr. Wardle hates natives, and the priest was more afraid of Mr. Wardle than of me') forces the man to show him the way out at gunpoint. 'Only my need for his services prevented my firing both barrels into the priest's back.' (*LH*, 369) Yet the narrator's horror is not really at the priest's devilish cunning so much as the Indian land itself, the jungle-grass that looks so seductively silvery when the wind blows yet is really a choking hot maze whose 'grass stems held the heat exactly as boiler-tubes do' (*LH*, 366) and the black well chuckling over its victims, from which only his probing gun preserves him.

The gun could be said to play a comparable role of mastery in 'The Mark of the Beast', in which the narrator and Strickland, the Indian expert, torture a mysterious leper with red-hot gun-barrels to save Fleete their fellow white from 'native' magic , which means that the weapon which is supposed to keep the user distant from its victim here brings the two into disgraceful intimacy. 'Although the Silver Man had no face, you could see horrible feelings passing through the slab that took its place, exactly as waves of heat play across red-hot iron – gun-barrels for instance.'(*LH*, 255–6). That the 'waves of horrible feelings' passing through the leper's slab of face should be replicated in the Englishmen's own weapon of mastery puts them on the same level with their victim and abolishes their technological superiority: the gun-barrels are simply red-hot iron, not a means of mastering a distant enemy.

For the great military advantage which guns offer is the power of rapid killing or wounding from a distance; and the more powerful the gun, the greater the distance that can be commanded. Use of guns implies a measuring eye, and for artillery, the capacity to measure and calculate degrees and distance – which is why the mapping of Britain and Ireland is carried out by the 'Ordnance Survey' ('ordnance' means 'field artillery' as opposed to 'small arms'). This originated in 1791 as a semi-military project directed by the 'Master-General of the Ordnance' in charge of artillery and engineering and carried out in England from 1840.[8] Yet the possession and use of those gun-barrels which look like such an obvious metaphor for the English colonizer's superior power over colonial India, turns out, in these much-too-close encounters with native land or people, to represent almost the reverse: a desperate hanging on to the insignia of mastery without in fact being able to master anything.

The nature of Kipling's colonial vision of a terrifying and hostile land which symbolically becomes the repulsive body of the conquered, can be seen with astonishing intensity in his own early account of a sacred place, the 'Gau-Mukh' ('Cow's Mouth')[9] in the ruined city of Chitor (the likely original of the 'Cold Lairs' in the *Jungle Books*). This first appeared in the Allahabad *Pioneer* newspaper, in 1887 as one of Kipling's 'Letters of Marque', a series of reports on his travels round independent states in Rajputana, written in the third person; a re-written version appears in the 1890 novel *The Naulahka*, co-written with Wolcott Balestier. Kipling calls himself an 'Englishman' whose travels in unvisited places give him an 'unholy knowledge' of the land (*FSS*, 203) far richer than that of 'globe-trotters' with their Baedeker guides. Awed by the splendour of the towers, halls and passages of Chitor and repelled by the 'slippery sliminess of the walls always worn smooth by naked men' (*FSS*, 98), he completes his visit by descending stone steps to the shrine:

> In a slabbed-in recess, water was pouring through a shapeless stone gargoyle, into a trough; which trough again dipped into a tank. Almost under the little trickle of water, was the loathsome Emblem

of Creation, and there were flowers and rice around it. Water was trickling from a score of places in the cut face of the hill: oozing between the edges of the steps and welling up between the stone slabs of the terrace. Trees sprouted in the sides of the tank and hid its surrounds. It seemed as though the descent had led the Englishman, firstly, two thousand years from his own century, and secondly, into a trap, and that he would fall off the polished stones into the stinking tank, or that the Gau-Mukh would continue to pour water until the tank rose up and swamped him, or that some of the stone slabs would fall forward and crush him flat.... And behind him the Gau-Mukh guggled and choked like a man in his death-throe. The Englishman endured as long as he could – about two minutes. Then it came upon him that he must go quickly out of this place of years and blood – must get back to the sunshine ... and the dak-bungalow with the French bedstead. He desired no archaeological information, he wished to take no notes, and, above all, he did not care to look behind him, where stood the reminder that he was no better than the beasts that perish. But he had to cross the smooth, worn rocks, and he felt their sliminess through his boot-soles. It was as though he were treading on the soft, oiled skin of a Hindu. As soon as the steps gave refuge, he floundered up them, and so came out of the Gau-Mukh, bedewed with that perspiration which follows alike on honest toil or – childish fear. (*FSS*, 101)

Harry Ricketts' recent biography of Kipling reads this 'moment of existential panic'[10] as an anticipation and possibly a source for Mrs Moore's moment of horror in the Marabar Caves: a confrontation with the Other represented by alien earth associated with a repulsive human body, which the Englishman can't comprehend or categorize. It seems to annihilate his history, taking him back to before A.D. (Anno Domini, 'the Year of Our Lord') by which his culture measures time; for the alien religion represented by the incense and flowers is stronger than his own. He feels he should not have come 'he had done a great wrong entering the heart and soul of Chitor'. He cannot apply the Western forms of knowledge and mastery – 'He desired no archaeological information, he wished to take no notes'. To be the object of archaeology the place would have to be safely dead, and it is alive with a hostile life; the pool may rise and drown him, or the rocks may crush, as if India itself – or herself? – were mutinying against the invader, as the sand resists Morrowbie Jukes by giving way beneath him.

The water 'trickling...oozing...welling' exceeds its containers, uncontrollably creating slime, like the 'trees sprouting' with a sinister life of their own that reminds him of his own body, of mortality. For the Gau-Mukh is sexualized in contradictory ways. On the one hand, the tank at the bottom of the hill with water trickling into a 'trough', and the 'glair' over the rocks, the slimy trail like a mucous membrane, sound like horrid female body fluids, and the threat of crushing and swallowing up the Englishman suggests the monstrous Kleinian mother who threatens to devour her son, taking him into her body of death (when the hero of *The Naulahka* visits the Gau-Mukh, its deathliness is actualized in a giant guardian crocodile who nearly snaps him up). But equally appalling is the masculine otherness represented by the 'loathsome Emblem of Creation' – i.e. the phallic Lingam – and the smooth rock whose resemblance to 'the soft, oiled skin of a Hindu' he can feel through the boot-leather of his protecting boot, just as the narrator of 'The Mark of the Beast' feels the leper's unclean skin through his own riding-boot. Surely the smooth naked skins of Hindus would not be so terrible unless they were also desirable? The whole experience of fascination and revulsion is well summed up by Julia Kristeva's description of 'abjection':

> A weight of meaninglessness, about which there is nothing insignificant, and which crushes me. On the edge of a non-existence and hallucination, of a reality that, if I acknowledge it, annihilates ....It is not lack of cleanliness and health that causes abjection, but what disturbs identity, system, order. What does not respect borders, positions, rules.[11]

This uncanny encounter with something both repulsive and fascinating, which one wants to reject and cannot because it is part of one's own identity, leaves the 'knowing' English writer baffled by an India which is unknowable just because it is much too close to home. That dilemma is very close to the anxiety articulated elsewhere in Kipling's writings that full comprehension of reality would be intolerable, 'lest we should hear too clear, too clear / And unto madness see!'(*W*, 614).

Yet Kipling's 'take' on colonial India is both too complicatedly various and too genuinely knowledgeable, as opposed to 'knowing', to be defined only by the opposition explored in this chapter between the Englishman stereotyping and cataloguing a 'knowable' Orient and a paranoid anxiety about the colonized 'Other' that finds its expression in horror-stories or Indian gothic landscapes. Although these oppositions would adequately contain 'The Strange Ride of Morrowbie Jukes', they have no space for classic stories like 'Without Benefit of Clergy' or 'The Bridge Builders', nor for the Indian societies represented in his greatest Indian fiction *Kim*. In order to read these it is necessary to look at other aspects of Kipling's writing: the idea of work and responsibility which drives so many of his colonial fictions; the ideal of masculinity which underpins the heroism of administrators and officers like George Cottar the 'Brushwood Boy' and is more subtly negotiated by the boy heroes Kim and Mowgli; and the approximation to 'vernacular' speech, both in the imagined language of Indians and the actual demotic of soldiers' Cockney, that allows his fictions to handle racial and class difference with a degree of ease and intimacy.

2

Imagining a Language: Kipling's Vernaculars

Vernacular *a.* and *sb.* 1601[f. L.*vernaculus* domestic, indigenous, f.*verna* a home-born slave, a native]. A. adj That uses the native or indigenous language of a country or district. 2. Of a language or dialect: That is naturally spoken by the people of a particular country or district; native; indigenous. 3. Of literary works: Written, spoken in, or translated into the native language of a particular country or people. B. *sb. 1.* The native speech or language of a particular country or district. 2. A native or indigenous language. 3. (*transf*) The phraseology or idiom of a particular profession, trade etc.[1]

INDIAN VERNACULARS: FAMILIARIZING THE FOREIGN

Difference of language marks off colonizer from colonized far more profoundly than skin colour. In Kipling's work, consistently with the word's etymology, 'vernacular' invariably denotes the native languages (usually Urdu or Hindustani) of colonized Indians, as opposed to English, the language of government and colonial authority. Recalling his early childhood in Victorian Bombay, he tells how 'we were sent into the dining-room after we had been dressed, with the caution "Speak English now to Papa and Mamma." So one spoke "English", haltingly translated out of the vernacular idiom that one thought and dreamed in.'(*SM*, 3). Because that 'vernacular idiom' (presumably Hindustani) which must have been Kipling's mother tongue, the first language he ever spoke, was the language of a subject race, his training as a 'Sahib' meant that he had to lose it. The reason why Kipling's loving parents sent him and his sister to suffer exile in England at the ages of five and three was the cultural imperative for children of their class and race to grow up speaking, thinking and dreaming in English – and not the halting English of Indian servants with their 'sing-song, *chi-chi* accents'[2], nor yet the fluent but accented English of educated Bengalis or Eurasians like Hurree Babu or Kim himself ('Oah yess,' *K*, 128), but the assured upper-class English tone and idiom of public schools, Pall Mall clubs and drawing rooms. Thanks partly to the harsh training that included learning much of the King James Bible by heart (a frequent punishment inflicted by his Southsea foster mother), Kipling's mastery of English would enable him to cross the linguistic divisions between the alien rulers and native ruled with seemingly effortless ease.

To imagine a language is, as Wittgenstein famously remarked, to imagine a world.[3] Kipling's grasp of the close relationship between language and social world which that aphorism implies, is made plain in that early letter to his cousin, written while he was still working as a journalist on the *Civil and Military Gazette*, advising the need to understand Indians 'as men with a language of their own which it is your business to understand; and proverbs which it is your business to quote... and byewords and allusions which it is your business to master; and feelings which it is your business to enter into and sympathize with', the object of this mastery being to ensure 'your' effective because sympathetic command: 'Then they'll believe you and do things for you'(*L* 1, 101). Kipling confirms this point by boasting how he successfully roused his Hindu printer to beat a deadline by first telling him in front of 'Mahommedan compositors' that a refusal would show him 'nearly as worthless as a Bengali babu' which stung the man's Punjabi pride, and later praising him for 'work[ing] like an elephant', icing the cake of flattery with the Punjabi proverb 'As is the shoulder of the elephant so is the weight of his labour' (*L* 1, 103).

There is an obvious analogy between the young man explaining how to master your Indian subordinates by 'little homilies' driven home by knowledge of their language and culture plus emotional shrewdness, and the writer of stories whose scope includes both the thoughts and speeches of colonial officials and their multitudinous vernacular-speaking subjects. To render these vernacular languages, which include Urdu, Hindustani, Pushtu (plus Arabic in 'Little Foxes' set in Ethiopia: *AR*, 1909), Kipling's stories deploy a stylized English idiom of his own with a deliberately archaic syntax and vocabulary whose speakers use 'thou', 'thee' and 'ye' for the second person singular and plural where modern English-speakers would say 'you', 'we be' for 'we are', and 'yea or nay' for 'yes or no', say 'bade' and 'wept' rather than the modern 'ordered' and 'cried', and even use the past-tense forms 'drave' and 'brake' for 'drove' and 'broke' – usages which were, even in Kipling's day, unknown outside the language of the King James Bible and William Morris' translations of medieval Icelandic. These archaisms also probably owe a good deal to the Victorian translations of the *Arabian Nights*, which Kipling as a child loved to listen to his 'beloved Aunt' reading 'as one lay on the big sofas sucking toffee, and calling our cousins "Ho, Son" or "Daughter of my Uncle" or "True Believer"' (*SM*, 12).

This fluent, natural-sounding archaic style is highly rhetorical, as is seen in its speakers' use both of the proverbs which, as he told his cousin, were so important in Indian conversations, and of allusive word-play which often has to be explained to English readers in brackets. So Mahbub Ali in *Kim*, on being told that his enemies 'all raged as though mad together' replies gleefully 'That is not so much *dewanee* [madness, or a case for the civil court – the word can be punned on both ways] as *nizamut* [a civil case]': (*K*, 202). Kipling's 'vernacular' speakers invent elaborate phrases for thanks or blessings, and even more elaborate curses like 'Go to Jehannum [=Hell] and abide there with thy reputationless aunt!' (*K*, 173), or 'May his sons turn Christian, and his daughter be a burning fire and a shame in the house from generation to generation!' ('Gemini', *ST*, 266). They often use vivid similes, as when a dismissed man describes how his English nemesis 'sat in the midst of three silver wheels that made no creaking, and drave them with his legs, prancing like a bean-fed horse – thus. A shadow of a hawk upon the fields was not more without noise than the devil-carriage of Yunkum Sahib.'('At Howli Thana', *ST*, 260).

Most of the above quotations of 'vernacular' speakers are taken from four early short stories narrated by Indian subordinates or outsiders in monologues addressed to a silent

'Sahib' listener in the early collection *In Black and White* (reprinted in *Soldiers Three*): an unscrupulous moneylender, an idle policeman sacked for dereliction of duty, a watchman guarding a river in flood, and the crazily vengeful horse-dealer of 'Dray Wara Yow Dee'. These compressed narratives and naïve self-revelations manifest the strong influence of Browning's *Men and Women* – not just in the revelation of their unsuspecting characters' minds through the way they tell their own stories or the role played by the silent listener, but in the exotic richness of their language, whose elaborate rhetoric represents a prose equivalent to the complex brilliance of Browning's poetry. Indeed these 'vernacular' speeches can at times rise to prose poetry, as when the speaker of 'Dray Wara Yow Dee' speaks of his longing for the hills of Afghanistan: 'There is a pleasant wind among the mulberry trees, and the streams are bright with snow-water, and the caravans go up, and the caravans go down, and a hundred fires sparkle in the gut of the Pass, and tent-peg answers hammer-nose, and pack-horse squeals to pack-horse across the drift smoke of the evening' (*ST*, 235). Later, when relating his mad quest for vengeance on his cuckolder across ravines and rivers and repeating his constant Urdu refrain, meaning 'all three are one', he evokes a nightmarish state of obsession:

> To the Uttock I went, but that was no hindrance to me. Ho! Ho! A man may turn the word twice, even in his trouble. The Uttock was no *uttock* [obstacle] to me; and I heard the Voice above the noise of the waters beating on the big rock, saying 'Go to the right'. So I went to Pindigheb, and in those days my sleep was taken from me utterly, and the head of the woman of Abazai was before me night and day, even as it had fallen between my feet. *Dray wara yow dee! Dray wara yow dee!* Fire, ashes and my couch – all three are one!

The effect of this combination of stylized, archaic language and syntax ('my sleep was taken from me' and 'even as it had fallen' for 'I could not sleep' and 'as though it fell'), formalized rhetoric, and word-play emphasized by italics or a bracketed English translation, is to evoke a world of unlettered, pre-industrial people – for few of Kipling's 'vernacular' speakers are literate; like Kim before the 'Sahibs' discover him they have to rely on paid letter-writers when they want to send a message. Unfamiliar with Western technology and laws, they may describe a tricycle with rubber wheels as a 'devil-carriage' and a railway train as a 'fire-carriage' ('At Howli Thana,', 'In Flood Time' *ST*, 260, 294) or passionately disregard British rule to pursue a blood feud ('Your Law! What is your Law to me? When the horses fight on the runs do they regard the boundary pillars?', 'Dray Wara Yow Dee' *ST*, 238). Yet they proudly possess a rich oral tradition, as manifested in their command of rhetoric and their love of proverbs, allusions and quotations, in an idiom both distant enough from modern English to signal cultural difference and easily intelligible to English readers – especially those familiar with the language of the King James Bible, as most of Kipling's original readers would have been from frequent experience of Sunday church-going.

Kipling's prose thus offers a seemingly miraculous entry to the speech and thoughts of people who are ordinary to themselves yet exotic to the English, like the old Indian living by a river who has never heard of Leander swimming the Hellespont, yet recalls how he long ago dared to swim the Great Flood to reach his secret lover. As the holy Gobind says, 'A tale that is told is a true tale as long as the telling lasts' (*LH*, x), and this verbal strategy represents a conjuring trick. Kipling has not so much 'imagined a language' and therefore imagined a world, as invented an artificial English equivalent to Indian language(s) and the minds and lives of those who speak them, inviting his readers to accept that artifice as a reality.

A similar idiom is used in the *Jungle Books* for the speeches of Mowgli and his animal friends and enemies, who talk with a skill and rhetorical vigour at least equal to that of humans: the Indian villagers whom Mowgli briefly joins, is rejected by and finally drives out of their homes, speak the same way, but with much less rhetorical verve. Thus Baloo, told by Mowgli that the *Bandar-log* [monkey-people] 'took pity on me', responds to this absurdity with contemptuous oxymoron: '"The pity of the *Bandar-log*!" Baloo snorted. "The stillness of the mountain stream! The cool of the summer sun!"' ('Kaa's Hunting', *JB*, 51); while Mowgli describes his enemy's outrageous lies with cheerful meiosis: 'And now...they are all sitting round Buldeo, who is saying that which did not happen' ('Letting in the Jungle', *SJB*, 80). Presumably because of the idiom's origin as an equivalent to 'native' speech, the Jungle People occasionally use

Indian words like *log* for 'people', or the Hindustani word for madness ('we call it hydrophobia, but they call it *dewanee* – the madness – and run'); while Mowgli, rejected by the Wolf-pack, tells them contemptuously that 'I do not call ye my brothers any more, but *sag*[dogs] as a man should' ('Mowgli's Brothers', *JB*, 4 and 38). Kipling thus turns the wild animals into 'Jungle *People*' (my italics), granting them speech, individuality and, where appropriate, wisdom like that of men, while at the same time marking off their world as separate from that of the English narrator and his audience.

By at once entering the minds of Indian men (and in the *Jungle Books*, the closed world of animals) and letting us listen to them – or more accurately, by *seeming* to do this – Kipling gives the illusion of undoing the curse of Babel, allowing his English readers to comprehend the strangeness of alien lives. This effect is elaborated in later stories where English officials find themselves entering the world of Indian lives, not as rulers but as companions or lovers. So in 'The Bridge Builders'(*DW*, 1898) the Scottish engineer Findlayson, architect of the Kashi bridge over the Ganges, is swept downriver by a great flood together with his foreman Peroo, and the two find themselves overhearing a *Punchayet* (meeting) of the gods of the Hindu pantheon in their animal forms as they debate whether to destroy the railway bridge as a machine-age insult to that ancient and terrible river-goddess Mother Gunga, or to disregard it as 'but the shifting of a little dirt'(*DW*, 32). The dialogue of the Gods is conducted in a formalized archaic speech: '"We be here", said a deep voice, "the Great Ones. One only, and very many. Shiv, my father, is here, with Indra. Kali has spoken already. Hanuman listens also"' (*DW*, 29). Since the Gods are (as they themselves remark contemptuously) thousands of years older than the white men's Christianity, their words must comprehend both the ancient Sanskrit from which modern Hindustani is descended and the contemporary language spoken between Findlayson and Peroo. This 'blurring' is made easy by the archaisms by which Kipling renders all Indian speech, so that the speeches of the Gods appear more solemn than but not essentially different from the exchanges between Peroo and Findlayson, the latter of whom is never seriously touched by his brush with India's numinous ancient night.

The 'vernacular' is much more seductive in John Holden's secret Indian household in 'Without Benefit of Clergy', where 'king in his own territory, with Ameera for queen' he follows Indian Muslim rules and customs including the ritual sacrifice of two goats at the birth of a son (thus covering his boots with blood and understandably shocking his colleagues at the English club). In the lovers' Urdu dialogues, the Englishman, whose exchanges with colleagues are formulaically slangy, ('Does that mean a wigging from headquarters?',) speaks with a lyricism equal to Ameera's, whether in joy – 'Yea. I love as I have loved, with all my soul. Lie still, pearl, and rest' – or in sorrow during their poignant exchanges after their child dies:

> 'Am I an alien – mother of my son?'
> 'What else – *Sahib*? Oh, forgive me – forgive...Do not be angry. Indeed, it was the pain that spoke and not thy slave.'
> 'I know, I know. We be two who were three. The greater need therefore that we should be one.' (*LH*, 151, 158, 154, 169).

It is moving and unexpected to find the man who 'could not declare his pain' in English (*LH*, 168), not only speaking with his Indian wife (as he regards her) on equal terms but finding this simple but telling figure of speech to define and comfort their shared pain. When he is speaking with Ameera, Holden enters a charmed world of direct feeling and eloquence that is otherwise closed to him, and that he will lose with her death. Similarly, an important part of the magic of the *Jungle Books* is the way we hear the 'Jungle People' speaking to one another in the language of orators while still remaining wild animals: '"Ye choose and ye do not choose! What talk is this of choosing? By the bull that I killed, am I to stand nosing into your dog's den for my fair dues? It is I, Shere Khan, who speak!" The tiger's roar filled the cave with thunder.' (*JB*, 6).

Even more flexibly than the 'Jungle People', the players of the 'Great Game' in *Kim* speak different languages and dialects at will, slipping from the formality of English to the ease and intimacy of 'native speech' (*K*, 181), as when Colonel Creighton wins Kim's confidence by his fluent mastery of the vernacular. When Hurree Babu congratulates Kim on his rescue of a colleague, the novel moves easily between three separate 'languages':

'I hear what you have done so well, so quickly, upon the instantaneous spur of the moment. I tell our mutual you take the bally bun, by Jove! It was splendid. I come to tell you so.'

'Umm!'

The frogs were busy in the ditches, and the moon slid to her setting. Some happy servant had gone out to commune with the night and to beat upon a drum. Kim's next sentence was in the vernacular.

'How didst thou follow us?'

'Oah. Thatt was nothing.' (*K*, 315).

This easy slippage from Hurree Babu's 'chi-chi' speech with its exaggerated imitations of middle-class English clichés ('our mutual', 'bally bun', 'instantaneous spur of the moment'), to the novelist's loving description of the sounds of a peaceful Indian night, then to Kim's fluent Hindi, and back again to the English-speaking Bengali's 'Thatt was nothing', produces *Kim*'s characteristic effect of maintaining an assured universal (i.e. English) perspective while delighting in Indian cultural, scenic and linguistic difference.

In Kipling's earlier stories, however, the relation between Standard English, colloquial English and 'the vernacular' is much more fissured and problematic. The 'Preface' to *Life's Handicap*, arguably his finest collection of Indian tales, defines the narrator as an intermediary between English and Indians, needed because 'the English do not think as natives do. They brood over matters that a native would dismiss to a fitting occasion; and what they would not think twice about a native will brood over till a fitting occasion: then native and English stare at each other hopelessly across great gulfs of incomprehension' (*LH*, ix). Given Kipling's habitual understatement, that jokily knowledgeable tone should warn the reader that those 'gulfs of incomprehension' can constitute a deadly abyss. So in the 'Return of Imray' an Indian servant confesses to killing his English master because 'he said he was a handsome child and patted him on the head; wherefore my child died. Wherefore I killed Imray Sahib in the twilight' (*LH*, 274). In 'The Mark of the Beast' the Englishmen can only deal with Hindu curse by torturing its instrument the leper; and in 'At the End of the Passage' Hummil's Indian servant shows an eerie understanding of the terror which killed 'this that was my master' (*LH*, 208).

39

Many of the stories in this collection make a point of contrasting the fluent, even flowery 'vernacular' idiom of Indians with the bluff colloquialism of English speakers, as in the very short but very telling story 'Little Tobrah' about a starving child acquitted (wrongly, we discover), of murdering his little sister. He is found stealing the uneaten grain in a horse's nose-bag and taken off by a shocked Englishman: '"Feed the little beggar, some of you, and we'll make a riding-boy of him! See? Wet grain, good Lord!"' (*LH*, 350). Once fed, the little boy tells the servants how smallpox killed his parents and blinded his sister, leaving the orphaned children to work beyond their strength, be cheated by a grain-seller (*bunnia*), lose their home and wander into famine country:

> 'I and the sister begged food in the villages, and there was none to give. Only all men said – 'Go to the Englishmen and they will give.' I did not know what the Englishmen were; but they said they were white, living in tents. I went forward; but I cannot say whither I went, and there was no more food for myself or the sister. And upon a hot night, she weeping and calling for food, we came to a well, and I bade her sit upon the kerb, and thrust her in, for, in truth, she could not see; and it is better to die than to starve.'
>
> 'Ai! Ahi!' wailed the grooms' wives in chorus; 'he thrust her in, for it is better to die than to starve!' (*LH*, 353).

By this point, Little Tobrah the beggar and criminal, has become a story-teller whose audience repeats his key line in a ritual sympathetic chorus. The brutal facts of starvation and murder are both softened by the women's response (itself a reminder that these miseries now lie safely in the speaker's past) and aestheticised by the skilful simplicity with which the boy tells of them; an English child talking like this would sound absurdly literary and precocious. The elegant parallelism of the climactic repeated phrase 'it is better to die than to starve' subtly redresses its own harshness, the uncontracted 'it is' (not the modern colloquial 'it's') and the repeated infinitive 'to die...to starve' sounding a note of formality and control in the face of desperation. The story is thus made both more exotic and less painful by its fluent old-fashioned idiom – not just in the obvious archaisms of 'bade' for 'told' and 'thrust' for 'push', but in the unusual syntax of 'on a hot night, she weeping and calling for food, we came': whose participial construction, resembling

40

the Latin ablative absolute ('these things being done'), suggests an inflected language with a different word order from that of English. The speakers of this language understand disaster fatalistically, as a normal part of life, as when the wives comment on the cheating grain-seller: '*Bapri-bap*... to cheat a child so! But *we* know what the *bunnia*-folk are, sisters' (*LH*, 351). Such things are clearly as normal and familiar to poor Indians as the hopeful custom of putting marigold flowers for the Gods upon the neck of the bullock to make it less stubborn. In this world of oppression, insecurity and famine, represented as always in Kipling's Indian fictions as an intermittent, unexplained disaster, the unnamed 'Englishman' can give Little Tobrah salvation and a second chance for life as his 'riding-boy,' precisely because this white *deus ex machina* is ignorant of and uninvolved in the catastrophes of 'native' life, in which the children were oppressed by the grasping native dealer, *not* the colonial Government demanding tax.

The hinted implication that the strength and power of the British rulers derives from their distance from Indian lives and customs as well as the wealth which allows them to be patrons to the needy, anticipates the much more emphatic handling of this theme in *The Second Jungle Book*, when Mowgli, having rescued his mother Messua from a murderous Indian mob, sends her to the protection of the English who are known to their Indian subjects as 'a perfectly mad people who would not let honest farmers burn witches in peace' ('Letting in the Jungle', *SJB*, 80). But this earlier story also emphasizes the Englishman's limitations, for though he can administer the forms of justice and find a place for the destitute boy, he knows little or nothing of what has really happened. The boy can tell his vernacular story to the grooms and their wives, because he knows that with them he is under the Englishman's protection, and yet safe from the English Law. And the Indian servants are familiar enough with hardship to understand the story and even to accept what the child has done, for none of Tobrah's listeners threatens to tell the Englishman that his new riding-boy has confessed to murdering his sister. In miniature, this story anticipates one of the great achievements of *Kim*, whose dramas are all between native speakers: to make the reader an honorary citizen of this hidden Indian world, knowing its laws, customs and speech.

41

DEMOTIC VERNACULAR

Kipling's writing 'in the vernacular' has another completely different dimension: his mastery of idioms that cross not racial and linguistic but class boundaries. No account of Kipling's vernacular usage can afford to neglect his use of demotic English slang, both in the cockneyfied *Barrack Room Ballads* and other poems 'spoken' by the private soldier, and in prose, the conversations of common men, especially the soldiers Ortheris, Mulvaney and Learoyd. (One might also add the comic German-English of 'Muller' in *Many Inventions* and 'Hans Breitmann' in *Life's Handicap*, the Scottish accents of the engineer McPhee in 'Bread Upon The Waters' [*TD*, 1904] and in poetry of 'McAndrew's Hymn', and the Sussex dialect speakers of the late stories 'Friendly Brook' [*D of C*, 1917] and 'The Wish House' [*DC*, 1926]). The demotic language of these poems and stories follows a long tradition of comic stylized speech, from Dickens via the nineteenth-century American humorists Bret Harte, Mark Twain, C.G. Leland of the 'Hans Breitmann Ballads', and Joel Chandler Harris of the 'Uncle Remus' stories – all of whom Kipling admired, especially Chandler Harris to whom he sent a fan-letter and a complimentary copy of the *Second Jungle Book* in 1895 (*L* 2, 217). (Another possible influence is Peter Finley Dunne's 'Mr Dooley' whose stagey Boston Irish wisdom ('Whin ye see one man hissin' 'miscreant' and the other 'thraitor', ye can bet they're two dimmycrats tryin' to reunite the party'[4]) sounds uncommonly like a more politically sophisticated Terence Mulvaney holding forth.)

But though American dialect humour certainly does celebrate variety of speech, it is worth noting that it does not so much celebrate difference as make a performance, however affectionately rendered, of mimicking the 'incorrect' departure of dialect from an accepted norm. The emphasis laid both by American humorists and by Kipling on the irregularity of dialect speakers, points to an important difference between his equivalent to Indian 'vernacular', a rhetorical yet classless idiom spoken indistinguishably by nobles and beggars, and the demotic slang of his English and Irishmen. This is obvious as soon as one compares, say, Little Tobrah relating his tragic story with Mulvaney recalling a battle with the 'Paythans':

'We opined out wid' the widenin' av the valley, an' whin the valley narrowed we closed again like shticks on a lady's fan, an' at the far ind av the gut where they thried to stand, we fair blew them off their feet.'

('With the Main Guard,' *ST*, 68–9)

Whereas Tobrah's Indian speech is represented by poetically archaic English, this uses a phoneticized transcription of irregularly accented spoken words. Mulvaney and the speaker of 'Gunga Din' *look* irregular on the page with their dropped consonants and mispronunciations – 'av' for 'of', 'thried' for 'tried', "eathen' for 'heathen' – as Kipling's Indians never do (unless they happen to speak English, like Hurree Babu's 'Oah. Thatt was nothing': *K*, 315). The irregularity of the soldiers' speech is emphasized in Kipling's poems when the speakers pepper their English with bits of italicized pidgin Hindustani: 'You 'eathen, where the mischief 'ave you been?/ You put some *juldee*[i] in it / Or I'll *marrow*[ii] you this minute / If you don't fill up my helmet, Gunga Din!' (*W*, 406). These emphatic irregularities and departures from the norm appear to correspond to Tony Crowley's Bakhtinian account of dialect being marginalized by Standard English,

> a monologic language which was thought of as pure, central to the English national life, superior to other languages, and carrying with it the mark of both rectitude and cultural status... It represented the linguistic embodiment of the authority of empire, and it sought to repress linguistic otherness by relegating all other languages to the state of non-recognition as forms of language proper.[5]

But this observation doesn't obviously apply to Kipling who, far from 'repressing' the linguistically 'other' speech of subaltern classes or races, makes their words integral to his fictions. Indeed, Kipling's rendering of working-class speech looks politically radical compared with the attitude of his contemporaries to working-class speakers in the late nineteenth and early twentieth centuries when, according to Crowley 'the figuration of the working class as unable to speak was a key trope', and 'the forces of monologism of the social order, which take

---

i   Be quick (Kipling's translation)

ii. Hit you (Kipling's translation)

standard spoken English, the language of the educated, to be "proper English", [had] the effect of silencing the working class by defining them as hopelessly inarticulate'.[6] It is the use of uneducated language in poetry that Robert Buchanan chiefly objected to in his attack on Kipling 'The Voice of the Hooligan' which finds Kipling's poems impossibly vulgar and uncivilized, 'cockney in spirit, in language, and in inspiration' with a 'disregard of all literary luxuries, even grammar and the aspirate. God, too, loomed largely in these productions, a cockney 'Gawd' again, chiefly requisitioned for purposes of blasphemy and furious emphasis.'[7] Kipling's sympathetic rendition of the voice of the coarsely aitch-dropping soldier can be read positively as a form of pluralist heteroglossia that enables the voice of the underprivileged, excluded from poetry by their low class and diction, to be heard – "It's Tommy this an' Tommy that' an' "Tommy, 'ow's yer soul?"/ But it's "Thin red line o' 'eroes" when the drums begin to roll'. (W, 399)

But given Kipling's firm assent to existing social hierarchies, it would be naïve to think that the inventing of an idiom for the Army private is the same thing as giving him a voice equal to Standard English. His conservatism does not only lie in what Isobel Armstrong calls Kipling's 'cunning populism ... celebrat[-ing] the resilience of the common soldier in colonial service with a patrician triumphalism',[8] making his soldiers say what conservative imperialists wanted to hear. The harshest criticisms made of the Empire in *Barrack Room Ballads* are in the complaints about the meanness of the pensions paid to the men who fought for it in 'Shillin' a Day', and the ingratitude of civilians 'makin' mock o' uniforms that guard you while you sleep' in 'Tommy'. The voices of monologues and ballads like 'The Road to Mandalay' and 'Gunga Din', which owe so much to the London music halls Kipling attended in 1891, and which themselves became favourite music-hall items, are not simple expression of demotic speech but a highly conscious *performance* of it for an appreciative audience; hence both their stylized and represen-tative effect. As Dixon Scott shrewdly observed in his 1912 essay, the price of the 'race and richness' of Kipling's demotic dialogue is the type-casting of its speakers: 'For dialect, in spite of all its air of ragged lawlessness, is wholly impersonal, typical, fixed, the code of a caste, not the voice of an individual.'[9]

44

I believe that much of Kipling's appeal for his lifelong admirer Bertolt Brecht lay not only in the fact that Kipling's poems speak a proletarian idiom, (Brecht was no Wordsworth desiring to write a humanist poetry in 'the language really used by men'[10]), but also in Kipling's self-consciously coarse and artificial imitation of the language really so used. Robert Buchanan's description of *Barrack Room Ballads* as 'a wild carnival of drunken, bragging Hooligans in red coats and seamen's jackets, shrieking to the sound of the banjo and applauding the English flag'[11] could well be an accurate description of the chorus of the 'Soldier's Song' in *Threepenny Opera*:

Soldaten wohnen	The Army's story
Auf den Kanonen	Is guns and glory
Vom Cap bis Couch Behar.	From Cape to Cutch Behar
Wenn es mal regnete	When they are at a loss
Und es begegnete	And chance to come across
Ihnen 'ne neue Rasse	New and unruly races
'ne braune oder blasse	With brown and yellow faces
Da machen sie vielleicht daraus	They chop them into little bits of
ihr Beefsteak Tartar.	beefsteak tartare ![12]

Unlike the Indian monologues of *In Black and White*, none of Kipling's English dialect speakers narrates a whole tale. The direct speech of the Indian 'vernacular' speakers needs no narrative intermediary because their own stylized, archaic English has done the explaining for them already, whereas the tales of Mulvaney and his companions are mediated by a civilian 'I', listening as an honoured guest of the soldiers; even 'On Greenhow Hill' (*LH*), though mostly told by the Yorkshire Learoyd, is framed by the omniscient narrator who begins and ends the story and at key moments comments on the speakers. The demotic speakers may have their own eloquence, especially when cursing – like Ortheris abusing the unfortunate new recruits: 'Well, you are a holy set of bean-faced beggars, *you* are' ('His Private Honour', *MI*, 130), or Mrs Sheehy putting a lifetime curse on Mulvaney: 'Clear-eyed you are? May your eyes see clear ivry step av the dark path you take till the hot cindhers of hell put them out! May the ragin' dry thirst that's in my ould bones go to you that you shall niver pass bottle full nor glass empty!'('The Courting of Dinah Shadd', *LH*, 65). But this speech is clearly demarcated from the main narrative's standard English. So in 'The Matter of a Private', about a hot-weather murder, when the miserable Simmonds' response to the bully's joke of training a parrot to call him 'Simmons, ye *so-oor'* (pig) – ' "I 'ear. Take 'eed *you* don't 'ear something one of these days" ' – gives little clue to the speaker's obsessional fury; and when we learn how 'fits of blind rage came upon Simmons and held him till he trembled all over, while he thought in how many different ways he would slay Losson' ('The Matter of a Private', *ST*, 80), the understanding of psychological vulnerability and the literary word 'slay' come from narrator, not the inarticulate Simmons. Similarly in 'The Record of Badalia Herodsfoot', when the curate entrusts the heroine with seventeen shillings to spend on the needy of the parish, the narrator knows her better than she knows herself:

> 'Ho yuss! 'Taint much, though, is it?' said Badalia, regarding the white coins in her palm. The sacred fever of the administrator, only known to those who have tasted power, burned in her veins. 'Boots is boots – unless they're giv' you, an' then they ain't fit to wear unless they're mended top an' bottom; an' jellies is jellies; an' I don't think anything o' that cheap pork-wine, but it all comes to something. It'll go quicker than a quartern o' gin – seventeen bob. An' I'll keep a book.' ('The Record of Badalia Herodsfoot, *MI*, 284)

However knowledgeable Badalia is about the expense of decent boots, the dubious value of cut-price port and the need to keep proper accounts when entrusted with money, it is the educated narrator who understands that she is one of the elect in whom burns the 'sacred fever of the administrator'.

The two forms of Kipling's vernacular, then, point in very different directions. The archaised 'vernacular', crossing the King James Bible with the 'Orientalised' English of the Victorian 'Arabian Nights', tends towards a classic realist 'transparency' that elides difference, offering readers a way to cross frontiers, not without noticing them – for the linguistic difference is foregrounded – but without the obstacles that exist in reality. This is what makes possible the imagined world of *Kim*, discussed in Chapter six, which appears to undo the curse of Babel by making its hero change languages as easily and as recognizably to the privileged reader, as he changes garments and identities. Conversely, the demotic language of *Barrack Room*

46

Ballads and in prose the tales of soldiers, sailors and Cockneys, by emphasizing its own irregular, fissured status looks forward to modernism. The deployment of coarsely demotic speech in serious poems like 'Danny Deever' or 'Follow Me 'Ome' in the 1890s was itself an innovation which would make possible later experiments like the pub conversation in Eliot's *The Waste Land* – and, very much later and in other hands, the far greater radicalism of *patois*, rap and dub poetry. Moreover, as I argue in more detail in Chapter seven, these demotic, formalized and thus deliberately artificial Cockney or Irish voices, all recognizable as 'Kiplingesque' yet none identifiable with Kipling himself, generate a modernist uncertainty and instability of meaning.

3

The Day's Work

I must work the works of him that sent me, during the day; for the night cometh, when no man can work. (John 9:4)

'Let the dirt dig in the dirt if it pleases the dirt' (*DW*, 32)

KIPLING AND THE POETRY OF WORK

C.S. Lewis's description of Kipling as 'first and foremost the poet of work'[1] clearly fits the monologue-poem 'McAndrew's Hymn' whose speaker finds the meaning of human existence in the working of his steam-engine – 'From coupler-flange to spindle-head I see Thy hand, O God / Predestination in the stride of yon connectin' – rod" (*W*, 120) and the tribute in 'The Sons of Martha', to the unsung heroes whose skill and endurance allow their fortunate fellows to take railways and electricity for granted: 'They finger death at their gloves' end where they piece and re-piece the living wires./ He rears against the gates they tend; they feed him hungry behind their fires' (*W*, 382). But Kipling's most far-reaching and nuanced exploration of man's destiny of labour and endurance is to be found principally in his prose fiction. In this chapter I examine the work ethic dramatized in two fictions: the novella *Captains Courageous* (1896), and the bleaker fable 'The Bridge Builders' (*DW*, 1898), which counterpoises confident English technological supremacy against the numinous, archaic world of Indian gods, in the context of other stories and poems dealing with this theme.

Kipling is fascinated, first of all, by manual skills of all kinds. Randall Jarrell wrote that 'if Kipling had written instructions on how to make a bed with hospital corners, or how to can gooseberries, I could read them with pleasure: as one of his characters says, "It was the tone, man, the tone!" '[2], a readerly fantasy which is plausible because Kipling's writing is so full of mundane tasks carried out with skill and despatch. When two Sussex woodmen deal with an overgrown hedge, 'Jabez ranged up and down till he found a thinner place, and with clean snicks of the handbill revealed the original face of the fence. Jesse took over the dripping stuff as it fell forward, and, with a grasp and a kick, made it to lie orderly on the bank till it should be faggotted'('Friendly Brook', *D of C*, 46). A ship's boy baiting the lines shows similar expertise: 'The hooks flew through Dan's fingers like tatting on an old maid's lap. "I helped bait up trawl ashore 'fore I could well walk", he said.'(*CC*, 75). Private Stanley Ortheris, showing off at target practice, likewise displays his expertise by an easy physical intimacy with his weapon: 'He weighed his rifle, gave it a little kick-up, cuddled down again, and fired' ('His Private Honour', *MI*, 147). The skills celebrated are not always manual; Kipling has equally admiring descriptions of an old blind miner saving himself and others in a flooded tunnel by a combination of attentive listening and tactile memory in 'At Twenty-Two' (*ST*, 287) and of the way Puck munches bread: 'He ate with a slow sideways thrust and grind, just like old Hobden, and like Hobden, hardly dropped a crumb' in 'Cold Iron,' (*RW*, 1909, 9). No doubt he would have written of making beds or canning gooseberries with equal flair and relish.

Kipling's animals too may show themselves to be virtuosi, like Kotick the seal 'backing water as a wave went over him, and steadying himself with a screw-stroke of his flippers that brought him up all standing within three inches of a jagged edge of rock'; while Mowgli's wolf brothers display similar mastery when they divide the cattle herd into bulls and cows by running 'ladies' chain fashion in and out of the herd, which snorted, and threw up its head, and separated into two clumps...No six men could have divided the herd so neatly'('The White Seal' and 'Tiger, Tiger !' *JB*, 106 and 88). What makes these actions admirable for Kipling is their combination of physical energy and control, a mastery which wild animals acquire by instinct but which humans have to learn by hard training.

Such enviable mastery confers authority on a person (almost always a man). A constant theme in Kipling's short stories is the narrator's respect for the working-class man who is an expert in his own field, like the lighthouse keeper explaining the way to tackle a strait in the Malay Archipelago – '"if you aren't full-powered, why it stands to reason you go round by the Ombay Passage, keeping careful to the north side. You understand, sir?" I was not full-powered, and judged it safer to keep to the north side – of Silence' ('The Disturber of Traffic', *MI*, 6). The narrator similarly respects Private Mulvaney's authority when reproved for incautiously poking a fire with Ortheris' bayonet: '"Fire takes all the heart out av the steel, an' the next time, maybe, that our little man is fightin' for his life, his bradawl'll break' ... 'Tis a recruity's thrick that. Pass the clanin' rod, sorr". I snuggled down abashed' ('The Courting of Dinah Shadd,' *LH*, 49). The point here is *not* democratic equality, (significantly, these working-class characters use the deferential 'sir' to address the gentry narrator,) but rather an intimation that the lower levels of the social hierarchy have their own authority. To ignore or despise an expert from a class below your own, as when the 'damned deevidend-huntin' ship-chandlers' on the Board of a shipping firm sack their engineer for telling them too bluntly that his ship needs expensive repairs and better rations for the crew ('Bread Upon The Waters', *DW*, 288), is to invite just and, anyway in a Kipling story, inevitable punishment.

Yet Kipling's profoundest admiration is not for practical skill so much as for the responsible exercise of authority. His greatest heroes are not manual workers but officials in charge of government and welfare: Scott in 'William the Conqueror' distributing rice during a famine without grumbling at impassable country roads, mutinous drivers, and his own malaria, 'things he did not find it necessary to report' ('William the Conqueror' II, *DW*, 219), or Orde the Deputy-Commissioner on his deathbed briefing his assistant to remit taxes in four villages – 'That's fair; their crops are bad' – in 'The Head of the District', (*LH*, 121). Similarly Findlayson and Hitchcock the civil engineers are heroes of labour who, in designing the bridge, negotiating contracts and masterminding their Indian work-force 'had been tried many times in sudden crises – by slipping of booms, by breaking of tackle, failure of cranes, and the wrath of the river – but no stress brought to light any man among them whom [they] would have honoured by working as remorselessly as they worked themselves' ('The Bridge Builders' *DW*, 4). Hummil in 'At the End of the Passage' refuses to apply for leave despite the hellish heat and an imminent mental breakdown, because he knows his work has to be done and if he goes, he would be replaced by a married couple, and 'it's murder to bring a woman here just now' (*LH*, 205). Such heroic dedication to duty is even occasionally found among women and Other Ranks. Badalia Herodsfoot, blinded and dying after her drunken husband's assault and yet finding strength to tell the parish worker that 'It's fourpence for Miss Imeny's beef-tea, an' wot you can give 'er for baby-linning' has a deathbed as heroic as Orde's ('The Record of Badalia Herodsfoot', *MI*, 107). And Findlayson's great labours in paper-work and directing men in 'The Bridge Builders' would be in vain without the practical skill of his Indian foreman Peroo. 'There was no one like Peroo, serang, to lash and guy and hold, to control the donkey-engines, to hoist a locomotive craftily out of the borrow-pit into which it had tumbled; to strip and dive, if need be, to see how the concrete blocks around the piers withstood the scouring of Mother Gunga'. Like Badalia, Peroo is a monument of integrity. 'No consideration of family or kin allowed Peroo to keep weak hands or a giddy head on the pay-roll. "My honour is the honour of this bridge," he would say to the about-to-be-dismissed.'(*DW*, 7).

To take such pride in your work defines any character as one of Kipling's elect. The work may well be un-thanked, as when the four English officials – doctor, surveyor, diplomat and engineer – persevere at the 'weary work' of administration in 'At the End of the Passage', risking assassination, cholera and sunstroke as a matter of course. It may not even be noticed: an early cynical story about Indian administrators warns that: 'Good work does not matter, because...another man takes the credit...Bad work does not matter, because other men do worse' ('Thrown Away', *PTH*, 17). Or it may be undone by official corruption or insensitivity, as when a pro-Indian Viceroy undoes Orde's dearly achieved legacy of law and order in 'The Head of the District', appointing the Hindu Bengali Grish Chunder De, M.A. as his successor to rule 'Mahommedan' tribes (*LH*, 125) and thus provoking the latter to unrest and rebellion. It may even lead to death, as it does for the doomed Hummil in 'At the End of the Passage'. Whether rewarded or not, the work must still be done because 'Man must finish off his work / Right or wrong, his daily work / And without excuses'. (*W*, 557)

The pride and consolation of these dedicated, un-thanked 'Sons of Martha' lies in their recognition by their peers – the expert inner circle which for Kipling represents the ultimate moral authority. The burdened officer knows that it is worth being overworked because 'there were men in the North who would know what he had done; men of thirty years' service in his own department who would say it was "not half bad"' ('William the Conqueror', *DW*, 218-19). Conversely, Findlayson knows that his colleagues will not condone failure: 'There were no excuses in his service. Government might listen, perhaps, but his own kind would judge him by his bridge, as that stood or fell.'('The Bridge Builders', *DW*, 20). To join this Inner Ring of overworked, incorruptible, implacable experts, it is necessary for a raw 'cub' to be licked into shape by acquiring the values hymned by the Glasgow engineer McAndrew: 'Law, Orrder, Duty an' Restraint, Obedience, Discipline!' (*W*, 126). As Lewis perceptively wrote, 'There is nothing Kipling describes with more relish than the process whereby the trade-spirit licks some raw cub into shape...Until he has been disciplined – "put through it" – licked into shape – a man is, for Kipling, mere raw material.' Lewis cites as evidence a passage from the 1891 political allegory 'A Walking Delegate', in which a vicious rogue horse (= a socialist agitator) calls the other work-horses to 'respec'...the dignity o' our common horsehood' and is answered by an old hand – or rather hoof:

> 'Horse, sonny, is what you start from. We know all about horse here, and he ain't any high-toned pure-souled child of nature. Horse, plain horse, is chock-full o' tricks an' meanness an' cussedness an' monkey shines...Thet's horse, an' thet's about his dignity an' the size of his soul 'fore he's been broke an' raw-hided a piece.'

Lewis comments that 'Reading "man" for "horse", we have here Kipling's doctrine of Man. This is one of the most important things Kipling has to say and one which he means very seriously, and it is also one of the things which has aroused hatred against him. It amounts to something like a doctrine of original sin'.[3] This is very shrewd, for the necessity of breaking in youngsters to work-harness *is* central to Kipling's thought. Even the playful *Just-So Stories* contain fables of domestic animals who try to resist their destiny of toil and end up punished for it by working harder than the others (the Camel), or being persecuted by men and dogs (the Cat). His own memoir repeatedly likens his own youthful experience of harsh discipline to 'rattling tins or firing under a colt's nose' or 'the curb that brings up a too-flippant colt' (*SM*, 11, 15). (Kipling's emotional investment in the idea of pain as the proper method of discipline misleads him here; cruel methods of training animals are counter-productive, and excessively 'raw-hided' [= 'whipped'] or frightened horses are notoriously vicious and unreliable.) Lewis, however, endorses Kipling's doctrine of discipline, agreeing that obedience to orders is necessary if the work of the world is to be done. 'If all men stood talking of their rights before they went up a mast or down a sewer or stoked a furnace or joined the army, we should all perish; nor while they talked of their rights would they learn to do these things'.[4]

Orwell, taking a similar line, gave Kipling credit for 'see[ing] clearly that men can only be highly civilized while other men, inevitably less civilized, are there to guard and feed them.'[5] Such insistence on the absolute necessity of work and discipline also goes far to explain why, despite his imperialist conservatism, Kipling was such a surprisingly popular writer in the Communist Soviet Union. He did at least take workers seriously.

But the duty or destiny of becoming the kind of worker praised by Kipling is not simply a matter of training and subjection to authority that anyone at all can undergo, for his Inner Ring of workers is also defined by class and race. In *Captains Courageous* the first words of approval for the hero when he accepts the captain's authority are 'You're white.' (*CC*, 32). In 'At the End of the Passage' an Indian who deserves promotion for 'work[ing] like a demon', is still only 'little Bunsee Lal' (*LH*, 189) whose opinion on his tasks is not sought. And for all Kipling's sympathy for the worker and the common soldier ('I came to realise the bare horrors of the private's life', *SM*, 56) and his praise of the N.C.O. in 'The ''Eathen' (*'And the backbone o' the Army is the Non-Commissioned Man!' W*, 453), Kipling's heroes are more often those who give orders than those who obey them. Of the bottom of the hierarchy, represented by the innumerable

Rivets in the allegory 'The Ship That Found Herself', he has little to say except the imperative 'Hold on' (*DW*, 92). When the rich boy in *Captains Courageous* comes to realize the labour and danger of dragging fish out of the sea by hard experience, the point turns out to be mainly that this training will make him a better commander of men when he grows up and inherits his father's industrial empire.

True, there is one moment in 'The Bridge Builders' when Kipling seems on the verge of acknowledging the claims to recognition of subordinate ranks and races. The Indian foreman Peroo's unease about putting the river 'Mother Gunga' between embankments is disregarded by the patronizing Findlayson:

> 'At sea, on the Black Water, we have room to be blown up and down without care. Here we have no room at all. Look you, we have put the river into a dock, and run her between stone sills.'
>
> Findlayson smiled at the 'we'.
>
> 'We have bitted and bridled her. She is not like the sea, that can beat against a soft beach. She is Mother Gunga – in irons.' His voice fell a little.

> (*DW*, 10)

Given that Findlayson's mastery will shortly be challenged by Mother Gunga in the form of a terrible flood that will wipe the complacent smile off his face, and quite possibly his bridge off the face of India, one can read this passage as 'placing' his racial and cultural arrogance, just as his human pride in his work will be 'placed' later in the story by the derision of the Indian gods. And since the long passage describing the multifarious processes of bridge construction quoted below (59) has already emphasized that the bridge is indeed the work of many sorts and conditions of men, both this exchange and the larger story potentially open up a space for the point made in Brecht's poem 'Questions from a worker who reads', about the elision of workers from historical records:

> Who built Thebes of the seven gates?
> In the books you will find the names of kings.
> Did the kings haul up the lumps of rock?
> And Babylon, many times demolished
> Who raised it up so many times?[6]

Kipling's story does not positively ask its readers to raise such questions. When, at the sounding of the alarm, the 'brown torrent' of men 'disappeared into the dusk of the river-bed, raced over the pilework, swarmed along the lattices, clustered by the crane, and stood still, each man in his place' (*DW*, 14), the ordered metaphorical 'torrent' threatened by the imminent literal one emphasizes how the brown people are controlled by the white men's disciplined command. Peroo himself is an aristocrat of labour, and the toil, anxiety and hardship which the story praises are those of the élite rather than the workmen who have suffered 'cholera... smallpox... fever... death in every manner and shape' (*DW*, 5) while hauling and hammering the bridge's component parts. That said, the potential space for questioning opened up within the story, both by the acknowledgment that these men exist and by the obvious shallowness of the Englishman's response to the Indian's perfectly valid 'we', makes Kipling a rather more complex 'poet of work' than might at first appear.

Complexity is not, however, the keynote of that most attractive of Kipling's celebrations of the work ethic, the novella *Captains Courageous* (1896). As a fable of education it is simple to a degree: Harvey Cheyne, the spoilt-brat son of a millionaire industrialist and a silly adoring mother, falls off the privileged liner and into the *We're Here*, a fishing schooner from Gloucester, Mass., where he is taught the values of hard work, integrity, self-respect and discipline. The crass teenager who despised the fishing-boats – 'Say, wouldn't it be great if we ran one down?'(*CC*, 4) becomes a reliable, experienced ship's boy with a job to do and pride in himself, returning to his parents transformed, a 'boy after his [father's] own hungry heart' (*CC*, 197). The interest of the story is Harvey's discovery of the delights and pains of work and of the freemasonry of initiate workers. As Mark Kinkead-Weekes says, 'Harvey is primarily there as a pair of ignorant eyes which gradually enact the process of seeing that Kipling expects from his reader'[7], as when he first sees the fishermen returning at sunset:

> 'I've never seen the sea from so low down,' said Harvey. 'It's fine.'
> The low sun made the water all purple and pinkish, with golden lights on the barrels of the long swells, and blue and green mackerel shades in the hollows. Each schooner in sight seemed to be pulling her dories towards her by invisible strings, and the little black figures

in the tiny boats pulled like clockwork toys.

'They've struck on good,' said Dan, between his half-shut eyes. 'Manuel h'aint room for another fish. Low ez a lily-pad in still water, ain't he?'

(CC, 33–4)

Clearly the young aesthete has everything to learn from his expert companion who knows the 'clockwork toys' as individual men and can gauge their catch at a glance, even at a distance. In this idyll of labour the open-eyed youth, eagerly receptive to experience in the Romantic tradition, is subjected to a demanding, but not harsh discipline. When he pitches cod into the hold his first evening, his back aches. 'But he felt for the first time that he was one of a working gang of men, took pride in the thought and held on sullenly.' (CC, 45) The next day, he learns what it means to land a hundred-pound halibut. 'He had seen halibut many times on marble slabs ashore, but it had never occurred to him to ask how they came there. Now he knew; and every inch of his body ached with fatigue'. (CC, 55)

Harvey is never bullied. He does get punched on his first day by the captain for insolence, but as Dan explains 'Dad did it for yer health' (CC, 28), and he does get names of ropes driven into him with blows, but realizes 'it was evidently all in the day's work' (CC, 70). On the other hand he is well fed, is paid a fair wage for an untrained boy, and above all enjoys companionship and respect from the crew and increasingly from the captain's son Dan. After a few weeks he feels that having a job to do on the ship is 'much better than being snubbed by strangers in the smoking-room of a hired liner' (CC, 106). When the ship is back in Gloucester and the great adventure ended, Harvey sobs 'as though his heart would break', and no one mocks him (CC, 179).

Even though the job is butchers' work – killing fish, cutting up and salting them – the ship Harvey tumbles into is a small utopia of hard work, mutual respect and kindness without softness. The captain-owner, Disko Troop, is a man of unmatched professionalism who, by his skill and knowledge, enables his crew 'for the fifth year running' (CC, 172), to fill their hold first of all the fishing-fleet and thus to return home first and get the best price for their cod. Disko's ship is a democratic place whose captain, first among equals, gives his orders with deceptive politeness: 'Don't you want to do so and so?' and

'Guess you'd better,' (CC, 118). His crew includes all sorts and conditions of men: Disko's own family, represented by his son Dan and his brother Salter, an Irishman, a Portuguese, a black Gaelic-speaking cook gifted with second sight, and Salter's unhandy protégé 'Penn', a casualty of those harsh natural forces which the fishermen endlessly contest and negotiate (Penn is actually a Moravian preacher who lost his memory after witnessing a dam-burst that drowned his wife and children). The men share the profits of the total catch in proportion to their own contributions which they tally themselves, and no one doubts their honesty: 'What's the sense of lying for a few old cod?' (CC, 42). This is not a pre-industrial world – the fish will eventually be carried on the railroads (some of which are owned by Harvey's father) to markets all over the USA – but the fishermen's methods are traditional, using only sail and oar. Fishing is done from the rowing-boats ('dories') by hook and line, and a man who catches 200 cod in a day does brilliantly. The world of steam trawlers and mile-long drift nets is very far in the future, and the fished-out North Atlantic of the twenty-first century not remotely imagined.

Although their catch of cod represents livelihood and a modest prosperity, the ship's kindly community is uncorrupted by market values; while they are at sea, money doesn't count among them. Their kindness to the lost Harvey and the vague, amnesiac Penn are matched by their unsentimental service to others in danger from the deep waters. When two stereotypically rash Irishmen anchor out of bravado over an underwater reef that is just about to 'break' in the swell, Long Jack rows up to cut their line just in time to save them from the 'foaming water, white, furious and ghastly' (CC, 159), and when the schooner *Abishai* is run underwater by its drunken crew, the *We're Here* immediately goes to help them – although the crew are frankly relieved to find no survivors: ' "Glory be!" said Long Jack. "We'd ha' been obliged to help 'em if they was top o' water" ' (CC, 98).

Danger and death are constant presences in this democratic pastoral, far more so than in any other of Kipling's books for children – quite apart from the routine butchery of fishing, which doesn't 'count'. Harvey witnesses death at sea on three occasions: first when the overloaded *Abishai* runs herself under ('even as the light passed so did the schooner. She dropped into a hollow and – was not,' CC, 98). Then a liner nearly runs down the *We're Here* and does destroy the *Jennie Cushman* without even knowing it, and the terrified Harvey sees not only the great ship bearing down on him but the remains of a boat and a man mangled by its propeller. Finally, after witnessing the sea-burial of a man killed during a storm, and accepting Dan's present of the dead man's sheath-knife, bought 'contrary to the general custom... at a sale of his kit', Harvey actually fishes up his body. It is a nasty sight 'erect and horrible... His arms were tied to his sides and – he had no face'(CC, 168), like an even more terrifying version of Wordsworth's early vision of the drowned man grappled up from Lake Windermere who 'bolt upright / Rose with his ghastly face, a spectre shape / Of terror even.'[8]

Some of these deaths and dangers are the result of human neglect or arrogance, like the foolhardiness of the Irishmen whom Long Jack saves from drowning themselves, or the drunken crew of the *Abishai* running the ship under – ' "That was liquor" ', Harvey is warned (CC, 101). But no skill or prudence could have turned away the liner that destroyed the *Jennie Cushman*, nor abolished the storm that drowned the Frenchman whose body Harvey fishes up. There are no limits to the sea's potential destructiveness, and only great skill and vigilance can keep ships fairly safe – which is why the names and uses of ropes are driven into boys with blows. The point is emphasized at the great annual Memorial Service at Gloucester, attended by all fishermen and their families, where the roll-call of the year's dead is ritually mourned: ' "14th February Schooner *Harry Randolph* dismasted on the way home from Newfoundland; Asa Musie, married, 32, lost overboard... 19th April, Schooner *Mamie Douglas* lost on the banks with all hands" ' (CC, 238). The catalogue of harsh reality makes Harvey's feeble mother collapse, whining ' "Why – why couldn't they put these things in the papers, where they belong?" ' (CC, 240). And all this human loss to put salt cod on the tables of the poor and halibut on the marble slabs of the wealthy.

Attractive and serious as this fable of redemption from frivolity by work and companionship is, it avoids asking the final reason for all this toil, danger and loss. The hard but rewarding work is presented simply as destiny for Disko and his crew, who show themselves men by accepting it and working as well as they can.

The work is apparently an end in itself; when Kipling does come close to examining the question of final ends, he becomes vague and contradictory, inviting C.S. Lewis' searching question 'How if this doctrine of work and discipline, which is so clear and earnest and dogmatic at the periphery, hides at the centre a terrible vagueness, a frivolity or scepticism ?'[9]

THE NIGHT WHEN NO MAN CAN WORK

Lewis' question applies with especial pertinence to Kipling's most elaborately extended fable of labour 'The Bridge Builders'. This begins optimistically, with the engineer looking proudly down at his almost-completed project:

> With its approaches, his work was one mile and three-quarters in length; a lattice-girder bridge, trussed with the Findlayson truss, standing on seven-and-twenty brick piers. Each one of those piers was twenty-four feet in diameter, capped with red Agra stone and sunk eighty feet below the shifting sands of the Ganges' bed. Above them ran the railway-line fifteen feet broad; above that, again, a cart-road of eighteen feet, flanked with footpaths. At either end rose towers of red brick, loopholed for musketry and pierced for big guns, and the ramp of the road was being pushed forward to their haunches. The raw earth-ends were crawling and alive with hundreds upon hundreds of tiny asses climbing out of the yawning borrow-pit with sackfuls of stuff; and the hot afternoon was filled with the noise of hooves, the rattle of drivers' sticks, and the swish and roll-down of dirt ... In the little deep water left by the drought, an overhead-crane travelled to and fro along its spile-pier, jerking sections of iron into place, snorting and backing and grunting as an elephant grunts in the timber-yard. Riveters by the hundred swarmed about the lattice side-work and the iron roof of the railway-line, hung from invisible staging under the bellies of the girders, clustered round the throats of the piers, and rode on the overhang of the footpath-stanchions; their fire-pots and the spurts of flame that answered each stroke showing no more than pale yellow in the sun's glare. East and west and north and south the construction-trains rattled and shrieked up and down the embankments, the piled trucks of brown and white stone banging behind them till the side-boards were unpinned, and with a roar and a grumble a few thousand tons more material were thrown out to hold the river in place. (DW, 1–3)

This lyrical prose-poem of labour is one of Kipling's great set-pieces, like the interior of the chemist's shop at night in 'Wireless', or the panorama of the Sussex downs seen from a motor car in 'They'. It is an intensely visual description, the narrator's gaze travelling over the bridge like a camera panning the piers, the railway line and the road above it defended by brick towers (and potentially by 'big guns'), and the great building site below and beyond. All the rhetorical strategies emphasize the magnitude and immediacy of the work, so that even the measurements of the bridge are slightly magnified by the style, 'seven-and-twenty brick piers' sounding more impressive than 'twenty-seven'. The 'hundreds upon hundreds of tiny asses' are not tiny at all, only dwarfed by their context , like the deliberately understated 'few thousand tons' of rock. Noises as well as sights are given (this movie has a sound-track): drivers' cries, engines grunting like elephants, trains shrieking and the stones falling 'with a roar and a grumble'. Individual tools and parts – the 'lattice-girder bridge, trussed with the Findlayson truss', 'footpath-stanchions' – are lovingly named, inviting us, even if we don't know what they mean, to pretend we do, and so to join the knowledgeable company of toilers. The bodily diction associated with the bridge – the ramparts' 'haunches', the 'bellies of the girders', and the 'throats of the piers' – all suggest the physical intimacy of the labourer with his work.

Yet conversely, the 'earth crawling and alive with...asses' and the metaphorical verbs used for the workers who 'swarmed ...hung...clustered' make one imagine them as ants or bees, suggesting how small they are in comparison with the great work. The image of a swarm of bees as an emblem of purposive activity goes back to Virgil's comparison, in Book I of the *Aeneid*, of the Tyrians building Carthage with bees in the spring (a potential irony here, magnified later when the works of man appear as a small affair beside 'the wreck of thy armies, Hanuman' [DW, 31] and are derided by the Indian gods). But now Findlayson, the bridge builder, looks 'on the face of the country that he had changed for seven miles.. and with a sigh of contentment saw that his work was good...raw and ugly as original sin, but *pukka* – permanent – to endure when all memory of the builder, yea, even of the splendid Findlayson truss, had perished'. The bridge which fills its designer with satisfaction, like that of God who created the world and 'saw that it was good' (Genesis 1:12), is also a reminder of man's Fall in being 'raw and ugly as original sin'. And the highly literary cadence of that last clause, contrasting with the Indian loan-word *pukka*, seems to allude to Prospero's warning at the end of *The Tempest* that 'the cloud capp'd towers...the great globe itself,/ Yea, all which it inherit, shall dissolve'[10]: a *topos* echoed by the final 'Riddle of the Gods', according to which the Gods like men are the stuff of dreams whose little life is rounded with the sleep of Brahm.

The challenge to Findlayson's bridge comes from India itself, in the flood which Peroo had superstitiously, and rightly, feared, threatening his whole *raison d'être*. When the river rises in anger and the bridge's defences disappear in 'spouts of foam', Findlayson can do nothing but watch helplessly and drug himself with the opium Peroo offers him. The register of the stories changes from realism to the romance of the 'vernacular' as the two dreamers are swept downstream and wrecked on an island where they witness a meeting of the Hindu gods in their animal forms, so that 'Mother Gunga' appears as a wrathful crocodile complaining that 'They have chained my flood, and my river is not free any more. Heavenly ones, take this yoke away!'(DW, 28–9). She has an ally in Kali the Tigress, the Goddess of death, but the other Gods are indifferent to the 'insult'. Indra the highest of the gods thinks it too trivial to notice:

> 'Does Mother Gunga die, then, in a year, that she is so anxious to see vengeance now? The deep sea was where she runs but yesterday, and tomorrow the sea shall cover her again as the gods count that which men call time. Can any say that this their bridge endures till to-morrow?' (DW, 30–1).

Ganesh and Hanuman feel a pitying amusement at the antics of the humans: 'It is but the shifting of a little dirt. Let the dirt dig in the dirt if it pleases the dirt' (DW, 32); Shiv fears no challenge: 'I have no anger; for when the words are said, and the new talk is ended, to Shiv men return at the last'(DW, 34), and Hanuman (thinking no doubt of his deeds in support of the hero Rama in the Hindu epic *Ramayana*), has a fellow-feeling with the humans

61

'remembering that I also builded no small bridge in the world's youth'. (*DW*, 31)

Yet the debate does not end here, with Findlayson's pretensions to technological mastery being dwarfed by the numinous divinities of the Hindu Pantheon, just as the ordered throng of men and animals at work on the bridge had been dwarfed by the sight of the wall of water bearing down on it. After the resentful Gunga has crawled back to her flood, Krishna, the only God to appear in human shape, tells the others that the new technology of bridges and railways does indeed pose a threat to their future. For these things represent a mastery of environmental forces to which humans were traditionally subject, which Hindu animism worshipped, and 'Now my people ... do not think of the Heavenly Ones altogether. They think of the fire-carriages and the other things that the bridge-builders have done' (*DW*, 40). Troubled by this news, the Gods ask Indra if it is true and are answered with the oracular 'Riddle of the Gods': 'When Brahm ceases to dream the Heavens and the Hells and the Earth disappear ... Brahm dreams – and till He wakes the Gods die not.'(*DW*, 42–3)

Kipling does not, in fact, let the forces of Ancient Night win out. The bridge survives, Findlayson forgets the whole thing ('the island was full of beasts and men talking, but I do not remember. A boat could live in this water, I think': *DW*, 44), and he and Peroo are taken off to safety in a local Rajah's up-to-date steam-launch. Moreover, when Peroo, the most intelligent person in the story, realizes that in daylight the terrible Gods mean nothing to Findlayson, he concludes that they can exist only because men dream them: 'Then it *is* true. When Brahm ceases to dream, the Gods go' (*DW*, 44). Not only the Ganges, but the gap of belief between Englishman and Indian has been bridged by English technology: Peroo the Indian sheds his superstition to enter Findlayson's own realm of materialism and technological mastery, and we last see him taking possession of the launch's steering-wheel and, in imagination, flogging the *guru* whose service he has outgrown. The dream of the divinities, whose vision reduced humanity to insignificance, has revealed itself as just that – a dream that is itself reduced to insignificance by the daylight reality of skill and labour. As Zohreh Sullivan says, 'the irony is clear; the gods exist as long as

Findlayson remains in his opium dream. And the colonialists exist as long as the natives remain asleep. Rationality, consciousness, enlightenment will gradually awaken the dreamers, and then the gods will die.'[11]

And yet these ironies do not still the question asked by Indra, the highest of the Gods: 'Can any say that this their bridge endures till tomorrow?' The story suggests that the real reason why men must attend to their duties is to avert their minds from an unimaginable eternity in which nothing they do can matter. The final significance of work seems to be for Kipling, as for Conrad's Marlowe, that it offers an escape from the nothingness of the night when no man can work, neither the colonial officer nor the native subaltern. Or, as his poem 'The Supports' has it, humans should be grateful 'for doing, 'gainst our will, work against our wishes – / Such as finding food to fill ever-emptied dishes,' because that keeps us sane:

Heart may fail, and Strength outwear, and Purpose turn to Loathing
But the every day affair of business, meals and clothing
Builds a bulkhead 'twixt Despair and the Edge of Nothing.

(W, 767)

The meanings of work in Kipling's writing are, then, neither single nor simple. Despite the scepticism at the heart of his doctrine of work, purposive labour is for him what gives meaning and energy to the lives of men (of women's work he has little to say). On one comparatively simple level, he enjoys and celebrates the processes of skilled labour, the mastery of techniques and the complexity of large-scale engineering projects. He also prizes work both for the shared pleasures of expertise and companionship known only to fellow labourers, as in the all-male idyll of *Captains Courageous*, and for the harsh discipline to which workers are subjected. The significance of his emphasis on the pain and discipline of work as well as the satisfaction of skills mastered can be clarified by comparing Kipling with the analysis of his near-contemporaries in Morag Shiach's recent important study *Modernism, labour and selfhood*. Shiach identifies the late nineteenth century, when Kipling was writing the works I discuss here, as 'the period when work begins to be grasped as the defining aspect of human individuality', and shows how, for these thinkers, 'labour is

63

understood as the energy of will, the process of growth and creativity that drives both the individual and the human species.'[12] For Kipling, labour is not so much a process of human creativity or (except perhaps in *Captains Courageous*) of growth, as of discipline and defence: a literal defence against the hostile natural forces personified by 'Mother Gunga': both a great river in furious flood and a devouring beast, and a psychological defence against both depression and 'the Edge of Nothing' and unmanly softness. And because he prizes work for its harsh training of men in the military virtues of strength, discipline and endurance, his celebration of labour also belongs to the idealization of masculinity discussed in the following chapter.

4

Being a Man

> Yours is the world and everything that's in it,
> And – which is more you'll be a Man – my son!
> 'Man goes to Man at the last.'

(SJB, 80)

Being a White Man was, as Edward Said wrote, 'an idea and a reality. It involved a reasoned position towards both the white and the non-white worlds. It meant in the colonies speaking in a certain way, behaving according to a code of regulations, even feeling certain things and not others. It meant specific judgments, evaluations, gestures. It was a form of authority before which nonwhites, and even whites themselves, were expected to bend.'[1] This imperial masculinity (or 'manliness') was defined as strength, authority and above all control: the control over subordinates earned by the White Man's (or the White Officer's) strength and knowledge, the control over nature exerted by English technological superiority, and above all the White Man's self-control that can 'force your heart and nerve and sinew / To serve your turn long after they are gone./ And so hold on when there is nothing in you / Except the will that says to you, "Hold on !"'(*W*, 556). That, anyway, is the ideal, acutely described by a catty Virginia Woolf as 'Mr. Kipling's officers who turn their backs; and his Sowers who sow the Seed; and his Men who are alone with their Work; and the Flag – one blushes at all these capital letters as if one had been caught eavesdropping at some purely masculine orgy'.[2]

Such manliness is certainly preached in several Kipling poems, notably 'The White Man's Burden', 'If' and 'The 'Eathen', and celebrated in fictions such as 'Only a Subaltern', 'The Brushwood Boy,' 'The Tomb of his Ancestors' and 'His

Private Honour'. Yet, as the post-colonial commentators Joseph Bristow in *Empire Boys* and Zohreh Sullivan in her study of Kipling have pointed out, the ideal of masculine authority in Kipling's stories is always in danger of subversion by weakness in young Englishmen destined to rule. Bristow and Sullivan argue forcefully that the colonial fantasy of controlled rational masculinity has to define itself not only against the unruly 'natives' but against the subject's own unmanly weakness. This feminine shadow-self can be subjected to the authority of control but never abolished, remaining a constant threat to the official masculine ideal. Hard-earned victory over weakness is indeed often the point of these stories; if the supposedly strong characters weren't also vulnerable, they would hold little narrative or psychological interest.

The idea of manhood, then, always implies the existence of its opposite. Masculinity must be defined against the feminine and/or the unmanly, and man as the universal subject must be defined against the inhuman and/or the bestial. Thus Mowgli in the *Jungle Books* is rejected by the wolves whom he regards as his brothers for being a man, but then finds that his humanity gives him power over the beasts to become 'Master of the Jungle' at least until puberty compels him to leave it. This latter notion of 'being a man' as opposed to 'being a White Man', which I discuss in the last part of this chapter, has interested post-colonial commentators on Kipling's fiction less than the tenets of imperialist masculinity, but is nonetheless an important aspect of his 'take' on human identities.

The definition of Kipling's ideal of 'being a man' is a complex matter. Virginia Woolf's statement that Kipling has 'not a spark of the woman in him'[3] is uncharacteristically crude and misleading. Though the young Rudyard would doubtless not have thanked his mother had he known that she wrote to his headmaster that the boy had 'a great deal of the feminine in his nature'[4], her insight is borne out not only by the ambiguities noticed by Bristow and Sullivan but politically by Kipling's chivalrous championing of Indian women , his 'pet subjects' as a journalist being infant marriage and enforced widowhood that forced women into prostitution.[5] Despite the obvious anti-feminism of tags like 'a young man married is a young man marred' (*ST*, 170) and 'A woman is only a woman, but a good

66

cigar is a smoke'(W, 40), his writing shows it has much sympathy with women's troubles, including their sexual transgressions, even if its notion of women's lives is largely limited to the conventionally feminine sphere of love, marriage and maternity.

In Kipling's fiction, the all-male worlds evoked seem to need a female presence mainly to define themselves against, and/or to escape from. For all the sentimentality of *'Mother O'Mine'* ('If I were hanged on the highest hill / Mother o' mine, mother o' mine! / I know whose love would follow me still': W, 638), motherhood in his work tends to mean, on the one hand, a constrictingly fussy social world, and on the other, the untameable hostility of the natural world which it is a man's part to outwit and endure. This duality is obvious in *Captains Courageous*, whose happy all-male camaraderie allows the boy Harvey to escape from the neurotic ineffectual mother who 'lived in fear of breaking his spirit' (CC, 15) into a world of disciplined masculine strength and skill, pitted against the great mother-ocean that threatens death while promising plenty. The sea's maternal ambivalence is emphasized at the start when the boy falls off the liner and 'a low grey mother-wave swung out of the fog, tucked Harvey under one arm, so to speak, and... the great green closed over him' (CC, 9). The sinister femininity of that 'mother-wave' anticipates the vision of the sea in the 'Harp-Song of the Dane Women' who fear they will lose their men to the 'old-grey Widow-maker': 'She has no strong white arms to hold you / But the ten-times-fingering weed to hold you / Out on the rocks where the tide has rolled you' (W, 528). Much later Harvey witnesses the sea's devastating femininity in the fury of the 'Virgin' rock 'breaking' in a swell: 'There was a deep sob and a gathering roar, and the Virgin flung up a couple of acres of foaming water, white, furious and ghastly' (CC, 159). And this image of the ocean as *femme fatale* is only the most extreme instance of feminized, threatening nature: like the engulfing terror of the 'Gau-Mukh' ('Cow's Mouth') shrine and other treacherous Indian sites that yield underfoot, discussed in Chapter Two, or the vengeful Mother Gunga and her fellow Goddesses Kali (Destruction) and Sitala (Smallpox), who unlike the more tolerant male Gods want to destroy bridge and people alike so as to keep the humans in proper awe of 'Us' in 'The Bridge Builders'.

67

That said, the ideal of masculinity is not a simple matter of heroic man mastering or outwitting a symbolically feminized nature. The complex nature of the masculine ideals explored in Kipling's work can be seen by examining two stories that dramatize and explore different ways of 'Being a Man': 'The Brushwood Boy', about the empire-building young Major Cottar whose identity is divided between disciplined daytime success and the freedom of his night-time dreams, and 'His Private Honour' which explores masculinity and class through a drama of tensions between officer and man, paralleled by equally complex tensions between experienced rankers and raw recruits.

In 'The Brushwood Boy', the final story of *The Day's Work*, George Cottar (named presumably for St George of England) first appears as a child of six 'telling himself stories as he lay in bed' which lead into a dream-world in which 'gilt-and-green iron railings, that surrounded beautiful gardens, turned all soft, and could be walked through' (*DW*, 361–2), containing a little girl who looks like Alice in Wonderland. Childhood ended, he attends a public school which is 'not encouraged to dwell on its emotions, but rather to keep in hard condition, to avoid false quantities, and to enter the army direct' (*DW*, 367). Here he flourishes, eventually 'blossoming into full glory as head of school, ex-officio captain of games, head of his house'. School is followed by a commission 'in a first-class line regiment' where he distinguishes himself by sportsmanship, study of tactics, and a gift for handling the men whom he successfully distracts from drink and gambling by teaching them clean-living boxing and wrestling: 'Oh, I sweated the beef off 'em, and then I sweated some muscle on to 'em. It was rather a lark'. This model officer 'seemed to know by instinct when and where to head off a malingerer; but he did not forget that the difference between a dazed and sulky junior of the upper school and a bewildered, browbeaten lump of a private fresh from the depot is very small indeed.' (*DW*, 370, 372). His virtue, his athletic prowess and his purity earn him the nickname 'Galahad', Tennyson's virgin knight who proclaimed 'My strength is as the strength of ten / Because my heart is pure'[6], though many women pine for him and at least one attempts a seduction which he is too innocent to understand.

Meanwhile, unknown to anybody but himself, Georgie at night inhabits his childhood land of dream, entered by 'a road that ran along a beach near a pile of brushwood' where a lamp shines on 'dark purple downs inland' (DW, 377). From here he sets out on a journey by a clockwork steamer that takes him to a 'Lily Lock' at the world's end and a place of instability from which he is rescued by an unknown companion who brings him back by a 'Thirty-Mile Ride' to the brushwood pile. The dreams sometimes separate him from his companion, 'a little girl in strapped shoes with her black hair combed back from her forehead' or threaten the two of them with the malignity of sinister undefined beings called 'They' or a 'Sick Thing' that portends 'some waiting horror'(DW, 380), but the pair always survive and find their way back to the brushwood pile.

Georgie Cottar gets to know this dream-country well enough to think of mapping it when his regiment is sent on a 'very ugly war' on the border (of India, presumably). Needless to say, his highly-trained troop distinguishes itself, and Cottar is promoted to 'brevet- major' and awarded the Distinguished Service Order. He also gets a year's leave to be spent in England at his family's country seat, which delights him: 'Perfect! Perfect! There's no place like England when you've done your work.'

'That's the way to look at it, my son.' After this paternal approval, Georgie's mother comes to 'tuck him up for the night And they talked for a long hour, as mother and son should, if there is to be any future for our Empire'. Satisfied that her son is still a virgin, the mother sets about organizing a house-party for him but of course he isn't tempted by its noise and racket. Then comes a family friend with a musical daughter of good family, naturally, and heiress to a fortune: 'Oh, Miriam's a dear girl.' Georgie is dubious:

'Sounds Jewish – Miriam'
'Jew! You'll be calling yourself a Jew next. She's one of the Herefordshire Lacys. When her aunt dies –' (DW, 389, 392).

Too naïve to realize how eligible the girl is, Georgie goes fishing to avoid her, arriving home just in time to hear her 'full, true contralto' singing a song about the geography of his own dream-country and the 'City of Sleep'. In the morning he recognizes the dark-haired beauty as his dream-companion, the little girl; they ride together, he makes himself known and the two ecstatically declare themselves lovers. End of story.

This, all too plainly, is a tale of disciplined daytime masculine virtue rewarded by unproblematic access to night-time feminine freedom, otherwise known as having your disciplinary cake and eating it. Georgie, the obedient pupil, clean-living athlete and military defender of Empire, owes his virtues and his success to a training which 'had set the public-school mask upon his face, and had taught him how many were the "things no fellow can do"' (DW, 368); yet the sexual and creative life represented by his dreams not only remains intact but is rewarded by the discovery that his dream-companion is also his ideal bride, the girl both of his dreams and his parents' daydreams.

Though the story centres very obviously on psychic division, this takes a boringly un-threatening form. Georgie's emotional life is happily and miraculously split into the all-male world of school and Indian Army where he achieves his career of predictable success (the cynical young narrator who wrote that 'good work does not matter because no one notices it' [PTH, 17] is silent here), and a night-time realm of chaotically exciting dreams governed by desires conventionally defined as feminine, shared with his literal and figurative soul-mate Miriam. When Zohreh Sullivan interprets the boy's dream-life as a potentially subversive 'obsession with the private and unconscious as a source of terror and fascination', arguing that 'the schizophrenic fragmentation of this text into the political world of action, war, colonial discipline and the sexual world of dream, desire, freedom and fear is repeated in both the form and the ideological content'[7], she makes 'The Brushwood Boy' sound much more interesting than it is. For, in the construction of Georgie's splendid masculinity, nothing important is sacrificed. The story does toy very briefly with otherness – not otherness of class and race in the Army, where Cottar treats the men he commands as junior boys and the colonized 'natives' do not appear, but otherness of race and gender in Miriam the dream-girl who might be Jewish but, of course, isn't. Those night-time dreams, far from threatening his daytime world, offer a refuge from its sexual temptations and an *entrée* to fulfilment in which he doesn't even have to court his lover because she instantly recognizes that 'You're the Boy my Brushwood Boy and I've known you all my life!' (DW, 402).

Whereas Major George Cottar belongs to a world of country houses and the 'Herefordshire Lacys', 'His Private Honour' deals with the world of the common soldier. It starts with the arrival of a batch of raw recruits being mocked by Private Ortheris for being dirty, untrained and (in one case) Jewish. The narrator explains approvingly that this is all part of their training: 'There is no scorn so complete as that of the old soldier for the new. It is right that this should be so. A recruit must learn first that he is not a man but a thing, which in time, and by the mercy of Heaven, may develop into a soldier of the Queen.' (*MI*, 130) After a poor performance at drill, the recruits are beaten by Private Learoyd who 'thrashed them one by one, without haste but without slovenliness; and the older soldiers took the remnants . . . and went over them in their own fashion.' (*MI*, 131). They then perform so badly on parade that the Colonel sends them back to squad-drill at the detested Fort Amara, which means more verbal and physical attacks from the old hands. The narrator watches them drill awkwardly under the nervous young Lieutenant Ouless who first swears and then lashes out with his riding-cane at the nearest soldier, ripping the tunic off the sturdy shoulders of blameless Private Ortheris. This rash act could lose Ouless his commission, but for the other man's loyalty and presence of mind. Despite the public, unmerited disgrace ('after seven years' service and three medals, he had been struck by a boy younger than himself!' *MI*, 148). Ortheris pretends that the ripped tunic is his own fault. The abashed Ouless then, most implausibly, asks the civilian narrator's advice and is preached an even less plausible sermon on self-reliance: 'He had a papa and mamma seven thousand miles away, and perhaps some friends. They would feel his disgrace, but no one else would care a penny'(*MI*, 142). The troubled boy walks off one way, and Ortheris goes another to sulk and work off his temper on the unfortunate recruit 'Samuelson', scattering the man's possessions in the dirt and kicking him when he tries to pick them up – thus laying 'Samuelson' open to more trouble from the NCOs.

This drama arouses amused sympathy in the narrator, who wonders how Ouless will deal with the matter and whether he will compound his sin by tipping Ortheris. Not so; when Ouless is next seen, a fortnight later, he is visibly 'a free man and an

71

officer' in command of a transformed squad of confident men at target practice, advising them to model their shooting on Ortheris. The narrator then hears from Ortheris how the young man ('´E's a gentleman. 'E's an officer too', *MI*, 148), offered him a private boxing-match to settle the score, and how his honour was satisfied by landing a blow 'on the nose that painted 'is little aristocratic white shirt for 'im,' – even though Ouless won the fight. The moral is pointed in a loaded exchange:

> 'It was your right to get him cashiered if you chose,' I insisted.
> 'My right!' Ortheris answered with deep scorn. 'My right! I ain't a recruity to go whinin' about my rights to this and my rights to that, just as if I couldn't look after myself. My rights! 'Strewth Almighty! I'm a man.'

(MI, 148–153).

This story has three intertwined strands, of which the two most obvious are the struggle of Private Ortheris to retain his pride after being struck in public and the eventually successful attempt by Lt. Ouless to achieve a true officer's authority, the similarity of the two names underlining the interdependence of these dramas. Third, and ideologically central, is the transformation of whining 'recruities' into seasoned soldiers like Ortheris who can proudly claim 'I'm a man!' Being a 'man' in this sense means being strong enough both to despise the rule-book because you can fight your own corner and to take punishment, whether deserved or not, without complaint. Such proudly self-respecting manhood implies the acceptance of social hierarchies, for the story is emphatically anti-democratic. True, Ouless offers Private Ortheris the opportunity to avenge his injury by fighting it out man to man, outside of the Army's boundaries; but of course it's not the private who wins. ''E wasn't so strong as me, but he knew more', says Ortheris (*MI*, 151), proudly displaying the gap where an eye-tooth was knocked out by the officer's left hook.

The title's theme of 'private honour' applies, then, to officer and man: Ortheris whose pride is mollified by the privilege (not the right) of private combat, and Ouless who proves himself a man of honour, first by his delicacy towards the affronted Ortheris (he neither ignored his own misdeed nor tried to buy the injured man off) and later by standing up to him in a fistfight. Ortheris' account of his opponent's anxious courage (''E sez to 'imself, more than to me, "I've got to go through it alone, by myself!" 'E looked so queer for a minute that I thought the little beggar was goin' to pray', *MI*, 151), prepares the reader for the narrator's satisfied verdict 'It was all right. The boy was proven' (*MI*, 153). In the background to these intertwined stories are the dimly-glimpsed recruits being knocked into shape and emerging as 'men made over again wearing their helmets with the cock of self-possession, swinging easily, and jumping to the word of command' (*MI*, 147). We are thus given to understand that the beatings and mockeries were all for their own good, training them to be like the disciplined Private Ortheris whose pride in being a 'man' is that he can stand up for himself.

The narrator's emphatic approval of this routine brutality was memorably attacked by C.S. Lewis, who commented on the account of Learoyd beating the recruits for their own good that 'Kipling seems quite unaware that bullying is an activity which human beings *enjoy*. We are given to understand that the old soldiers are wholly immune from this temptation; they threaten, mock and thrash the new recruits only from the highest possible motives. Is this naivety in the author? Can he really be so ignorant? Or does he not care?'[8]

The answers to these questions are almost – but not quite – a simple: Yes, he doesn't care and No, he is not ignorant.[9] Harsh discipline gets frequent praise in Kipling's work; even in the relatively gentle *Captains Courageous*, boys have the names and uses of the ship's ropes beaten into them, evidently with the narrator's approval. And despite the sympathy for vulnerable youths shown in 'Thrown Away' or 'In the Matter of a Private', part of Kipling's writing plainly *does* identify with and enjoy the idea of rough men bullying their victims. The narrator's evident satisfaction in the methodical thrashing of the bewildered recruits resembles the sadism so memorably – and not unjustly – mocked in Max Beerbohm's devastating parody 'P.C. X. 36' in which the usual Kipling 'I' plays sycophantic audience to a brutal policeman who arrests Father Christmas for suspected burglary and beats him up, 'and the kick that Judlip then let fly was a thing of beauty and a joy for ever'.[10] Moreover, the approved brutality of 'His Private Honour' is compounded by the anti-semitic scapegoating (not noticed by Lewis), of

'Samuelson', the only man in the story with no 'private honour'.
The bullying starts when a contemptuous Ortheris first sees the
new men:

> 'Fried fish an' whelks is about your sort. Blimey if they haven't
> sent some pink-eyed Jews too. You chap with the greasy 'ed, which
> o' the Solomons was your father ?'
> 'My name's Anderson,' said a voice sullenly.
> 'Oh, Samuelson ! All right, Samuelson ! An 'ow many o' the likes o'
> you Sheenies are comin' to spoil B Company ?'
>
> (*MI*, 130).

The nickname defines this man whose Hebrew name (which
would certainly not be 'Samuelson') we never learn, and who is
not heard to speak again in the story, his role being simply to be
victimized. When Ortheris takes out his shame and anger at
having been hit in public by persecuting the Jew, it is not the
victim but the bully for whom the narrator feels sympathy and
anxiety: 'Learoyd . . . must have been a great comfort to Ortheris
– almost as great a comfort as Samuelson, whom Ortheris
bullied disgracefully. If the Jew opened his mouth in the most
casual remark Ortheris would plunge down it with all arms and
accoutrements, while the barrack-room stared and wondered.'
(*MI*, 145).

This is Kipling's 'knowing' narrator at his moral and
ideological worst. Unlike those wondering Tommies, *he* understands and sympathizes with Ortheris taking out his temper on
the other man, and invites us to join him – for although the
phrase 'bullied him disgracefully' looks at first glance like
condemnation, it carries the sly intimation 'But you can
understand him, can't you?' Whereas 'dishonourable' is always
a serious condemnation in Kipling's writing, 'disgraceful'
implies unorthodoxy rather than sin – as when at the end of
'The Mark of the Beast' the narrator and Strickland are seized
with cathartic laughter at the thought that 'we had disgraced
ourselves as Englishmen for ever' (*LH*, 258). The contrast with
Ortheris' lapse into resentful class-consciousness for which he is
reproached by the narrator and (off-stage) Mulvaney, is striking:

> 'I'm a private servin' of the Queen, an' as good a man as 'e is,' I
> sez, 'for all 'is commission an' is airs an' 'is money,' sez I.'
> 'What a fool you were,' I interrupted. Ortheris, being neither a

menial nor an American, but a free man, had no excuse for yelping. 'That's exactly what Terence said.'

(MI, 152)

Yet when Ortheris relates how 'I give Samuelson a little more trouble with 'is kit...I give 'im one or two for 'imself, and arxed 'im very polite to 'it back,' (MI, 150), nobody tells him he's a petty-minded brute for taking out his bad temper on a helpless man. That 'discovery for literature of the underdog' for which Craig Raine praised Kipling[11] is conspicuous by its absence; 'Samuelson' forfeits sympathy simply by being vulnerable and a Jew, his point of view remaining invisible. (If he had fought back, Ortheris would presumably forgive his Jewishness; Samuelson would then replicate Ortheris' own happy ending by graduating from Other as victim to Self as a potential bully, happy to avenge his own grievances on the next lot of unfortunates).

This unthinking racism – so much the more unpleasant for clearly reproducing common attitudes and not being intended with any particular malice – tempts me to misquote Kipling's own lines: 'If Kipling was what Kipling seems... 'Ow quick we'd drop 'im! But 'e aint' (W, 485). My point is not that Kipling was uniformly racist and never let 'lesser breeds' speak, for there are many sympathetic counter-examples to demonstrate the reverse (notably the Jew Kadmiel in 'The Treasure and the Law' (PPH) and the entire Indian cast of Kim); but rather that the ideal of tough masculinity explored and dramatized in 'His Private Honour' depends on class and race subjection. The boast 'I'm a man!' implies acceptance of one's place in a social hierarchy, potentially undermined by the officer's illegal blow, but stabilized first by the lower-class victim finding his own release by bullying a racial inferior, and later by the man-to-man fight which the officer wins.

This interdependence of an idealized masculine self with a hierarchy of race and class recalls, despite the very great difference of form and subject matter, Kipling's justly famous 'Ballad of East and West', in which an English officer and an Afghan horse-thief Kamal discover friendship by respecting one another's courage and chivalry. The ballad tells how, when 'Kamal' the border-thief steals a prize bay mare, the Colonel's son (not named) follows them into enemy territory. When his

75

own horse collapses from exhaustion the Colonel's son, having lost a pistol to Kamal and being threatened with the prospect of being a meal for the jackals and crows, 'lightly' responds by promising vengeance: 'Do good to bird and beast/ But count who come for the broken meats before thou makest a feast'. His jesting defiance wins the tribute 'May I eat dirt if thou hast hurt of me in deed or breath' from Kamal, and the Colonel's son responds in kind: 'Take up the mare and keep her – by God, she has carried a man!' Kamal instead gives back the mare with the 'lifter's dower' of his own jewelled accoutrements, and when the Colonel's son in turn offers him the gift of his remaining pistol Kamal, not to be outdone in generosity, whistles up his 'only son' to be the companion and fellow soldier of the Englishman. The two young men return to 'Fort Bukloh', and the boy who was last night a 'Border-thief' is now 'a man of the Guides.' The poem ends as it began:

> Oh East is East and West is West and never the twain shall meet
> Till Earth and sky stand presently at God's great judgment seat,
> But there is neither East nor West nor Border nor breed nor birth
> When two strong men stand face to face, though they come from the ends of
> the earth!

(W, 234)

Despite that stirring proclamation of equality, it is noticeable that in this tale Kamal comes out the loser. In exchange for the Englishman's pistol (admittedly a heavily symbolic gift, but hardly a rare object to a Border bandit) he not only surrenders the mare and her trappings, but as a gesture of reciprocation – 'Thy father has sent his son to me, I'll send my son to him' – gives up his son to the enemy British, his final words being the wry 'Belike they will raise thee to Rissaldur [sergeant] when I am hanged at Peshawar!'. The recognition of one another by 'two strong men' means that Kamal's tall wild boy who 'trod the ling like a buck in spring and looked like a lance in rest' must lose his wildness by becoming an anonymous member of a troop of military athletes . All of which shows with transparent clarity how the establishment of a masculinity recognized by the imperialist English implies the subjection of the colonized to the rulers' own laws and customs. Where the racial 'Other' is feminine she cannot be assimilated in the same way and is therefore likely to end up mutilated like Bisesa in 'Beyond the Pale' (*PTH*) dead like Ameera in 'Without Benefit of Clergy' (*LH*), or at best rejected like 'Lispeth' and the Burmese mistress in 'Georgie Porgie' (*LH*).

ANIMAL *VERSUS* MAN

A more subtle and interesting notion of being a 'Man' can be seen in the Mowgli stories of the two *Jungle Books*. Because the magical appeal of these stories for children lies partly in the hybrid nature of the hero who can both travel between and be master of the animal and human worlds, the idea of 'Man' is not based anything like so strongly on notions of gender and hardly at all on race. Unlike the Irish Kim, Mowgli is, by origin the Indian boy Nathoo from a Hindu village. Although the local villagers will reject him and he will cause both the village and its cultivated hinterland to be destroyed by the wild beasts, he will eventually rejoin his Hindu mother among the ploughed lands when he grows up and leaves the Jungle in 'The Spring Running'.

The Jungle animals are humanized by being given the speech, memory, individual characters, societies, customs, and above all the 'Jungle Law', a civil code governing the wolves as 'citizens' of the 'Free People' with maxims such as 'When ye fight with a Wolf of the Pack, ye must fight him alone and afar / Lest others take part in the quarrel, and the Pack be diminished by war'. This Law represents the ultimate social authority: '*But the head and the hoof of the Law and the haunch and the hump is – Obey!*' (*SJB*, 30–2). The society of the animals, with its law, culture, unquestioned hierarchy (and even its own mythology in 'How Fear Came'), is made to seem considerably superior to that of the cruelly superstitious mob of Hindu villagers. Thanks to his induction in the Jungle Law by Father Wolf, Mother Wolf, Baloo and Bagheera, Mowgli becomes a noble savage, superior not only in grace and strength but in forbearance to the villagers. He is patient when the children tease him for not playing games or flying kites, because 'luckily, the Law of the Jungle had taught him to keep his temper, for in the Jungle life and food depend on keeping your temper...but only the knowledge that it was unsportsmanlike [sic] to kill little naked cubs kept him from picking them up and breaking them in two' (*JB*, 95). As anyone who has watched a documentary film of carnivores in the wild will be aware, this 'knowledge' of decent behaviour clearly differentiates Kipling's Jungle and its Law from zoological realities.

Yet their capacity for speech and obedience to the Law does not completely anthropomorphize the animals. Although Mowgli's friends and enemies in the Jungle do each represent aspects of humanity in Baloo's teacherly benevolence, Bagheera's strength and cunning or Shere Khan's bullying rage, yet the beasts retain their animal qualities. As Daniel Karlin says 'there is something *other*, something recalcitrantly estranged from human experience, in the silky violence of Bagheera, the silence and lordship of Hathi, and the cold, ageless, fathomless wisdom of Kaa'.[12] And although the boy Mowgli 'would have called himself a wolf if he had been able to speak in any human tongue' (*JB*, 27), none of the animals ever forgets that he is a 'Man'. As Hathi's fable of the Fall 'How Fear Came' emphasizes, Man's aggression and ingenuity have made him the most feared predator 'through the noose, and the pitfall, and the hidden trap, and the flying stick, and the stinging fly that comes out of white smoke [Hathi meant the rifle]' (*SJB*, 26). The wise Akela sees from the start the value of Mowgli's human intelligence: " 'Men and their cubs are very wise. He may be a help in time of need" ' (*JB*, 22) It is the boy's intelligence, memory and presence of mind that enable him, when kidnapped by the *Bandar-Log*, to direct his friends to help him in 'Kaa's Hunting'. These qualities enable him as a youth to plan and carry out the trampling to death of Shere Khan by frightened cattle, and the destruction of the hateful village by the Jungle, and in 'Red Dog' to lead the wolves' victorious resistance to the far more numerous invading dholes. As Akela tells him, ' "Thou art a man, or else the Pack had fled before the dhole" ' (*SJB*, 257).

Mowgli's humanity also, as Bagheera warns him, leaves him vulnerable both to the wolves' envy and since, unlike them, he does not act by instinct, to his own folly or oversight:

> 'The others they hate thee because their eyes cannot meet thine – because thou art wise – because thou hast pulled out thorns from their feet – because thou art a man.'

'I did not know these things,' said Mowgli sullenly; and he
frowned under his heavy black eyebrows.
'What is the Law of the Jungle? Strike first and then give tongue.
By thy very carelessness they know thou art a man.' (*JB*, 31)

Man may be clever but he is full of weaknesses. Thanks to his
own early experience of captivity, the panther readily recognizes human fallibility. Mowgli's open inconsistency and
furious 'Am I to give reason for all that I choose to do?' later
moves him to the comment 'There speaks Man! Even so did men
talk round the king's cages at Oodeypore' and the muttered
aside that for all Man's wisdom he is 'of all things the most
foolish' (*SJB*, 66). In 'The King's Ankus', Kipling's brilliant re-
writing of Chaucer's *Pardoner's Tale*, the six men who kill one
another to possess a useless but precious object display a kind of
greed and violence baffling to both Mowgli and Bagheera who
merely kill from hunger. Far worse is the mob-violence of the
credulous villagers who stone the innocent Mowgli as a jungle-
demon, and would also have burned Messua as a witch for
being kind to him if she had not escaped to the protecting
English (yes, colonial attitudes do persist even in the *Jungle
Books*) who 'do not suffer people to burn or beat each other
without witnesses' (*SJB*, 81). Yet Mowgli the hero is Indian, not
English, and will ultimately return to Messua and her domestic
shrine. Moreover, it is partly Mowgli's human fallibility that
makes him lovable. There is a telling episode in 'Mowgli's
Brothers' when, after his intelligence, courage and Promethean
ability to steal fire and handle it have enabled him to outwit and
master Shere Khan the tiger and the Wolf-Pack, Mowgli is
overcome by mortal grief:

'Am I dying, Bagheera?':
'No. Those are only tears such as men use', said Bagheera. 'Now I
know thou art a man, and a man's cub no longer. The Jungle is shut
indeed to thee henceforward. Let them fall, Mowgli. They are only
tears.' So Mowgli sat and cried as though his heart would break; and
he had never cried in his life before. (*JB*, 40)

Since the Jungle where no one weeps, here represents the
enchanted world of childhood, the implication of Mowgli's tears
that prove him 'a man-cub no longer' is that to be an adult man
includes both experiencing grief and giving it passionate

expression. To be a man means, then, not only the capacity to pursue vengeance more terribly because more cleverly than any beast, but as Mowgli's weeping shows, to be shaken by love and pain. This is a very long way from the ideal of masculinity as the exercise of strength and self-control that enables Ortheris to boast 'I'm a man!' Viewed against Ortheris' macho pride or the impeccable virtue of Major 'Galahad' Cottar, this fantasy children's book seems, strangely, to manifest the more adult and complex notion of 'Man'.

5

Kim

This was life as he would have it – bustling and shouting, the buckling of belts, and beating of bullocks and creaking of wheels, lighting of fires and cooking of food, and new sights at every turn of the approving eye. The morning mist swept off in a whorl of silver, the parrots shot away to some distant river in shrieking green hosts: all the well-wheels within earshot went to work. India was awake, and Kim was in the middle of it, more awake and excited than anyone.

(*K*, 103–4)

Kim is the Kipling book that people like who don't like Kipling.[1]

A COLONIAL FICTION

Kim (1901), the most enchanting of Kipling's fictions and the only one ever to be compared with the great traditional names Dickens, Shakespeare, or Chaucer,[2] is that rare thing, a colonial fiction that takes ethnic and cultural otherness as a source of pleasure, not anxiety. As Angus Wilson wrote,

> Kipling's passionate interest in people and their vocabularies and their crafts is, of course, the essence of the magic of all his work. But in all the other books it tends to be marred by aspects of his social ethic – by caution, reserve, distrust, mastered emotion, stiff upper lips, direct puritanism or the occasional puritan's leer, retributive consequences, cruelty masquerading as justifiable restraint or bullying as the assertion of superiority. None of these is present in *Kim*.[3]

Not all readers and critics will agree with this account. The post-colonial critics Zohreh Sullivan and Joseph Bristow find Kipling's inner contradictions and his imperialist politics lurking beneath his loving portrayal of India's rich diversity, while

Thomas Richards reads *Kim* as an imperialist fantasy of comprehensive knowledge. Given that the boy hero's growth to the verge of manhood culminates in becoming a successful spy for the British Government as well as a devoted disciple to the Buddhist priest, lovers of this novel clearly do have serious critiques to answer. But before discussing these, it is useful to begin with a summary of the novel.

The boy Kim is a hybrid, born Irish and bred Indian. 'Though he was burned black as any native; though he spoke the vernacular by preference and his mother-tongue in a clipped uncertain sing-song' (*K*, 1), he is a white boy whose real name is Kimball O'Hara. His mother is long dead of cholera; his father, an ex-colour sergeant of the 'Maverick' regiment turned drunk, railwayman and opium smoker, has also died of his addiction, leaving the boy his identity papers (including Kim's birth certificate) and a confused prophecy that his son will be made great by men worshipping a 'Red Bull on a green field'(*K*, 2). When the novel opens Kim is playing king-of-the-castle on the great gun Zam-Zammah with two other Indian boys, but abandons the game at the approach of a strange Chinese-looking priest, the gentle, unworldly Buddhist Teshoo Lama from Tibet, whose friendship will transform both their lives. Kim guides him into Lahore Museum the 'Wonder House' and overhears the conversation with the white-bearded Curator (an idealized portrait of Lockwood Kipling the author's father, who really was the curator of Lahore Museum) in which the lama explains his quest to Benares and beyond in search of the 'River of the Arrow' which will free him from the Wheel of Things.

Fascinated by the old priest and deciding that he needs a protector, the street-wise Kim joins his pilgrimage, leading him first to the Kashmir Serai where the Afghan horse-dealer Mahbub Ali entrusts the boy with a message, supposedly the 'pedigree of a white stallion' but actually, since Mahbub Ali is an intelligence agent, a secret report to the 'Indian Government' (*i.e.* the British Government of India), to be delivered in Umballa City. Aware of imminent danger as he spies on Mahbub being robbed by a prostitute, Kim pilots the old man towards Lahore station and the '3.25 a.m south-bound' (*K*, 38) towards Umballa where, unknown to the lama, Kim delivers his message and overhears the Governor-General's decision to declare war. The two set out on their pilgrimage, the lama in search of his River and Kim of his Red Bull, through gardens, fields and villages until they join the 'Grand Trunk Road' going southwards.

Kim soon finds his 'Bull', the crest of the 'Maverick' regiment which arrives to pitch camp and set up their flag; while spying (again) on the officers' mess, he is caught by the regimental chaplains who identify him by his papers as a white boy and decide to make him a soldier. Conversing with difficulty with the two English priests who regard him as a heathen and do not speak his language (Kim acts as interpreter), the lama, though grieved and dismayed at losing his *chela* [disciple], accepts that Kim must go with the 'Sahibs'. He nevertheless intervenes to save Kim from the grim prospect of a 'Military Orphanage' and a life of soldiering, by arranging to pay for his education at St Xavier's Public School in Lucknow, described as 'the best schooling a boy can get in India' (*K*, 133). Through the lama's generosity and the influence of Colonel Creighton of the 'Ethnological Survey' (meaning also the Secret Service) whom Mahbub advises that the boy is a promising intelligence agent, Kim is dispatched to his public school. He joins the officer-class of the ruling race (for which the envious drummer-boys beat him), and is just able to take farewell of the lama before 'the "Gates of Learning" shut with a clang' (*K*, 174) behind him.

But Kim's transformation into an Anglo-Indian schoolboy is very partial, for he longs for his old Indian street-life. 'Kim yearned for the caress of soft mud squishing between his toes, as his mouth watered for mutton stewed with butter and cabbages, for rice speckled with strong-scented cardamoms, for the saffron tinted rice, garlic and onions, and the forbidden greasy sweetmeats of the bazaars' (*K*, 178 – wonderfully exotic for English readers in 1901, when rice meant rice pudding, saffron and cardamoms were strange, onions were suspect and garlic unspeakable). Disguised as a Hindu boy by a friendly prostitute, he rejoins Mahbub, whose life he saves after overhearing a plot to murder him, and is further inducted into the secrets of the 'Great Game' by a series of mentors: Mahbub himself on his travels, then Lurgan Sahib, seller of curios at Simla, whose attempt to subject him to the 'native magic' by hypnotism Kim successfully resists, and last the Bengali Hurree Chunder Mookerjee, who instructs him in the usefulness to spies of medicine and the 'art and science of mensuration' (*K*, 231) as performed unobtrusively by treading distances and calculating them on a rosary (a method based, as Thomas Richards has shown, on General Montgomerie's historic network of spies disguised as monks who, from 1862, secretly surveyed Tibet).[4] This sets the pattern of Kim's education: application to school work, especially mathematics, during term-time and successful immersion in native life in the holidays combine to make him a master of disguise, intrigue and manipulation.

Kim leaves school at sixteen, for a post as 'chain-man' in the 'Canal Department' (clearly a cover for intelligence work) after six months' leave to spend as *chela* to his lama. Equipped for the Road by two of his mentors, Mahbub and Hurree, who gives him the password by which Government spies recognize each other, he finds his lama at the Jain temple in Benares that has been the old man's base during Kim's schooldays. The two set out again in search of the sacred River which the old man believes he will only find in Kim's company. He is delighted when Kim cures a child of malaria but is less pleased when, meeting a distressed 'Mahratta' who is really another spy on the run and recognizing him by their shared code-word, Kim changes the man's identity by disguising him as a *saddhu* (holy man) – somewhat to the disapproval of the lama, who of course does not realize that Kim has thereby saved the man's life. Drawn northward by the lama's love of the Hills – for after all, his River may be anywhere in northern India – they drift towards Saharunpore as guests of a generous old lady, among whose household Kim unexpectedly finds Hurree who asks for his assistance in dealing with some Russian spies on the north-east frontier.

The lama needs little persuasion to revisit his beloved Hills, and with Kim he penetrates to the heart of the Himalayas where Hurree has already found the Russians and is making himself useful to them. When the two sides meet, the lama is expounding his chart of the 'Wheel of Life' to Kim; impressed with this picturesque tableau – ' "Look! It is like the picture for the birth of a religion – the first teacher and the first disciple" ' (*K*, 342). The Russian demands to buy the chart and, when the lama refuses, strikes him; in the resulting *mêlée* their servants desert them and Kim, alerted by Hurree, steals their diplomatic correspondence. Tempted, however briefly to revenge himself for the blow by ordering a lynching which the hillmen would be only too happy to carry out, realizing that he has let himself be seduced from his quest by love of his homeland, and weakened by the blow and his own spiritual crisis, the lama is now wholly dependent on Kim, whose beauty and charm prompt the 'Woman of Shamlegh' to help them by providing a litter and servants to carry it. They return to the Plains, Kim supporting the old man in mind and body and carrying the stolen documents. It is a weary march, on which exhaustion reduces the boy to a near-breakdown, even as the love between him and the lama grows deeper and stronger. But they reach the estate of the old lady at Saharunpore, who heals Kim with rest, massage and food, and Hurree Babu arrives to collect the stolen documents, congratulating them both on a most successful *coup*. Restored to himself, Kim meets the lama whose spiritual journey is at last accomplished; separating himself from Nirvana for Kim's sake, he is rewarded by finding his River:

> 'Come!'
> He crossed his hands on his lap and smiled, as a man may who has won salvation for himself and his beloved.

(K, 413)

Kim thus has a twofold plot: on the one hand, the pilgrimage in quest of salvation, undertaken by the lama and assisted by Kim who is drawn to the old man both out of protective love and for the pleasure of journeying through North India, and on the other the spy thriller in which Kim is the resourceful charmer, adventurer and master of disguises. The double narrative corresponds to the Indian and British poles of Kim's dual identity: the Indian self which both reverences a holy man and takes an expert delight in begging and journeying with him, and the English (or rather Irish) self which delights in duplicity and intrigue and is an ideal recruit for the 'Great Game' of spying, played in the service of the British Empire. These selves quite literally speak and think different languages: 'fluent and picturesque' vernacular and the 'tinny, saw-cut English of the native-bred' (K, 167, 119). The Kim who resists Lurgan Sahib's attempt to subdue him by hypnotism, switches from thinking in 'Hindustani' to mentally reciting 'the multiplication-table in English' (219), and the devout *chela* instructed in the lama's wonderful chart of the Wheel is five minutes later drawing a pistol from his robe and 'thinking hard in English, "This is dam'-tight place, but *I* think it is self-defence"' (347).

Yet the two halves of Kim's identity do not produce the conflict in himself or the novel that might be expected from an author whose work is so often characterized by division and contradiction. They harmonize practically because Kim's street-boy ability to pass as an Indian, his attention as a beggar to people's expressions and intentions, and his charmingly manipulative social skills learnt in the same school, are all essential to his work as a spy. And they harmonize ideologically, because the story's narrator takes for granted the benevolence and legitimacy of the 'Indian Government' (i.e. the colonization of India by the English) on whose behalf the 'Great Game' is played, while the boy hero isn't interested in politics but in adventure and intrigue for their own sakes. During their adventures in the Hills, Kim shows himself as both a devoted disciple and an efficient spy, sometimes in the same moment; yet as Edmund Wilson complained, the novel nowhere intimates that Kim is betraying the innocent old man by using their pilgrimage as a 'cover' for Intelligence[5]. On the contrary, for Kipling it is the *Pax Britannica* which Kim's participation in the 'Great Game' plays a small but significant part in sustaining, that secures the safety and civility of the India in which the lama is free to wander. The point is made in an early exchange between the lama and an old soldier who responds to the lama's question 'What profit to kill men?' with a sentiment that clearly has the author's approval: 'If evil men were not now and then slain it would not be a good world for weaponless dreamers'. The retired *rissaldur* (sergeant) then gives as his example an account of his own experience of the Indian Mutiny of 1857, and of the bloody reprisals that followed its suppression in terms defined by imperialist English like Kipling, phrased in the archaised rhetorical English by which Kipling represents Indian 'vernacular':

> A madness ate into all the Army, and they turned against their officers. That was the first evil, but not past remedy if they had then held their hands, but they chose to kill the Sahibs' women and children. Then came the Sahibs from over the sea and called them to most strict account.... Of six hundred and eighty sabres stood fast to their salt – how many, think you? Three. Of whom I was one, (*K*, 73–4).

Kipling's portrayal of the old loyalist's pride and courage is charming and convincing enough to divert our attention from the fact that, as Edward Said forcibly pointed out, the old soldier's view of the Mutiny as an episode of treacherous 'madness' and the massacres that avenged it as a 'strict account' would *not* have been shared by most Indians, who saw the 'Rebellion' as a nationalist uprising against British rule and would have regarded him 'as (at the very least) a traitor to his people'.[6] *Kim*'s representation of the English rule of India as harmonious, benevolent and uncontested (except by the ineffective Russian spies) is seductive because it is articulated not by Anglo-Indian spokesmen as in the early propagandist story 'The Enlightenments of Pagett, M.P.' (*ST*) but by Indians themselves. Yet it is unrealistic because it suppresses any acknowledgment of the serious Indian opposition to English rule that in reality existed, and was gathering strength during Kipling's own years in India in the late 1880s (the Indian National Congress, for example, was founded in 1885) during which the action of *Kim* takes place.[7] When the highly educated Hurree Babu gets drunk on Russian vodka and abuses a 'Government which had forced upon him a white man's education and neglected to supply him with a white man's salary... the tears ran down his cheeks for the miseries of his land', (*K*, 389), the whole point is that his complaint is a practical joke on the Russians. Of course they are duly taken in, and the delight which Hurree takes in manipulating them as the disaffected 'Mohendro Lal Dutt. M.A, of Calcutta'(*K*, 383) and in the success of his intrigue ('onlee me could have worked it – ah – for all it was dam' well worth', *K*, 357), make it hard to imagine that his charade could represent the real grievance of real people, still less the real threat to the British Raj that Indian economic and political discontent finally proved to be. The novel seems completely untroubled by its sins of what Kipling elsewhere calls '*suppressio veri* and *suggestio falsi*' ('suppressing truth and suggesting lies': *S & C*, 27), because as Edward Said explains, Kipling was innocent (or more accurately, oblivious) of any attempt to deceive.

> The conflict between Kim's colonial service and loyalty to his Indian companions is unresolved not because Kipling could not face it, but because for Kipling *there was no conflict*; one purpose of the novel is in

fact to show the absence of conflict once Kim is cured of his doubts, the lama of his longing for his River, and India of a few upstarts and foreign agents. That there *might have been a conflict* had Kipling considered India as unhappily subservient to imperialism, we can have no doubt, but he did not; for him it was India's best destiny to be ruled by England.[8]

To recognize how deeply Kipling's imperialist beliefs are interwoven with the narrative harmonies of his fiction does not, as Said emphasized in his own critical account of this 'great work of art',[9] mean that those who dispute Kipling's beliefs can take no pleasure in the novel. On the contrary, a critical account of *Kim* needs to begin by acknowledging the glowing lyricism of its love for the India of Kipling's childhood, for the people and for the land itself, the 'broad smiling river of life' which is also the dust that heals Kim at the end: 'no new herbage that, living, is half-way to death already, but the hopeful dust that holds the seeds of all life' (*K*, 86, 404). Its double love story - love for a land and love between people – is intimated in Mahbub's question 'Who are thy people?' and Kim's often-quoted answer: 'This great and beautiful land', followed immediately by 'And further, I would see my lama again' (*K*, 193). These two people of utterly different age, race, experience and belief nevertheless find their hearts drawn together to become one another's salvation. Angus Wilson calls their Don Quixote / Sancho Panza relationship 'an allegory of that seldom portrayed human ideal, the world in the service of spiritual goodness, and, even less usual, spiritual goodness recognizing its debt to the world's protection'[10] – even though neither of the two ever fully understands the other. For the lama remains ignorant throughout of Kim's activities as a spy (he believes that Kim will 'take service under the Government as a scribe', *K*, 273); and conversely, the comedy of Kim's response to his master's culminating discovery of his River shows how far he is from sharing his master's visionary quest to be free of the Wheel of Things, or even his Buddhism:

'*Allah kerim* ! Oh, well that the Babu was by! Wast thou very wet?'
'Why should I regard?' (*K*, 412)

The novel is irradiated throughout by Kipling's own love for 'the great and beautiful land' of India, represented both by the lama's spirituality which no Englishman in Kipling approaches, and by the diverse scenes encountered by the hero – as Abdul R. JanMohammed observes, 'the narrator seems to find as much pleasure in describing the varied and tumultuous life of India as Kim finds in experiencing it'[11] – however possessive, patronizing and wilfully self-deceiving that love may now look to postcolonial readers. To mine *Kim* for evidence either of its colonial fear and suspicion of 'natives' as Zohreh Sullivan's brilliant but one-sided reading in *Narratives of Empire* does, or of Kipling's imperialist anxiety about maintaining white superiority in response to the Boer War, as Joseph Bristow does in *Empire Boys*, means neglecting this novel's exceptional pleasure and serenity (Said's point that '*pleasure*...is an undeniable component of *Kim*'[12] is essential to remember). It tends therefore to produce strained readings, as when Sullivan argues that a 'hierarchy of natives [is] set up and stereotyped early in the text', ensuring that because Kim's father died of the opium addiction he acquired from an Indian woman, 'we learn, along with Kim, something significant about the natives: they are to be controlled and kicked...because if allowed control, their unrestrained ways can lead to the death of fathers'.[13] Yet Father Victor's remarks ' "It's very much what his father would have done – if he was drunk...The Regiment will take care of you and make you as good as man as your – as good as a man can be" ', (*K*, 124, 127), clearly indicate that the late Sgt. O'Hara was already a drunken wastrel on the way down. Of course this makes the dead Irishman a daring, drunken rule-breaker according to colonial stereotype, but it doesn't follow that the Indian 'natives' are to blame for his self-destruction.

Similarly, Joseph Bristow interprets the episode when a British drummer-boy jeers at Kim – 'You talk the same as a nigger, don't you?' (*K*, 145) – to mean simply that Kim does indeed look like a 'nigger' (*i.e.* Indian) but is in fact white, so that the scene 'aims to manipulate sympathy for Kim's peculiar hybrid role...No one else is vilified as harshly as Kim in this upsetting exchange of words, and no one can be blamed for how he looks and acts, like a native'.[14] But the drummer-boy *is*, quite plainly, blamed and mocked both by the narrator and Kim for his bullying ignorance and coarseness: 'He styled all natives "niggers", yet servants and sweepers called him abominable names to his face and, misled by their deferential attitude, he never understood. This somewhat consoled Kim for the beatings' (*K*, 150). In Kipling's fiction, calling Indians 'niggers' invariably convicts a white speaker of crass ignorance and vulgarity – *not* because the word was regarded as objectionable, but because it more 'properly' denoted Africans or (as we should now say) African-Americans. Hence the narrator's contempt for the stupid Army captain who 'called all natives "niggers", which besides being extreme bad form, shows gross ignorance' in 'On the City Wall' (*ST*, 336) or the raw soldiers in 'The Drums of the Fore and Aft' who idiotically think of Afghans as 'niggers – people who ran away if you shook a stick at them', (*WWW*, 327.) The drummer-boy, a 'fat and freckled person ... [whom] Kim loathed from the soles of his boots to his cap-ribbons' (*K*, 141) here represents everything repellent about the graceless, ignorant English.

That said, the imperialist attitudes and racist essentialism emphasised by Sullivan, Bristow and others certainly do exist in *Kim*. They are present in the narrator's frequent 'Orientalist' generalizing remarks about Indians being untruthful (Kim can 'lie like an Oriental'), unregulated ('all hours of the twenty-four are alike to Orientals') and incorrigibly lazy, so that Mahbub 'an Oriental, with an Oriental's views on the value of time', breaks camp 'swiftly – as Orientals understand speed – with long explanations, with abuse and windy talk, carelessly, with a hundred checks for little things forgotten' (*K*, 33, 36, 31, 203). Hurree Babu's nervousness about the Russians – 'I-I do not want to consort with them without a witness ... they may beat me' is likewise explicable by his race: 'I am Bengali – a fearful man' (*K*, 319). We are told that Asiatic people are timelessly dishonest (Kim taking a percentage on the lama's ticket exacts 'the immemorial commission of Asia') and religious: 'All India is full of holy men stammering gospels in strange tongues; shaken and consumed in the fires of their own zeal; dreamers, babblers and visionaries: as it has been from the beginning and will continue to the end' (*K*, 38, 46), the echo of the familiar Church of England formula 'As it was in the beginning, is now and ever shall be' giving that last sentence a religious authority.[15] Conversely, we are told that Kim thinks and behaves as he does because of his 'white blood' which 'set(s) him upon his feet' when he talks of war, where a 'native would have lain

down' passively, makes him resist the spells of the witch
Huneefa ('How he fought!... That was his white blood'), and
less heroically, leaves him terrified by a cobra which the lama
accepts calmly as a fellow-creature: 'No native training can
quench the white man's horror of the Serpent' (*K*, 65, 255, 61).
Moreover Kim's Irish descent is several times invoked to
explain his qualities of curiosity ('Kim's mother had been Irish
too' says the narrator sagely), his reckless adventurousness ('he
was Irish enough by birth to reckon silver the least part of any
game') and his hot-tempered aggression when the Russian hits
the lama: 'The blow had waked every unknown Irish devil in
the boy's blood' (*K*, 17, 51, 346). In her elegant Lacanian
explication of Kim surrendering the Imaginary world of his
Edenic relation to Mother India for the Law of the Father
articulated in the controlling gaze of the white man's knowledge, Zohreh Sullivan relates this stereotyping, judging aspect
of *Kim* to the hero's own identity as a white man, enhanced by
the education he receives as a 'Sahib' which enables him to
measure and (in part) control the land whose government he
serves. This is convincing, and makes good post-colonial sense
of the ethnological side of the Secret Service; yet however right
Sullivan is about the novel's themes, her reading makes the
novel sound more schematic and Kim's loyalties more firmly
English than they really are. It is telling that Kim, for all his
public-school education, never comes to speak like the narrator:
his English idiom whether spoken aloud or thought inwardly,
remains as 'native-bred' ('yess, smashed'; '*thatt* is all right', *K*,
219, 362) as Hurree Babu's.

The novel is, throughout, much more lively and individual
than its stereotypical generalities might lead one to expect,
contradicting Dixon Scott's criticism that Kipling's characters
are all type-cast and never develop. This plainly isn't true of the
self-questioning hero wondering 'Who is Kim?' on the verge of
adulthood, or of the lama experiencing his spiritual crisis. The
characterization of the Indian players of the 'Great Game' is
more problematic, especially Hurree Babu who can easily be
made to appear a comic, over-educated coward and the butt of
the narrator's contempt. Bristow calls him 'a comic amalgama-
tion of European and Indian attitudes: prayers to the gods of
Hinduism on the one hand, and enthusiasm for the positivism

91

of Herbert Spencer on the other. The novel insists on the ludicrous incompatibility of these differing systems of belief. In fact, this incongruity is supposed to provoke laughter... Hurree Babu is often mocked.'[16]

Hurree is certainly comic in his girth, his educated but mispronounced English ('*Thatt* is the question, as Shakespeare hath it',) and his self-confessed cowardice ('I am a fearful man', *K*, 314, 320). He bears a certain resemblance to the sinister Gunga Dass in 'The Strange Ride of Morrowbie Jukes', known to Jukes before their incarceration in the accursed pit as a 'portly Government servant with a marvellous capacity for making bad puns in English' (*WWW*. 175), sharing with Dass several conventional 'Babu' qualities: low cunning, high education, physical cowardice, portliness, fluent but heavily accented English, a liking for puns ('There is no hurry for Hurree', *K*, 321), and a nodding acquaintance with liberal-progressive Victorian philosophy. 'I am good Herbert Spencerian' (*K*, 319) parallels Dass's Benthamite jibe that 'greatest good of greatest number is political maxim' (*WWW*, 189) – *except* that Dass is hateful, whereas Hurree is represented as likeable, even admirable in his courage and wiliness. His educated intelligence enables him to 'play' the enemy spies like an expert fisherman playing a salmon and to think up his own side's tantric password 'Son of the Charm' and its bogus ethnological origin. '"You see, it was me invented all this. Colonel Creighton he does not know"'. Despite Hurree's girth and his professed cowardice, he proves both a tough mountaineer whose 'marches... would astonish folk who mock at his race' and a daring spy whose bold manipulation of the enemy impresses even Kim. '"He makes them a mock at the risk of his life – *I* never would have gone down to them after those pistol-shots – and then he says he is a fearful man."' (*K*, 260, 383, 402).

Hurree's attitudes and ambitions as an intellectual are more problematic. He is an erudite ethnographer whose desire to become a Fellow of the Royal Society moves Creighton, who nurses a similar ambition, to fellow-feeling and approval; but his comic boast (which ought to draw a sigh of fellow-feeling from many an aspiring academic) that 'I have contributed rejected notes to the *Asiatic Quarterly*' (*K*, 258) implies that an Indian intellectual wanting to be an F.R.S. is an absurdity like the 'letter-writer who can write English veree well' boasting the qualification 'Failed Entrance Allahabad University' (*K*, 146–7). Yet this mockery clearly does not imply that Asians cannot be scholars, for the lama's great learning as well as his spirituality are always treated seriously, both by the narrator and by the sympathetic English characters. The Curator of Lahore Museum sees he is 'no mere bead-telling mendicant, but a scholar of parts', and much later we are told reverentially how the old priest speaks 'as a scholar removed from vanity, as a Seeker walking in humility, as an old man, wise and temperate, illumining knowledge with brilliant insight' (*K*, 11, 305) – a description borne out by the lama's un-superstitious, subtly self-searching interpretation of the torn chart of the Wheel as a warning and admonition to himself at the story's crisis in the Himalayas. Because Hurree has learned from his English teachers to remind himself that 'you cannot occupy two places in space simultaneously. Thatt is axiomatic', the English axioms cut him off from understanding either the Buddhist monk's quest for freedom from 'the illusion of Time and Space and of Things', or the Hindu *bairagi* whose wisdom comforts the lonely Kim: 'It is a long road to the feet of the One, but thither do we all travel' (*K*, 357, 411, 266). Of course, Hurree's materialism and worldliness have their practical uses; besides masterminding the plot against the Russians, it is he who rescues the lama from drowning in his River of healing. Nevertheless, his adoption of English thought is represented as a serious loss to him, not a gain. Hence his comic mixture of Indian superstition and Spencerian scepticism:

> 'How am I to fear the absolutely non-existent?' said Hurree Babu, talking English to comfort himself. It is an awful thing to dread the magic that you contemptuously investigate – to collect folk-lore for the Royal Society with a lively belief in the Powers of Darkness. (*K*, 257)

Unlike Kim who, thanks presumably to his 'white blood' as well as his training at St Xavier's, could see through those Powers of Darkness to the plain daylight by reciting the English words 'twice three was six, and thrice three was nine', or the lama who can disregard them in his contemplation of the Causes of things, serenely contemptuous of 'silly devils – not one of whom is worth a grain of dust in the eye' – and of caste as illusions: ' "Low-caste I did not say, for how can that be which is not?" ' (*K*, 219, 323, 61), Hurree finds not salvation but comfort – and not much of that – in his English-language question 'How am I to fear the absolutely non-existent?' His predicament – not so far from Kipling's own, outside the charmed world of *Kim* – ought to elicit sympathy and might, in a different fiction, make him a tragic figure. But unlike the hero wondering 'Who is Kim – Kim – Kim?', and again 'I am Kim. And what is Kim ?' (*K*, 265, 403), Hurree is forever defined – and indeed defines himself – as a comic trickster. His other literary cousin besides Gunga Dass is Shakespeare's Falstaff, for Hurree is Falstaffian in his bulk, his cunning, his cowardice which is, however, deceptive: Shakespeare's Falstaff pretends to be a hero and is really a coward, whereas Hurree insists that 'I am – oh, awfully fearful! – I remember once they wanted to cut off my head on the road to Lhassa. (No, I have never reached to Lhassa.) I sat down and cried, Mister O'Hara, anticipating Chinese tortures,' (*K*, 320) and yet proves coolly daring in an emergency – or as he would say a 'dam' tight place'. He shares with Falstaff the status of a 'low' character, which both not only accept but enjoy, Hurree playing his role as a self-confessed coward and comic character part ('I am only Babu showing off my English to you. All we Babus like to show off', *K*, 260) with a conscious relish like Falstaff waddling in front of his page 'like a sow that hath overwhelmed all her litter but one'.[17]

It is the sly gusto of Hurree's role-playing that makes him such a good impersonator, capable of deceiving even the quick-witted Kim, and able to turn any occasion to advantage, as when, posing as a guide 'discours[ing] of botany and ethnology with unimpeachable inaccuracy', he brings his enemies where he wants them, to the lama and Kim. ' "Ha!" said Hurree Babu, resourceful as Puss-in-Boots. "That is eminent local holy man...He is expounding holy picture – *all* hand-worked." '(*K*, 342). The fairy-tale comparison is apt , since Puss-in-Boots is the trickster-servant whose cunning secures his master's ascendancy as 'Marquis of Carabas', a most fitting role for a Bengali 'subaltern'. More subtly, by parodying his own hybridity in his pose of incompetent native guide, Hurree's masquerade enables him to manipulate his credulous victims in the service of his real master, the British Government. Unlike Dass, Hurree the trickster offers no threat to the Sahibs' rule. Taking almost as much pleasure in the comedy of his own performance as the narrator does ('Yess, and they gave me a certificate. That is creaming joke', *K*, 400) he seems like Kim to regard the successful playing of the 'Great Game' as an end in itself. Like the old Indian soldier remembering the Mutiny in terms defined by the occupying power, Hurree is at once a convincing character and a misleading guide to the common attitudes of the nineteenth-century Indians to the 'Orientalist' colonial power that cast them in the roles of loyal comic servants.

AN INDIAN PARADISE

The attitudes that underpin the vision of a harmoniously ruled India in *Kim* are certainly imperialist. But to read it as an endorsement of white superiority is to ignore both the warmth and serenity of its portrayal of India and the fact that its Indian characters are far more complex and interesting than its English. Significantly, of the two characters from Kipling's earlier fictions who reappear in *Kim*, 'Strickland' the police expert on native life and the wronged 'Lispeth' of *Plain Tales from the Hills*, far more attention is given to the 'native' woman. Strickland makes a single brief appearance as a secret agent cleverly making himself look stupid (*K*, 297) – just another useful example to Kim, the apprentice spy. But Lispeth, the beautiful Kashmiri girl adopted by missionaries who let her be jilted by a visiting Englishman (*PTH*, 7), reappears in *Kim*'s nearest approach to adult heterosexual romance as 'no common bearer of babes' the rich and still 'aught but unlovely' ruler of Shamlegh town, which she holds from the Rajah. Reminded by the beauty of this 'priest with a Sahib's face' of her lost lover and the days when 'I made music on the *pianno* in the Mission-house at Kotgarh', she accepts his refusal – tempered mischievously with an English kiss and 'Thank you verree much, my dear' (*K*, 377, 379) – with dignity and generosity, ordering her 'husbands' to carry the litter of the weakened lama back to the Plains. The novel accommodates her sexual desire for Kim without fuss – '"There is nothing I would not do for thee." He accepted the compliment calmly, as men must in lands where women make the love' (*K*, 364) – though admittedly it does make Lispeth a rather conveniently good loser. As with the old *Rissaldur* whose opinions and loyalties coincide with Kipling's own, the novel here avoids a potential conflict by making an Asian character think and behave in a way that suits its own book; a more determined or successful wooing would have represented a real problem to both of Kim's loyalties instead of a poignant might-have-been. Yet with neither character is there any sense of strain or falsification. The honourable old soldier, open-handed alike to stray toddlers, to mendicants and to grown-up sons in need of a good horse, and the proudly embittered yet generous Woman of Shamlegh give no impression of being cut to fit an ideological pattern.

A key difference between *Kim* and any other of Kipling's Indian fictions lies in its two heroes: the boy and the old man. The lama's Buddhist philosophy is completely outside English experience, his holiness being recognized by Indians but simply not understood by the English characters (nor, it must be said, by Hurree Babu, the most Anglicized of the Indians). As Mark Kinkead-Weekes and, more recently, Clara Claiborne Parks[18] have argued, his Buddhist rejection of the world as 'illusion', and especially his spiritual crisis in the wake of the blow struck by the Russian, when he recognizes he has yielded to bodily illusion in his beloved Hills, represent a profound opposition, not only to the activity of Kim's brilliant intelligence *coup* but to the pleasure in India's 'great and beautiful land' (*K*, 193) and its people that informs the novel. Repenting that 'I delighted in life and in the lust of life. I desired strong slopes to climb...I measured the strength of my body, which is evil, against the high Hills', the lama recognizes the blow as 'a sign to me, who am no better than a strayed yak, that my place is not here' (*i.e.* among the Hills). The hard lesson that 'Thou canst not choose Freedom and go in bondage to the delight of life' (*K*, 373) is at once placed against, and 'places' the novel's delight in India and in the lively worldliness of Indians like the Woman of Shamlegh, the Kulu Sahiba and Mahbub Ali, as well as Kim's English-speaking identity as a trained spy. The potential conflict between the lama's quest to be free of worldly illusion and the novel's (and the boy's) delight in life, is only – and barely –

resolved by the lama's achieving his Quest through the selfless love for his disciple that allows him to find his River of healing. The 'Holy One' represents a vision that is 'other' and yet entirely respected.

Conversely, the street-wise hero (who unlike the Abbot of Such-Zen 'acquiring merit' by taking the begging-bowl, really *is* a street-beggar) is also a child in the Romantic tradition of joyous innocence eagerly encountering the world. Writing of children almost always brings out a tone of warmth and tenderness in Kipling's work, especially his Indian fictions, as in the portrayal of the doomed small boy in 'The Story of Muhammed Din' (*PTA*) or Tota in 'Without Benefit of Clergy' (*LH*), whose English father unforgettably answers his Indian mistress's speculation whether the *'white mem-log* [women]' are as happy as she, '"I know they are not. They give their children over to the nurses"', (*LH*, 160). The ease, gentleness and intimacy with which Kipling's Indians treat their own and others' children appear in the holy man Gobind in *Life's Handicap* (who seems in retrospect like an early sketch for the lama), telling a satisfying folk-story about a cheating money-lender forced by the god Ganesh to endow a mendicant priest with a '*lakh* [100,000] of rupees' to a small naked child nestling in his quilt: 'When I came to the Chubara [the monastery] the shaven head with the tuft atop, and the beady black eyes looked out of the folds of the quilt as a squirrel looks out from his nest, and Gobind was smiling while the child played with his beard' (*LH*, 326). *Kim* consistently shows Indian adults behaving tenderly towards small children: the grizzled old soldier comforting a frightened toddler – '"Little one – little one – do not cry"', and the Jat farmer cajoling his sick child to take his medicine – '"Do not spit it out, little Princeling! King of my heart, do not spit it out, and we shall be strong men, wrestlers and club-wielders, by the morning"' [78, 270]. Even the lama, to his own embarrassment, is found comforting a child with a nursery rhyme, and Kim himself prompts a little boy to reveal his world of magical play in which he makes 'clay men and horses' and 'Sír Banas, he makes them all alive at the back of our kitchen-midden' (*K*, 292). These exchanges belong to a far warmer and kindlier world of feeling than that of the distant, disciplinarian English.

One need not be a psychoanalyst to see that the invention of Kim the dauntless, parentless street-boy enabled Kipling to revisit and repossess the India of his childhood, that Eden of 'light and colour and golden and purple fruits' and Hindu temples with their 'dimly seen, friendly Gods' where, like his hero, he was fluent in 'the vernacular that one thought and dreamed in' and used 'English' only haltingly when prompted by the servants 'Speak English now to Papa and Mamma' (*SM*, 1–3). Having no Papa and Mamma to exile him – for his own good, of course – to the lonely hell of the 'House of Desolation' in Southsea and the harsh discipline of a public school, Kim, like Mowgli in the *Jungle Books*, is the adopted child of a wonderfully 'other' world that nurtures him even more wisely and lovingly than the parent with whom Kipling discussed its composition when he 'took it to be smoked over with my Father.' (*SM*, 139). For the orphaned Kim is looked after by everyone he knows, from the native policeman who 'grinned tolerantly; he knew Kim of old' to the woman who fills his begging-bowl (*K*, 5, 20). And as Mowgli is guided in the Jungle world by the different wisdom of Baloo, Bagheera and Kaa, so Kim's growth to maturity is watched and guided by those splendid if mutually contradictory figures of authority, Mahbub Ali and the lama. The Pathan horse-dealer and Buddhist priest, each in his different way, regard the boy as a son, as does the 'Sahiba' who nurses Kim out of his breakdown at the end of the book; as Mahbub jealously grumbles ' "Hmph! Half Hind seems that way disposed" ' (*K*, 405). Colonel Creighton of the Secret Service, the object of much post-colonial scrutiny,[19] is a cold fish in comparison; respected not loved, he holds little importance once Kim is launched on his education.

Kipling, the poet of the work ethic, thus most surprisingly creates a hero who 'did nothing with an immense success...he lived a life wilder than the Arabian Nights, [though] missionaries and secretaries of charitable societies could not see the beauty of it (*K*, 3–4). Even when Kim falls into the hands of Fr. Victor and the Revd. Bennett, chaplains of his father's regiment, he avoids the life of drill and uniformity by which Kipling's 'cubs' are usually licked into shape. Thanks to the lama's generosity and Creighton's influence, his public-school education at St Xavier's School allows him the status and training of a 'Sahib' and future officer without the usual pains of exile and harsh discipline. No turning out to 'footer', on pain of three strokes of a ground-ash wielded by an athletic prefect, for Kim, who obeys his English teachers only because it suits him and out of term-time promptly disappears into the life of his beloved bazaars and the tutelage of Mahbub Ali and 'my lama'. The contrast with George Cottar, that boring paragon whose hidden dream-life as the 'Brushwood Boy' runs alongside but never enters his existence as a model officer and gentleman, could hardly be more striking. Like Mowgli, until he leaves the Jungle, Kim is free of Adam's curse 'in the sweat of thy face shalt thou eat bread' (Genesis 3: 19) for his future lies in a 'Great Game' played by disguise and intrigue: an endless source of adventures.

Although Kim's Irishness, his physical beauty, his 'low-caste' (*K*, 3) hybrid identity, and his street-wise charm make him a quite different person from Rudyard Kipling, the two are alike in more than their names. Kim, like his creator, leaves school at sixteen after a display of schoolboy brilliance, though his teachers know 'the rush of minds developed by sun and surroundings, as they know the half-collapse that sets in at twenty-two or twenty-three'; which sounds like an allusion to Kipling's own breakdown in 1891.[20] And Kim who can talk to anybody, grasp any speech he hears or overhears, in whatever language it is spoken, carry a map in his head and describe exactly objects he has briefly glanced at, can slip in and out of identities as he chooses, and to whom fortune (or the plot) offers a series of lucky chances at exactly the right moments, might well have said, as Kipling in old age wrote of himself, that 'every card in my working life has been dealt me in such a manner that I had but to play it as it came' (*SM*, 1). The impression of identification and intimacy with the hero is subtly enhanced by the fact that 'Kim' is so named only by himself and the narrator – and so also the reader. Though he tells Father Victor that ' "they call me Kim Rishti ke. That is Kim of the Rishti ... *Eye*-rishti" ' – "Irish – oh, I see" ' (*K*, 121), he is called 'Little Friend of all the World' by Mahbub Ali and (initially) the lama, and 'O'Hara' by the English clerics and soldiers; as a young man he is called '*Chela*' by the lama and 'Mister O'Hara' by Hurree Babu. Moreover, Kim's chameleon ability to slip between different costumes, adopt different identities and above all to speak different languages parallels Kipling's own invention of a rhetorical, archaised English equivalent to the 'vernacular' which enables the narrative to move easily and interchangeably between the narrator's own Standard English and the 'fluent and picturesque' (*K*, 167) Indian vernaculars spoken by his characters (including the lama's Urdu, Kim's Hindustani, Mahbub's Pushtu and the policeman's Punjabi). The scene where Kim interprets between the English priests and his lama emphasizes his duplicitous linguistic skills:

> 'Now I make pretence of agreement, for at the worst it will be but a few meals eaten away from thee... However it goes, I shall run back to thee when I am tired. But stay with the Rajputni, or I shall miss thy feet... Oah yess,' said the boy, 'I have told him everything you tell me to say.' (*K*, 127–8)

The invention of the 'vernacular', with its characteristic rendering of Indian speech through a stylized linguistic archaism that implies both difference and kinship, allows the reader to enter with Kim into the crowded third-class railway compartment of the railway train (known to Indians as the '*te-rain*' [*K*, 38] – clearly a loan-word from English) where priest and disciple converse throughout the journey with a banker, an Amritsar 'courtesan' making eyes at a soldier on leave, a respectable Hindu farming couple and a Sikh carpenter, making us free of the interchanging tensions and harmonies of the different castes and genders, and even privy to family relationships; as when a farmer's wife, having offered Kim and the lama shelter at a relative's house, deals with her husband's objection to her filling the place with 'wastrels'. '"Thy cousin's younger brother owes my father's cousin something yet on his daughter's marriage-feast," said the woman crisply. "Let him put their food to that account"' (*K*, 50) – a snippet that implies much about the complex finances of extended families and the potential dominance of strong-minded Indian wives. This affectionate depiction of ordinary peoples' speech, at once strange to a modern English reader and completely intelligible, continues into the idyllic night scene in the family's courtyard where the children are *not* sent upstairs to bed while the lama describes his beloved Hills and discusses the casting of horoscopes and nativities with the family's priest, 'each giving the planets names that the others could not understand, and pointing upwards as the big stars sailed across the dark' while the 'children of the house tugged unrebuked at his rosary; and he clean forgot the Rule which forbids looking at women' as he speaks of his beloved Hills, 'blocked passes, the remote cliffs where men find sapphires and turquoises' (*K*, 55).

The pleasure of these dialogues is matched by the novel's painterly descriptions of Indian scenes like the dawn seen by the train passengers – 'Golden, rose, saffron and pink the morning-mists smoked away across the flat green levels. All the rich Punjab lay out in the splendour of the keen sun' (*K*, 44), or the night-piece when the lama converses by firelight with the old lady behind the curtains of her litter:

> The lama, very straight and erect, the deep folds of his yellow clothing slashed with black in the light of the *parao* fires precisely as a knotted tree-trunk is slashed with the shadows of the low sun, addressed a tinsel and lacquered *ruth* which burned like a many-coloured jewel in the same uncertain light. The patterns on the gold-worked curtains ran up and down, melting and re-forming as the folds shook and quivered in the night wind; and when the talk grew more earnest the jewelled forefinger snapped out little sparks of light between the embroideries. (*K*, 101)

Darkness, the 'uncertain' firelight, patterns that don't stay still, the unseen face and jewelled hand are here no fearful mysteries to be opposed by the daylight certainties of English reason. The richly changing colours have both a Shakespearean glamour, echoing Cleopatra's barge that 'burned on the water'[21] and the freshness of the country where, as Kipling wrote in a late poem of longing for a warmer place, 'There isn't any Door that need be shut!' (*W*, 812). Most beguiling of all is the great description of the Great Trunk Road full of all sorts and conditions of Indian humanity: the 'long-haired, strong-scented Sansis', the stiffly walking jail-bird, 'the memory of his leg-irons still on him', the 'Akali, a wild-eyed, wild-haired Sikh devotee...with polished steel quoits glistening on the cone of his tall blue turban', the gang of 'strong-limbed, big-bosomed, blue-petticoated' women labourers belonging to a 'caste whose men do not count' and the 'gaily dressed crowds of whole villages turning out for some local fair', described in loving detail:

> the women, with their babes on their hips walking behind the men, the older boys prancing on sticks of sugar-cane, dragging rude brass

models of locomotives such as they sell for a halfpenny, or flashing the
sun into the eyes of their betters from cheap toy mirrors. These merry-
makers stepped slowly, calling one to the other or stopping to haggle
with sweetmeat-sellers, or to make a prayer before one of the wayside
shrines – sometimes Mussulman, sometime Hindu – which the low-
caste of both creeds share with beautiful impartiality.' (K, 86-8)

Although that last sentence, loosely equating caste (unknown to
Islam) with class, marks a distance between the narrator and the
people he describes, its language and tone – the tender archaism
of 'the women with their babes', the light-hearted mock-
disapproval for the small boys teasing 'their betters' with
mirrors, and the unanxious acceptance of 'pagan' prayers as
'beautiful', clearly make the description strongly affirmative.
Kipling's description of this 'wonderful spectacle.. such a river
of life as nowhere else exists' (K, 81) is striking for an endless
delight taken in human difference and in the small diverse
details of custom and behaviour that, as Said observed, recalls
Chaucer: 'Kipling has the Middle English poet's eye for
wayward detail, the odd character, the slice of life, the amused
sense of human foibles and joys.'[22] True, Kipling even when
celebrating this rich diversity of Indian life remains a knowing
writer who surveys the 'wonderful spectacle' from above.
Thomas Richards argues persuasively that such passages,
including both Kim's boyish pleasure in new sights and
Kipling's own ethnographic knowledge of names and histories,
represent a colonial fantasy of the 'comprehensive knowledge
on which English hegemony rests';[23] but here it is a loving
knowledge.

By contrast with this colourful Indian world, the English
soldiers and clerics who lay claim to Kim as a white boy look
emotionally impoverished, stupid and brutal, their 'dull fat eyes'
(K, 168) seeing only their own superiority. The Anglican
chaplain Bennett not only comes in for bitter disapproval of
the 'triple-ringed uninterest' with which he dismisses the holy
lama as a 'heathen' *fakir*, but is shown up as a racist fool in his
naïve reliance on Kim once he knows the boy is white:

'The old man doesn't look like a villain'
'My experience is that one can never fathom the Oriental mind.
Now, Kimball, I wish you to tell this man what I say' (K, 125).

The kindlier Father Victor at least understands the lama's goodness and his pain, but being unable to speak the vernacular thinks of the Buddhist scholar as a street-beggar. As Mark Kinkead-Weekes points out in a subtle reading of *Kim*, the Catholic priest shows his limitations by using the Muslim term *'Kismet'* to a Buddhist 'to whom he might as well have talked of Mesopotamia' (*K*, 127). Even more telling is his repeated exclamation 'Powers of Darkness!' (120, 123, 124, 131).[24] Kipling had used a couplet from Bishop Ken's 'Evening Hymn' ('May no ill dreams disturb my rest / Nor powers of darkness me molest') as the ironic epigraph to his early ghost-story 'The Phantom Rickshaw' (*WWW*, 123), and Hummil in 'At the End of the Passage' who is being slowly trapped in the 'Dark Places' of Indian nightmare quotes the same lines with equally bitter irony (*LH*, 194, 208). But as with the drummer-boy's crass 'You talk like a nigger, don't you?' (*K*, 145), the point in *Kim* is the way that the ill-chosen words 'place' their English speakers as examples of (to borrow a term from Father Victor's own Catholicism) invincible ignorance. For in this scene the lama not only questions the white men who have claimed Kim: 'You take him from me and you cannot say what you will make of him. Tell me before I go, for it is not a small thing to make a child' (132), but intervenes to save Kim according to the tenets of his own faith:

> 'It is no wrong to pay for learning. To help the ignorant to wisdom is always a merit.' The rosary clicked furiously as an abacus. Then he faced his oppressors.
> 'Ask them for how much money do they give a wise and suitable teaching? And in what city is that teaching given?' (*K*, 133)

Nowhere else in Kipling's work are white men called 'oppressors' without irony. And the 'weaponless dreamer' who has so often on the journey seemed lost and bewildered, more of a child than the street-wise Kim, manages to impose his will on the foreign priests, even before he is helped by the influential Colonel Creighton (and, at a further remove, Mahbub Ali). Though he accepts Kim should be educated as a Sahib, when Kim later objects that 'to abstain from action [is] unbefitting a Sahib,' the old man answers with Buddhist authority, 'To those who follow the Way there is neither black nor white, Hind nor Bhotiyal. We be all souls seeking escape' (*K*, 303).

6

Kipling's Poetry: Victorian to Modernist: 'He Do The Police In Different Voices'

It's Tommy this and Tommy that and 'Chuck 'im out, the brute',
But it's 'Saviour of 'is country' when the guns begin to shoot.

('Tommy', *W*, 399)

I could not dig: I dared not rob:[1]
Therefore I lied to please the mob.

(*Epitaphs of the War:* 'A dead statesman' *W*, 390)

We fainted with our chins on the oars and you did not see
  that we were idle, for we still swung to and fro.
  Will you never let us go?
The salt made the oar-handles like shark-skin; our knees
  were cut to the bone with salt-cracks ; our hair was stuck
  to our foreheads; and our lips were cut to the gums, and
  you whipped us because we could not row.
  Will you never let us go?

('Song of the Galley-Slaves' *W*, 671)

AMBIGUOUS CONSERVATISM

The ambiguous status of Kipling's poetry is aptly summed up by Dan Jacobson's exasperated tribute to 'Kipling, a poet I cannot abide yet cannot stop reading'.[2] Kipling is not always recognized as a poet at all, yet his endlessly popular 'If –' was in 1995 voted the 'Nation's Favourite Poem'; more tellingly still, he is one of the few English poets besides Shakespeare whose words have entered common usage. George Orwell's 1941 remark that

104

'Nothing could exceed the contempt of the *New Statesman* for Kipling, but how many times during the Munich period did the *New Statesman* find itself quoting that phrase about paying the Dane-geld?'[3] remains pertinent today, Kipling's poems – or bits of them – having taken on a life of their own, often in ways that would have greatly surprised their author. If you type well-known phrases from Kipling's verse into the search engine 'Google', you find them cited on both extreme right-wing websites and others of utterly different persuasions. 'Never the twain shall meet' from the 'Ballad of East and West' (*W*, 234) has been used as the title for articles on gender relations, on bipolar mental disorder, on overspending, on school syllabi, and on the arts/science division in intellectual life, not to mention a book on telecommunications. And by a nice historical irony, the phrase 'Lest we forget', from 'Recessional' (*W*, 329) has become a favourite title of websites commemorating history's victims – not just the dead of the First and Second World Wars, a usage of which Kipling would have approved, but African-American slaves and Britain's heritage of radical democracy,[4] which he surely would not. One wonders whether Kipling himself or the authors of these websites would be the more disconcerted by this information.

The political attitudes articulated in Kipling's poems are various and ambivalent. He invented the voice of the engineer McAndrew hymning 'Law, Orrder, Duty an' Restraint, Obedience, Discipline' (*W*, 126), and the Sergeant warning *'Keep away from dirtiness – keep away from mess,/Don't get into doin' things rather more-or-less!'* (*W*, 453) – but also the 'Voice of the Hooligan' speaking cheerfully for the soldier who gets into street-fights ('Belts, belts, belts, an' that's one for you! Belts, belts, belts an' that's done for you!' *W*, 415), and who, even more shockingly, boasts how 'If you treat a nigger to a dose o' cleanin' rod, / 'E's like to show you everything 'e owns' (*W*, 410). 'Recessional' makes the English superior to 'lesser breeds without the Law' (*W*, 329) and 'The White Man's Burden' calls the 'sullen' natives 'half devil and half child' (*W*, 323); yet other poems speak so eloquently for the put-upon common man that Craig Raine has hailed Kipling as 'the discover[er] for literature of the under-dog'.[5] And Kipling's formal qualities seem equally contra-dictory. His thumping rhythms and mechanically patterned metres seem to belong to a stereotypical Victorian poetry, bounded at the shallow end by W.S. Gilbert's comic verse and at the deep end by the organ-voice solemnities of Tennyson in patriotic 'Rise, Britons, rise, if manhood be not dead'[6] mode; yet he was admired, quoted and rewritten by the modernist poets T.S. Eliot, Bertolt Brecht and Ezra Pound,[7] and has had a persistent influence on English poets from Auden onwards. His voice is echoed in Auden's early hortatory 'Get there if you can and see the land you once were proud to own', and more obliquely in 'Roman Wall Blues' whose speaker grumbling that 'I've lice in my tunic and a cold in my nose' nicely subverts the pieties of Parnesius in *Puck of Pook's Hill*; while Auden's 1939 elegy 'In Memory of W.B. Yeats' pays ambivalent tribute to the lasting power of his language: 'Time that with this strange excuse / Pardoned Kipling and his views'.[8]

Donald Davie pointed out how deeply indebted Tony Harrison, John Betjeman and Kingsley Amis were to 'Kipling['s]...greatness and fecundity as a poet', and more recently Harry Ricketts finds his influence on the poems of Gavin Ewart and Wendy Cope.[9] And James Fenton's political poem 'The Ballad of the Imam and the Shah' brilliantly uses a Kiplingesque ballad-narrative with a thumpingly repetitive refrain to articulate a relentless machine of persecution endlessly reproducing itself: 'The song is yours. Arrange it as you will./ Remember where each word fits in the line./ And every combination will be true / And every permutation will be fine: *From policy to felony to fear... From poverty to malady to grave / From malady to agony to spite / From agony to misery to hate / From misery to policy to fight!*'[10]

Auden compared Kipling's mechanical competence to a sergeant drilling the awkward squad: 'Under his will, the vulgarest words learn to wash behind their ears and to execute complicated movements at the word of command'.[11] But by no means all of Kipling's poems are in fact 'thumpers'. Many of the 'Epitaphs of the Great War', and the 'Puck' poems including 'The Way through the woods', 'Eddi's Service' and 'Cities and Thrones and Powers' are quietly poignant, as are his rare free verse lyrics (all written in conjunction with short stories), like the 'Song of the Galley-Slaves' quoted above from 'The Finest Story In The World', or 'Mowgli's Song' on the death of Shere

Khan in *The Jungle Book*, or the 'Runes on Weland's Sword' from
Puck of Pook's Hill:

> The Gold I gather
> Comes into England
> Out of deep Water.
>
> Like a shining Fish
> Then it descends
> Into deep Water.

(*W*, 670)

In short, Kipling's poetry is, like the prose writing with which
it is so often intertwined, far more various, agile and interesting
than is commonly recognized. But it is necessary here to
distinguish between the different *kinds* of contradiction and
argument generated by Kipling's poetry. Some of his apparent
contradictions arise because the sheer bulk and range of his
poems make them too diverse to fit into any one, or even two or
three, genres or tendencies. The demotic coarse vitality of
Barrack Room Ballads is countered by the solemnity of patriotic
hymns like 'Recessional'. The swashbuckling narratives of
pursuit or slaughter like 'The Ballad of East and West' or 'The
Ballad of Boh Da Thone' contrast with the compassionate
minor-key song of the Vikings' wives left behind to wait and
worry: 'Then you drive out where the storm-clouds swallow /
And the sound of your oar-blades falling hollow / Is all we have
left through the months to follow' (*W*, 528). The crassly populist
'Holy War',[12] which ropes John Bunyan of *The Pilgrim's Progress*
into English war propaganda ('The Pope, the swithering
Neutrals./ The Kaiser and his Gott,/ Their roles, their goals,
their naked souls,/ He knew and drew the lot': *W*, 290) is
opposed by the measured gravity of the 'Epitaphs of the War'.
And so on; one could go on enumerating these contrasting
genres – *except*, strikingly, for the one category that most readers
expect in the work of any poet since Wordsworth and don't find
in Kipling: the subjective lyric of personal experience.

Although 'Kiplingesque' poetry has an instantly recognizable
style – usually but not invariably that of *Barrack Room Ballads* in
which demotic Cockney (or occasionally Irish) speech with
dropped aitches is shaped into elaborate stanza form, often with

a refrain – it is almost never possible to identify its speaker with Kipling's own voice. Except perhaps in elegiac war poems like 'Mesopotamia 1917' or 'The Children', and even here he writes principally as a public man, Kipling hardly ever speaks in his own person. Even in those very rare poems that speak of his own sorrows, Kipling preferred to be indirect. The nearest he came to writing an elegy for the son he lost at the Battle of Loos is the dialogue-poem 'My Boy Jack', which transmutes his own agonized anxiety about John, 'missing believed killed', into the voice of a worried mother[13] asking vainly 'Have you news of my boy Jack?' (W, 216). Similarly with Kipling's grief for his daughter Josephine, the 'Best Beloved' of the *Just-So Stories* who is commemorated in the moving poem 'Merrow Down', where she becomes the fictional 'Taffimai' whose ghost flits ahead of her father as poignantly as the elusive children of the ghost story 'They':

> For far – oh, very far behind,
>   So far she cannot call to him
> Comes Tegumai alone to find
>   The daughter that was all to him.

(W, 597, JS, 139)

This absence of directly personal lyrics from Kipling's *œuvre* partly explains why more people don't read him; a post-Romantic literary culture that still tends, even in these postmodernist days, to associate poetry with self-expression, has problems with a poet who so resolutely avoids doing any such thing. But another difficulty is, undoubtedly, the conservative political allegiance that for so long made readers uncertain of his aesthetic status: should he be read as Orwell's 'gutter patriot'[14] or Craig Raine's 'voice of the underdog'? Furthermore, is he a poet or a versifier?

The question of Kipling's poetic stature is much less problematic now than it was just after he died, when Cyril Connolly damned him as a poet admired only by stuffy schoolmasters and Edmund Wilson observed that 'the more serious-minded young people do *not* read him; the critics do not even take him into account.'[15] T.S. Eliot's preface to *A Choice of Kipling's Verse* (1941) ponders elaborately and at length whether Kipling should be considered a poet or a versifier, resolving the question with the rather fence-sitting answer that Kipling should be considered a writer of great verse which occasionally rises to the intensity of poetry. George Orwell's better-known verdict 'a good bad poet' defines the appeal of Kipling's coarse populist vitality as ' almost a shameful pleasure, like the taste for cheap sweets that some people carry into middle age'.[16] These anxieties about Kipling's aesthetic status nowadays look rather dated, belonging as they do to a historical moment in which Kipling fell foul of a critical consensus in favour not only of liberal politics (which still broadly holds) but of *avant-garde* aesthetics. Eliot's defensiveness is notably absent from the prefaces to recent anthologies of Kipling's poetry by Craig Raine (1992) who makes a strong case for him as both a master of subtle metre and a modernist poet, and Harry Ricketts (2004) who points out how widely and deeply Kipling influenced twentieth-century English poets.[17] Twenty-first century poetry readers who regard rap and dub poetry as lively contributions to literary culture and admire 'performance poets' like Linton Kwesi Johnson, Jean Binta Breeze and John Hegley, are not likely to share Orwell's and Eliot's worries about according vernacular language, demotic vitality and the exploitation of cliché and formula the status of 'poetry'.

But the question of how to judge Kipling's political work remains difficult to resolve. The element of right-wing politics in his poetry is undeniable: he was an imperialist spokesman, he did write some virulent poems preaching the doctrines of the political Right such as the hysterical 'Ulster 1912' ('We know the wars prepared/ On every peaceful home,/ We know the hells prepared/For such as serve not Rome': W, 233), and the viciously anti-semitic satires 'Gehazi' and 'The Waster'. There is genuine power as well as nastiness in these political poems, arising from Kipling's profound identification both with the administrators of the Law (nearly always capitalized in his poems) and with the outlawed anarchy that threatens it. Hence the deep ambivalence of 'The Gods of the Copybook Headings', a powerful reactionary poem which contrasts the fashionable hopes for progress represented by the 'Gods of the Marketplace', with the unfashionable but inescapable laws of the 'Gods of the Copybook Headings' whom humans have, from the beginning of Time preferred to ignore:

With the Hopes that our World is built on they were utterly out of touch.

They denied that the Moon was Stilton; they denied she was even Dutch.

They denied that Wishes were Horses; they denied that Pigs had Wings.

So we worshipped the Gods of the Market Who promised these beautiful things.

(W, 793)

The 'beautiful things' are pacifism, sexual emancipation and socialism, each resulting in, respectively, war, sterility and poverty. David Gilmour[18] convincingly reads this poem as a humorous political allegory, in which the 'Cambrian' era represents Lloyd George and Liberal disarmament, 'the first Feminian sandstones' mean women's emancipation, and the 'Carboniferous Era' when 'we were promised abundance for all / By robbing selected Peter to pay for collective Paul' alludes to trade unionism amongst coal miners. Yet the poem's scope goes beyond these specific political issues with its final prophecy of 'terror and slaughter'. It is dated, like many of Kipling's public poems, with the year of its composition: 1919, when the First World War officially ended with a post-war settlement at Versailles, General Dyer ordered the shooting of Indian civilians in the Amritsar massacre, Kipling's enemies triumphed in the post-War elections, the Liberal Party granted women the vote, and – even more disastrously from Kipling's Unionist point of view – Sinn Fein's electoral victory in Ireland spelled the beginning of the Irish Free State. These events are not accorded detailed allusions, but their threatening presence can be sensed in the deadly serious ending, hammered home by the biblical allusion to the biblical maxim 'The dog is turned to his own vomit again; and the sow that was washed to her wallowing in the mire' (Proverbs 26, v. 22):

As it will be in the Future, it was at the Birth of Man –
There are only four things certain since Social Progress began,
That the Dog returns to his Vomit and the Sow returns to her Mire
And the burnt Fool's bandaged Finger goes wabbling back to the Fire,

And that after this is accomplished, and the brave new world begins
Where all men are paid for existing and no man must pay for his sins,

110

As surely as Water will wet us, as surely as Fire will burn,
The Gods of the Copybook Headings with terror and slaughter
return!

(W, 793)

As with Yeats' dark foretelling 'The Second Coming', there is a
good deal of prophetic truth in this poem. (It was read by W.H.
Auden in 1939 to a very surprised New York audience, and the
'Copybook Headings' probably influenced the reflection in his
own 'September 1st, 1939', that as 'all schoolchildren learn,/
Those to whom evil is done / Do evil in return'[19]). But this
doesn't stop it from also being a savagely entertained revenge
fantasy of violence and castration ('the burnt Fool's bandaged
Finger...wabbling back to the Fire') invoked in the name of
permanent truth. The sermon on order and stability is thus
subverted by its own violent images and thumping repetitive
rhythm, which arouse those ferociously destructive energies
whose suppression the poem is so loudly demanding.

Yet, against Kipling's reactionary hatreds must be set his
poetry's extraordinarily wide imaginative sympathies, its identification with the common man and (though less often)
woman, its epigrammatic shrewdness, and above all, the way
it speaks for rebels and outlaws. This identification with the
outsider enables Kipling to voice the misery of exploited outcasts
in 'Song of the Galley Slaves' and in 'A Pict Song' the bitterness
of the downtrodden:

Rome never looks where she treads.
Always her heavy hooves fall
On our stomachs, our hearts or our heads;
And Rome never heeds when we bawl.

(W, 248)

It should also be remembered that Kipling's best-known
'Barrack Room Ballad' ends with the English soldier's admission
that the despised, ill-treated Indian is 'a better man than I am,
Gunga Din!' (W, 408). Though Kipling is never a political radical,
his *Departmental Ditties* (1885) even evince a wry sympathy for
the Indian peasant enjoying the dubious colonial blessings of
'Jails – and Police to fight,/ Justice – and length of days,/And
Right – and Might in the Right' (W, 39). The author of *Kim*, who
celebrated multi-racial difference and satirized the Revd.

111

Bennet's racial arrogance and religious bigotry, also wrote the moving epitaph for a Hindu sepoy in France, 'This man in his own country prayed we know not to what Powers./ We pray Them to reward him for his bravery in ours' (*W*, 387), and the ironic 'Jobson's Amen' satirizing the parochialism of English Christianity ('*Blessed be the English and everything they own,* / *Cursed be the Hereticks who bow to wood and stone!*', *W*, 503), and most delightfully, the tongue-in-cheek 'We and They':

> Father, Mother and Me,
> Sister and Auntie say
> All the people like us are We,
> And everyone else is They.

(W, 764)

Kipling's poems, as Craig Raine has emphasized, constantly speak of and for ordinary people, 'the mere uncounted folk / Of whose life and death is none / Report or lamentation' (*W*, 500) as well as for the 'Sons of Martha', fated to labour unrewarded and unthanked. His Army poems speak not for the officer class to which he belonged by birth and education but for the rank and file 'Tommy' who is humiliated in London pubs where 'The publican 'e up and sez, "We serve no red-coats here", /The girls be'ind the bar they laughed an' giggled fit to die' (*W*, 398), who goes out to battles where 'some was crimped and some was carved,/ And some was gutted and some was starved,/ When the Widow give the party' (*W*, 421), who grieves for a dead friend in 'Follow me 'Ome' and who sardonically describes being paid off: ' 'Ere's ... fourpence a day for baccy – an' bloomin' generous, too; /An' now you can make your fortune – the same as your orf'cers do.' (*W*, 430) The civilians for whom Kipling speaks include a discarded woman pleading vainly for matrimony: 'I want the name – no more – / The name, an' lines to show,[20] An' not to be an 'ore .... / Ah Gawd, I love you so!' (*W*, 456) and a rebellious veteran who can't take post-war civilian life:

> 'Ow can I ever take on
> With awful old England again,
> An' 'ouses both sides of the street,
> An' 'edges both sides of the lane,
> An' the parson an' gentry between,
> An' touchin' my 'at when we meet –

112

Me that 'ave been what I've been?

(*W*, 461)

The significance of these demotic and marginalized voices is not only that they counter any simple political notion of Kipling as the bard of Authority. By multiplying and destabilizing the single voice of authority, their heteroglossia represents a significant early contribution to modernist poetry.

KIPLING'S MODERNISM

To describe Kipling as a modernist poet may look paradoxical, given that much of his poetry, including *Barrack Room Ballads*, appeared before 1900. His favoured verse genres are the ballad, the demotic 'music-hall' monologue, and the hymn, all accepted 'Victorian' modes, and he liked to use the elaborate stanza-forms associated with Swinburne and the comic poems of W.S. Gilbert. His public poems like 'Recessional' or 'The White Man's Burden' (both published in *The Times*) vocalized conservative and imperialist pieties and his poems for children invoke a semi-mythical traditional England. One could make the case for Kipling's traditionalism from the poem 'Minesweepers', dated 1914, a fine example of his formal skill:

> Dawn off the Foreland – the young flood making
>> Jumbled and short and steep –
> Black in the hollows and bright where it's breaking –
>> Awkward water to sweep.
>> 'Mines reported in the fairway.
>> Warn all traffic and detain.
> 'Sent up – *Unity, Claribel, Assyrian, Stormcock* and *Golden Gain*.'
>
> Noon off the Foreland – the first ebb making
>> Lumpy and strong in the bight.
> Boom after boom, and the golf-hut shaking
>> And the jackdaws wild with fright !
>> 'Mines located in the fairway.
>> Boats now working up the chain.
> Sweepers – *Unity, Claribel, Assyrian, Stormcock* and *Golden Gain*'.
>
> Dusk off the Foreland – the last light going
>> And the traffic crowding through,

113

And five damned trawlers with their syreens blowing
   Heading the whole review!
   'Sweep completed in the fairway.
   No more mines remain.
Sent back – *Unity, Claribel, Assyrian, Stormcock* and *Golden Gain.'*

                               (W, 261)

Two voices speak here, each stanza opened by a literary observer given to strongly visual, emphatically alliterative adjectival phrases like ' black in the hollows and bright where it's breaking', followed by a naval officer's voice reporting each stage of the manœuvre in that three-line refrain, ending with the listed names of whose incantatory music the speaker is apparently unaware: 'Sweepers – *Unity, Claribel, Assyrian, Stormcock* and *Golden Gain'.* The poetry of that simple statement comes partly from a lilting rhythm which answers the two previous trimeter (three-foot) lines; if you discount the light first syllable of 'Assyrian' and allow the second light syllable of 'Golden Gain' to make the final foot an amphimacer (= long, short, long) instead of the usual spondee (=long, long), the line becomes a (very) rough accentual hexameter.[21] The names too are rich in patriotic and literary connotations: *Unity* states the poem's key theme of the trawlers completing their mission undamaged, *Claribel* and *Assyrian* respectively echo a Tennyson lyric and Byron's line 'The Assyrian came down like a wolf on the fold' (celebrating, appropriately enough, the defeat of an invading enemy), and *Stormcock* evokes the missel-thrush singing with 'blast be-ruffled plume' in Thomas Hardy's 'The Darkling Thrush'.[22] The final *Golden Gain* echoes the *Golden Hind* in which the Elizabethan hero-adventurer Sir Francis Drake circumnavigated the world, changing it into the clinching '*Gain*' whose end-rhyming emphasis triumphantly denies the possibility of *loss* that just one missing name would mean. The sea's tossing violence and the exploding mines do nothing worse than shake a golf-hut and frighten birds, thanks to the Royal Navy's courage and skill which is both celebrated and imitated in the poem's own verbal performance, each refrain's chiming closure proclaiming that the English tradition represented by its literary-historic allusions and orderly music remains and will remain unbroken. Both the pleasure of the poem and its ideological limitations lie in their reliance on protective formal boundaries, as in Kipling's remembered childhood games: 'The magic, you see, lies in the ring or fence that you take refuge in' (*SM*, 10). If this poem, articulating patriotic ideology and aesthetics in an original form (Kipling seems to have invented this stanza) which is none the less traditionalist, adequately represents Kipling's poetic achievement, then he cannot remotely – can he? – be considered a modernist poet.

Yes, he can. Kipling may be in one sense a Victorian poet, but those affinities with modernism in his poetry, which could be guessed from the admiration of Eliot and Brecht, are in retrospect becoming more and more apparent as the history of poetry in the last century is increasingly understood in more nuanced and complex ways than the old simple opposition between Victorian or Georgian traditionalism and a modernist *avant-garde*. Kipling's modernity is not merely a matter of themes, like the fascination with modern technologies of communication that inspired his celebration of the sub-Atlantic telephone cable with its ominous vision of 'The great grey level plains of ooze where the shell-burred cables creep,'(*W*, 124), anticipating Thomas Hardy's imagined sea-worms crawling over the wrecked *Titanic* in 'The Convergence of the Twain', or the deep intuition he shares with Conrad and Eliot of the chaos and anarchy lying not far below the 'certain certainties' of civilized England. His modernity lies more subtly in the interpretative uncertainty generated by the multiple voices and registers that speak his poems, even 'Minesweepers' with its literary and Service voices, and its musical form jarred by those triumphant 'five damned trawlers with their syreens blowing'. The voices of this poetry are all stylistically recognizable as 'Kiplingesque' yet none identifiable as the expression of Kipling's true self. 'He Do The Police In Different Voices', T.S. Eliot's original title for *The Waste Land*,[23] would fit Kipling splendidly – especially given his political role as the singer of hard-fisted authority.

There are many recognizable 'Kiplingesque' voices: in *Barrack Room Ballads* the voices of common soldiers; in his dramatic monologues the voices of the Glasgow engineer McAndrew, pondering the meaning of his life in and of the unscrupulous old ship-builder Sir Anthony Gloster on his deathbed; in *The Jungle*

Book the voices of the monkeys jeering 'Don't you envy our pranceful bands?/ Don't you wish you had extra hands?'(*W*, 544), of Chil the kite about to prey on the corpses of his wolf friends – 'These were my companions going forth by night / *For Chil! Look you, for Chil!*/ Now I come to whistle them the ending of the fight' (*W*, 532) or of Mowgli about to destroy the hated village, chanting 'The trees – the trees are on you!/ The house-beams shall fall; / And the *Karela*, the bitter *Karela* / Shall cover you all!' (*W*, 640).

Robert Browning's influence on Kipling is evident, and not only in the obvious homage of the two dramatic monologues 'McAndrew's Hymn' and 'The Mary Gloster' (the latter of which, spoken by the dying 'robber-baron' shipping magnate, Sir Anthony Gloster to his silent son 'Dickie', whom he despises and possibly wants to murder, amounts to a late Victorian re-writing of Browning's poem 'The Bishop of St Praxed's Orders his Tomb'). Kipling's creative relationship with Browning goes deeper than imitation or even intertextual rewriting. He learnt from the Victorian poet not just to mimic voices not his own, but in ways comparable to the young Eliot's *Love Song of J. Alfred Prufrock* musing 'I grow old . . . I grow old,/ I shall wear the bottoms of my trousers rolled' or Ezra Pound's 'Sestina: Altaforte' beginning 'Damn it all! all this our South speaks peace'[24] to ironise both a speaker and his (or occasionally her) world. This is also true of Kipling's prose: the superficially knowing, ironical 'I' whose narratives frame so many early Kipling stories is as much a fictional construct, and as much 'placed' by the violent or mysterious events he describes, as Browning's self-deceived artist 'Andrea del Sarto' or the venomous monk who speaks in 'Soliloquy of the Spanish Cloister'.

There is, likewise, an element of modernist uncertainty in the way Kipling's stage Cockney or stage Irish poems make a point both of their own demotic realism and of their artificiality. This conscious artifice, combined with the talent for aphorism in lines that have become familiar to the point of cliché – 'You're a better man than I am, Gunga Din', or 'Them that asks no questions isn't told no lies' (*W*, 408, 655) – can make the reader of Kipling's poetry want to echo the old joke about Shakespeare's *Hamlet*, 'It's much too full of quotations'. This is also true in a literal sense, Kipling being a brilliant stylistic magpie who borrows at will from the Bible, from Anglican hymn-books, from the music-hall monologue, and from English literature.

> *Ah! What avails the classic bent*
> *And what the cultured word,*
> *Against the undoctored incident*
> *That actually occurred?*

(W, 340)

That epigram about the limits of realism, itself a parody of Walter Savage Landor's once-famous anthology-piece 'Rose Aylmer',[25] shows both the ear for cliché and commonplace that made Orwell class Kipling as 'a good bad poet' and a subversive yet oddly directionless irony that leaves one uncertain how far Kipling 'means' what he says. Such poetry exactly fits Roland Barthes' well-known definition of a 'text' in *The Death of the Author*: 'a multi-dimensional space in which a variety of writings, none of them original, blend and clash...a tissue of quotations drawn from the innumerable centres of culture'.[26]

This indeterminate textuality can be found in Kipling's secular hymns, including some of his most famous public poems. A hymn is a communal form of verse voicing shared beliefs, to be spoken – or rather sung – by a consensual 'we' (as opposed to the individual 'I' of subjective lyrics). It also belongs to that Evangelical Christianity which was forced on Kipling as a bullied child in the Southsea 'House of Desolation' and which he rejected in adult life while using its language to vocalize the patriotic and imperialist beliefs of an idealized national community. For 'Recessional' and 'The White Man's Burden' (W, 328, 323) draw very closely on their Anglican originals. Kipling himself attested that 'Recessional' was modelled on 'the simple jog-trot of 'Eternal Father, strong to save',[27] and a look at the first stanzas of each shows how closely he kept to his original:

'Recessional'	'Eternal Father'
God of our fathers, known of old,	Eternal father, strong to save
Lord of our far-flung battle-line	Whose arm doth bind the restless wave
Beneath whose awful hand we hold	Who bid'st the mighty ocean deep
Dominion over palm and pine,	Its own appointed limits keep,
Lord God of Hosts, be with us yet	O hear us when we cry to Thee
Lest we forget – lest we forget !	For those in peril on the sea.

117

The similarity is not just the obvious formal one of octosyllabic stanzas rhyming *ababcc* or even the repeated refrain invoking divine authority. It lies also in the invocation of a geographical vista dominated by a Father-God whose strength is manifested in His mighty 'arm' and 'awful hand', setting limits alike to natural chaos and to human endeavour. Kipling's own ambivalence about the Christianity in which, as the present Archbishop of Canterbury aptly put it, he 'sometimes passionately believed and sometimes passionately disbelieved'[28] doesn't prevent the poem from drawing on the energies of Victorian orthodoxy. Similarly with 'the White Man's Burden' which draws equally closely on the hymn 'Stand up, stand up for Jesus', not only in rhyme and metre but in its tone of strenuous uplift and the commands repeated by the first line of each stanza: 'Stand up – stand up for Jesus!' 'Take up the White Man's burden! '

These secular hymns draw on a popular and solemn but unintellectual language of belief to articulate imperialist pieties. But there are also subversive hymns in Kipling's *œuvre*, including the splendid mockery of hymn-singing in the story 'The Village That Voted The Earth Was Flat', where, after the music-hall impresario 'Bat' Masquerier has successfully brought his cast of actors dressed up as the 'Flat Earth Society' to get the villagers of Huckley drunk and persuade them to join the Cause, the members of the *real* Flat Earth Society then turn up with a portable harmonium, singing:

> Hear ther truth our tongues are telling,
> > Spread ther light from shore to shore,
> God hath given man a dwelling
> > Flat and flat for evermore.
>
> When ther Primal Dark retreated,
> > When ther deeps were undesigned,
> He with rule and compass meted
> > Habitation for mankind!

> (*D of C*,199–200)

This sounds so authentic, right down to the phonetically transcribed 'ther' for 'the', that when the envious 'Bat' mutters ' "Curse Nature, she gets ahead of you every time. To think *I* forgot hymns and a harmonium!" ', one could almost forget that

118

Kipling invented this hymn (which surely rings so true because the language of piety and the imagery of control imposed on chaos came so easily to him). But there is no mockery in the dark 'Hymn to Physical Pain', first published with the late story 'The Tender Achilles' (*LR*, 1932), which thanks Pain the 'Dread Mother of Forgetfulness' for 'wip[ing] away our soul's distress / And memory of her sins' by all-consuming physical agony:

> Thine is the weariness outworn
> No promise shall relieve
> That says at eve 'Would God 'twere morn!'
> At morn, 'Would God 'twere eve!'
>
> And when Thy tender mercies cease
> And life unvexed is due,
> Instant upon the false release
> The Worm and Fire renew.

(W, 787–8)

One may guess that this expression of anguish owes much to Kipling's own experiences: the pain he suffered from 1915 from an undiagnosed stomach ulcer, the unhealed wound of his son John's disappearance and death in the Battle of Loos, and perhaps also the memory of the breakdowns he experienced both in childhood and as a young man. Yet the ascription to the fictional Dr. Wilkie, the 'tender Achilles' of the accompanying story's title, and the use of the first person plural 'we' both distance and generalize its anguish. Though the poem alludes overtly to the Old Testament curses 'The worm shall not die, neither shall their fire be quenched' (Isaiah 66: 24) and 'In the morning thou shalt say, Would God it were evening! and at even thou shalt say, Would God it were morning!' (Deuteronomy 28: 67), there is no sense here of an angry punishing God. This isn't a theological poem; it merely uses the idiom of piety as Kipling elsewhere uses the idioms of soldiers, exiles and engineers – as a language of extremity rather than belief.

These secular hymns, then, work by staging a rhetoric of belief with which the author cannot quite be identified. Even more subversive are the parody and pastiche which consequently play a key role in Kipling's poetry, from the early schoolboy pastiches and the parodies written with his sister 'Trix' and collected in *Echoes*, to the late sequence 'The Muse

119

Among The Motorists'. Like Kipling's hymns, these highly accomplished parodies often betray serious concerns, including an ever-present sense of crisis, danger and sorrow: for instance in the wryly sympathetic description of the Indian peasant in the early satiric sequence 'A Masque of Plenty', which re-writes the lament for the tragic contradictions of mankind's existence in Swinburne's *Atalanta in Calydon:*

> His speech is a burning fire;
> With his lips he travaileth;
> In his heart is a blind desire,
> In his mind foreknowledge of death.
> He weaves, and is clothed with derision;
> Sows, and he shall not reap;
> His life is a watch or a vision
> Between a sleep and a sleep.

Kipling's version turns the abstractions and metaphors into harsh material facts:

> His speech is of mortgaged bedding,
> On his kine he borrows yet,
> At his heart is his daughter's wedding,
> In his eye foreknowledge of debt.
> He eats and hath indigestion,
> He toils and he may not stop;
> His life is a long-drawn question
> Between a crop and a crop.

(W, 39)

Insisting on the poverty, debt and unending labour that make a subsistence farmer's life wretched, the young Kipling mocked not only the big empty words of poetic universality but the imperialist boast of enlightened rule as equally irrelevant to the peasant. It is almost as if his creative Daemon had anticipated Sara Suleri's post-colonial observation that 'the canonicity of English literature was primarily formulated in the laboratory provided by colonial terrain',[29] for of course Kipling's radicalism is also limited by depending on the authority of the canon that it mocks; the joke on Swinburne loses its edge if no one recognizes the original. And his relation to Swinburne is not only negative, for he draws on the older poet's acknowledgement of human sorrows even while mocking his abstractions.

The harshness of this poem is characteristic; Kipling's parodies often combine comic mimicry of form with a startling narrative brutality. This gleeful cruelty is a common feature of English comic verse in the pre-First World war era, a golden age for blackly humorous verse. Death, torture, cannibalism and dismemberment are the principal jokes of such comic classics as Hilaire Belloc's *Cautionary Tales* (1908) Harry Graham's *Ruthless Rhymes for Heartless Homes* (1899), as well as W.S. Gilbert's earlier *Bab Ballads* (1868) or W.M. Thackeray's comic verses. The jokes in 'The Muse Among the Motorists' follow suit, often turning on fatal car crashes – as in the two exquisite poems entitled 'Arterial (Early Chinese)':

> I
> Frost upon small rain – the ebony-lacquered avenue
>   Reflecting lamps as a pool shows goldfish.
> The sight suddenly emptied out of the young man's eyes
>   Entering upon it sideways.
> II
> In youth, by hazard, I killed an old man.
>   In age I maimed a little child.
> Dead leaves underfoot reproach not:
> But the lop-sided cherry-branch – whenever the sun rises,
>   How black a shadow!

> (W, 677)

This is an extraordinarily accomplished pastiche – presumably of Arthur Waley's translations of early Chinese poetry, perhaps also of the Pound of *Cathay*. If one didn't know the author, these poems would look like Imagist epiphanies turning on the disjunction between the 'timeless' pastoral of Chinese poetry and the modernity of the motor-car, articulated in the opposition between the still images of cherry trees and goldfish and the story of rapid blinding, maiming and death. Both poems play with the idea of the controlling gaze, most clearly in the first stanza's inspired conjunction of the shining shapes of goldfish glimpsed underwater and black ice reflecting street-lights (which in Kipling's day would be yellow gas-lamps whose low intensity left much of the road in darkness) – all suddenly wiped out when the careless aesthete, so delighted with the beauty and his own sensitivity in perceiving it, is knocked unconscious or dead. Vision is restored in the second poem

121

where grief and sorrow are once again aestheticized by being 'seen' as timeless images from nature: dead leaves, the shadow of a broken branch.

These parodies are in part exercises in disavowal, in that their voices are not Kipling's own. The same is less obviously true of his public 'hymns', even when they articulate opinions he is known to have held; their organ-voice solemnities speak for a collective 'we' who cannot finally be identified with Kipling himself, any more than the Tommies or the galley-slaves of the ancient world quoted at the head of this chapter. Such speaking for others can be seen as an exercise of power over them, since it implies standing in the place of others and defining their point of view; yet even here, the phonetically transcribed demotic language and the elaborately stylized metres and rhymes insist on their own artificiality, marking the difference between poetry and truth. The 'certain certainties' of Kipling's poetry are not as certain as all that, once you look at them closely.

7

Communications, Modernity and Power

He pressed a key in the semi-darkness, and with a rending crackle
there leaped between two brass knobs a spark, streams of sparks,
and sparks again.

'Grand, isn't it? *That's* the Power – our unknown Power – kicking
and fighting to be loose,' said young Mr. Cashell. 'There she goes –
kick, kick, kick into space. I never get over the strangeness of it when
I work a sending-machine – waves going into space, you know.'

('Wireless', *TD*, 227)

We declare that the splendor of the world has been enriched by a
new beauty: the beauty of speed

(Marinetti, 1909)[1]

KIPLING AND MACHINERY

The excitement of the young radio expert exchanging Morse
messages with his opposite number in Poole along the South
Coast, the awe at the unknown, immensely powerful force of
electricity giving out 'streams of sparks' and 'kicking and
fighting to be loose', the sense of uncharted possibilities –
'there's nothing we shan't be able to do in ten years' (*TD*, 226),
all combine to make Kipling's short story 'Wireless', one of the
earliest literary responses to the new 'Marconi experiments' in
radio, a proto-modernist text. Kipling was among the first
English writers to respond creatively to the revolutionary
technologies of the early-twentieth century – radio, cinema,
motor cars and air travel. His enthusiasm for communications
technology is almost comparable to that of the Futurist

123

Marinetti, whose manifesto announcing a modernist aesthetic of mechanical speed and brilliance that would celebrate 'the nocturnal vibration of the arsenals and the workshops beneath their violent electric moons: the gluttonous railway stations devouring smoking serpents...great-breasted locomotives, puffing on the rails like enormous steel horses with long tubes for bridle, and the gliding flight of aeroplanes whose propeller sounds like the flapping of a flag and the applause of enthusiastic crowds'[2] could have applied to Kipling's own fables of railway trains and air travel.

Yet 'Wireless' is as much a Victorian ghost story as a modernist fable of technology: its central drama is not young Mr Cashell's conquest of space by radio, but the drugged consumptive chemist's assistant John Shaynor unconsciously speaking with the voice of a Keats struggling to write the 'Eve of St Agnes' and 'Ode to a Nightingale'. Shaynor never knows that he has spoken with Keats' voice or written Keats' lines (albeit in doggerel versions), while the narrator, who does know and is frightened by his own knowledge, can do nothing but wait and listen. The unknown 'Power' evoked here thus represents both the potential to transform human life and experience through the scientifically based technologies of the early-twentieth century, *and* an irrational, supernatural inspiration that men can neither understand or control – a near relation of those 'Powers of Darkness' so often apostrophized in the early 'Indian Gothic' tales.

Kipling's lifelong interest in systems of communication appears as early as the comic poem 'A Code of Morals' in *Departmental Ditties* (1886), in which an anxious husband's Morse message sent by heliograph (an early telegraph using sunlight flashed by mirrors) warning his wife not to dally with 'General Bangs – a most immoral man' (*W*, 13) is unfortunately intercepted by the General himself. It reappears in the excited lyricism of 'The Deep-Sea Cables' about the laying of telephone cables across the sea-bed of the Atlantic, the ultimate 'waste of slime' where 'the words of men flicker and flutter and beat' (*W*, 174), in later poems about electric dynamos and air travel, and in the many short stories he wrote about steamships, railways and telecommunications. He owed the scale of his success as an internationally famous and discussed writer not only to his own talent, great as it was, but to the existence of an expanding publishing industry circulating its products world wide at the moment when he began to make his career as a London-based professional writer in 1889. At the peak of his reputation in 1895, Kipling became an international celebrity of a kind previously unknown in Victorian England; when he lay dangerously ill with pneumonia on the disastrous family trip to New York in 1899, his condition was headline news all over the world, and his recovery brought a telegram of congratulation from Kaiser Wilhelm.[3] As Lockwood Kipling shrewdly observed in 1890, his son's worldwide fame would not have been possible a generation or even ten years previously:

> Owing to the recent developments & organising of journalism, syndicates and what not, each new boom is more portentous, more wide-spread and more voluminous in print than the last and it will be literally true that in one year this youngster will have had *more said about his work, over a wider extent of the world's surface* [my italics] than some of the greatest of England's writers in their whole lives. Much of this of course is merely mechanical, the result of the wholesale spread of journalism and the centralising tendencies of it.[4]

In other words, Kipling's success was not only due to his talent; it was also a product of the literary-economic conditions which created a 'boom' in new authors, of mass-produced newspapers and reviews, and of their circulation by sea and railway.

Technologies of communication profoundly affected not just Kipling's literary reputation but the course of his life. His childhood, schooldays and early manhood would all have been different without the development of the steamship, the railroad, the electric telegraph, and the large-scale printing press. It was the existence of P. and O. steamers sailing regularly from England to India, carrying mail as well as passengers, that enabled his parents to settle in Bombay and later Lahore while still keeping in touch with their families by letter, and to send their children 'Home'. A steamer took the young Rudyard from paradisal Bombay to the 'House of Desolation' in Southsea for six years, until his mother was alerted to his misery by a letter from her sister (also carried by mailboat) and came from India to rescue him; another steamer took the sixteen-year-old boy back to India to start work as an apprentice journalist. Travel by steamship was to be the adult Kipling's preferred form of escape and recuperation from overwork and psychic distress, described by Zohreh Sullivan as a form of manic defence against his original trauma. 'The original passage away from childhood's India and the return...[was] followed by a furious and compulsive need to travel by ship from land to land – repeated journeys from India to England, Japan, America, Canada, South Africa, New Zealand and Australia'.[5] It is no wonder then that steamships should reappear so often in his prose and poetry, as do the telegraph and the railway.

As an apprentice journalist, the young Kipling had to depend on the telegraph for international and local news in order to supervise and proof-read the production of the Lahore *Pioneer* (in which his early stories first appeared), and his first short story collections were published and distributed by the 'Indian Railway Library'. The railway train is crucial alike to the plot and theme of 'The Man Who Would Be King', in which 'the beginning of everything was a railway train upon the road to Mhow from Ajmir'. The journalist-narrator is asked by a fellow-passenger to deliver a message three days later to a passenger 'coming in the early morning of the 24th by the Bombay Mail' (*WWW*, 208) thus enabling the two adventurers' decision to leave British India to carve out their own colony beyond the Afghan border in Kafiristan. The fact that this incident is closely based on a real-life experience described in a letter to his cousin Margaret Burne-Jones, in which a fellow passenger asked Kipling to deliver a mysterious message to a stranger (*L* I, 101), is perhaps less significant in this story than the way the train represents the possibilities of conquest, chance and mobility open to colonists. In the more benign world of *Kim*, the invention of the *'te-rain'* is un-threateningly progressive, allowing people who would otherwise be separated by caste, sex or race to meet harmoniously (on the whole) in the temporary space of railway carriage, while moving swiftly towards their goals; in this earlier, harsher story, the railway, the newspaper office and its telegraph explicitly represent the white man's just and reasonable jurisdiction, as opposed to the half-modern, half-medieval world of the 'Native States' which 'are the dark places of the earth, full of unimaginable cruelty, touching the Railway and the Telegraph on one side, and, on the other, the days of Harun-al-Raschid' (*WWW*, 205).

The Telegraph is, we note, of equal importance as the Railway; it is the telegraph beside which the journalist has to wait for the news of Government decisions and of international incidents, and which enables officers and administrators in the provinces to keep in touch with central authority. In stories about endangered outposts or artefacts like 'His Chance in Life' and 'The Bridge Builders', the telegraph is instrumental in giving administrators and officers early warning of danger and summoning immediate help.

Kipling, then, understood very well that control of communications was essential to military superiority. He was not, however, at all interested in the relationship between the technology he praised and the industrial capitalism which invested in it. He hardly ever mentions the mechanical process of production except in the post-war 'The Gardener', where a bereaved mother feels herself becoming an object on an assembly-line, just as when she saw 'the progress of a shell from blank-iron to the all but finished article. It struck her at the time that the wretched thing was never left alone for a second; and "I'm being manufactured into a bereaved next of kin", she told herself, as she prepared her documents' (*DC*, 406). For Kipling, technological progress is a matter of civil engineering (bridges, roads, aqueducts, canals) or of communications technology (steamships, railroads, telegraphs, radio, air transport), not of factories producing goods. This is made very clear in the children's poem 'The Secret of the Machines' which boast that they can send a message 'half across the world' in an instant, or bring down water 'from the never-failing cisterns of the snows' to irrigate orchards and produce water-power:

> It is easy! Give us dynamite and drills!
> Watch the iron-shouldered rocks lie down and quake,
> As the thirsty desert-level floods and fills,
> And the valley we have dammed becomes a lake

> (*W*, 730)

What the machines of the poem *don't* do, for all their tireless power and pride, is to make goods or other machines (machine tools are not part of Kipling's world), nor, although they can 'see and hear and count and read and write' (*W*, 729) do they produce services. For Kipling, the work of telecommunications,

127

large-scale transport or engineering, is all done for its own sake, not for gain and certainly not for shareholders. (In 'Wireless', the radio enthusiast is, significantly, quite uninterested in the commercial possibilities of his hobby.)

Nothing he writes about the benefits of technological innovation approaches the sophistication of Conrad's *Nostromo* (1900), with its subtle perception of the interdependence of foreign investment, wealth-creating capitalism, and the growth of a 'progressive' liberal state. His engineers dedicate their lives to road-building not for belief and still less for money; they work for 'simple service simply given to [their] own kind in their common need' (*W*, 383; no wonder that Kipling's poetry was popular in the Soviet Union!), or like Findlayson in 'The Bridge Builders' for the proud satisfaction of a job well done.

Similarly with journalism, which for Kipling represents a grubby vocation rather than a living: his Fleet Street farce 'The Village That Voted the Earth Was Flat', is full of insight into the connexions between political influence and journalism and the power of a self-generating publicity machine to make fiction turn into fact, but no awareness of newspapers as profit-making institutions. Unlike Theodore Dreiser whose novels famously register the transformation of bourgeois lives by market values, Kipling is not at all interested in production and consumption, still less in buying and selling – low activities associated with Jews like Mr M'Leod the fur trader of 'The House Surgeon' (*TD*) or, less benignly, the managerial Steiner in 'Bread Upon the Waters' pandering to his share-holders' desire for profits at the expense of his employees' health and safety – or at best, the likeable but unscrupulous American arms dealer Laughton O. Zigler in 'The Captive' (*AR*). And neither, as Auden observed, does he write of science: 'Kipling is interested in engineering, in the weapons that protect man against the chaotic violence of nature, but not in physics, in the intellectual *discovery* that made the weapons possible.'[6]

If Kipling is not interested in science and despises production for profit, what then excites and interests him about technological progress? The answer seems to lie in the thrill of power, the reassurance of discipline, and the pleasure of knowledge. Part of Kipling's response to the power of machinery is an almost childish awe and satisfaction in the sheer scale of industrial processes and communications technology: newspaper presses devouring 'their league-long paper bale' (*W*, 534) or airships travelling in the future at a barely imaginable '320 m.p.h' in 'With the Night Mail' (*AR*). The bigger and faster a process, the more it earns his impressed approval, as in the fable of modernization 'Below the Mill Dam', where the mill-wheel is converted from its lazy old-fashioned repetition of names from the Domesday Book into the enterprise and energy of an electricity-generating turbine 'good for fifteen hundred revolutions a minute' (*AR*, 392). This gawping at sheer size at times results in weaknesses, like the over-elaborate detail in which *Captains Courageous* specifies the arrangements by which a millionaire travels by his railroad from San Francisco to Boston in three days. 'The train would take precedence of one hundred and seventy-seven others meeting and passing; despatchers and crews of every one of those said trains must be notified. Sixteen locomotives, sixteen engineers and sixteen firemen would be needed', etc., etc. for three tedious pages (*CC*, 186–8). This enthusiasm for scale and magnitude does represent a thematic engagement with modernist processes of mass production and transport technology, but of a kind that now looks very dated indeed. We who can take 7-hour flights from London to New York, are not going to be impressed by that three-day journey across the USA, still less by the airships crossing the Atlantic at 'an honest two hundred and ten knots' in the futurist fable 'With the Night Mail' (*AR*, 129).

Yet there is also a clear element of scientific modernism in Kipling's perception that the power of machinery is born of knowledge, and in his loving technical explanations. He seems to enjoy new processes for their own sake, as in the famous description of the early cinema by a fascinated viewer: 'I'd never seen it before. You 'eard a little dynamo like buzzin', but the pictures were the real thing – alive an' movin' ('Mrs Bathurst', *TD*, 356). 'Wireless' has an explanation, based on the author's conversation with Marconi himself,[7] of how the reception of 'Hertzian waves' from the transmitter on the pole outside causes the nickel-dust in a glass tube to 'cohere' for just long enough to conduct the current of electricity 'a little while for a dot and a longer while for a dash', (*TD*, 225) so as to harness – though never to tame – the unknown 'Powers' of radio and electricity.

And in 'With the Night Mail', his elaborate description of a perpetual-motion gas machine, driven by pressured gas which is condensed by the imaginary 'Fleury's Ray' to a liquid and recycled, has a real lyricism:

> From the low-arched expansion-tanks on either side the valves descend pillar-wise to the turbine-chests, and thence the obedient gas whirls through the spirals of blades with a force that would whip the teeth out of a power saw. Behind, is its own pressure held in leash or spurred on by the lift-shunts; before it, the vacuum where Fleury's Ray dances in violet-green bands and whirled turbillons of flame. The jointed U-tubes of the vacuum-chamber are pressure-tempered colloid (no glass would stand the strain for an instant) and a junior engineer with tinted spectacles watches the Ray intently. It is the very heart of the machine – a mystery to this day...how the restless little imp shuddering in the U-tube can, in the fractional fraction of a second, strike the furious blast of gas into a chill greyish-green liquid that drains (you can hear it trickle) from the far end of the vacuum through the eduction-pipes and the mains back to the bilges' (AR, 20).

As this passage shows, what most profoundly excites Kipling about machinery is the idea of barely controlled forces: the half-understood 'Power' sparking from a battery, the 'imp shudder-ing in the U-tube', perilously contained and exploited by elaborate mechanisms but always ready to escape or explode. The danger and excitement of the just-tamed powers that drive machinery offers the thrill of mastery of the environment, the ability of humans to exert their will over brute nature, almost to be godlike and certainly to be free of reverence to the gods. For as Krishna warns the Hindu Gods in 'The Bridge Builders', men who have seen fire-engines and engineering works 'do not think of the Heavenly Ones altogether. They think of the fire-carriages and the other things which the bridge-builders have done' (DW, 40). This mastery, hymned in 'The Secret of the Machines' with its boast of effortlessly flattened mountains, or more soberly celebrated in 'The Sons of Martha' doing the world's work of building railways and aqueducts, represents machinery as an unlimited extension of existing human capacities:

> We can pull and haul and push and lift and drive,
> We can print and plough and weave and heat and light,

We can run and race and swim and fly and dive,
We can see and hear and count and read and write!

(W, 729)

The machines, in other words, can do anything humans can do, only better, faster and more powerfully. This notion of machinery corresponds to Tim Armstrong's description of modern technology as a 'prosthesis' – that is, an extension of existing skills or abilities beyond what is possible for human dexterity and/or strength. On the one hand, this evident superiority of the 'prosthesis' testifies negatively to human lack and incapacity compared with mechanical power; but it also 'involves a more utopian version of technology, in which human capacities are extrapolated ... [and] technology offers a re-formed body, more powerful and capable, producing in a range of modernist writers a fascination with organ-extension, organ-replacement, sensory-extension'.[8] This last, however, cannot be said of Kipling who, even in his most futurist moments, as in the stories of a twenty-first century world run by the 'Aerial Board of Control', still represents its new technology in terms of manual control; the engineer watches 'Fleury's Ray' much as a Victorian fireman would watch the pressure-gauge on a steam engine. When the air pilot takes his dirigible through an electric storm 'the fierce sparks flying from his knuckles at every turn of the hand ... [while] we were dragged hither and yon by warm or frozen suctions, belched up on the top of wulli-was, spun down by vortices and clubbed aside by laterals' (AR, 131) he is evidently a fellow of the heroic sailors in sea-yarns who stay at the ship's tiller through typhoons and hurricanes.

The pilot's courage and skill marks him out as a member in good standing of Kipling's all-male world of hard-working, brave, lonely administrators and technicians, who spend their lives guarding their fellow humans (whom they rather despise), and whose rewards are the satisfaction of a job well done and the approving camaraderie of their equally hard-pressed peers. Kipling's love of machinery and technology is one aspect of the harsh masculine work ethic discussed previously (see chapters 4 and 5); he loves machines partly because of the ferocious discipline which they impose on those who tend and use them. As they warn the children with evident relish, 'We are not built to comprehend a lie,/ We can neither love nor pity nor forgive./

131

If you make a slip in handling us you die!' (W, 730). This harsh discipline of mechanical laws is praised in 'The Sons of Martha' (alluding to the woman in the Bible who was 'careful and troubled about many things' Luke 10: 41), about the unthanked men who 'take the buffet and cushion the shock'. The fact that 'they do not preach that their God will rouse them a little before the nuts work loose./ They do not teach that His Pity allows them to drop their job when they dam' well choose' (W, 383) earns Kipling's most admiring praise.

The world of these dedicated men is emphatically all-male; 'Martha's Daughters' would presumably be anxious housewives like their biblical foremother. And 'men' means 'white men' here; for, especially in the twentieth-century writings that appeared after Kipling had moved emphatically Rightwards, it is a 'given' that subaltern races have no more part in the exclusive world of dedicated male toilers and mysteries of disciplined control of the environment than do women of any race. There is a striking contrast between the narrow racial world of the futurist anti-democratic fable 'As Easy as A.B.C.' and the more flexible 'Indian' stories, which had room for the enterprising girl 'William' in 'William the Conqueror', Peroo discovering scepticism along with engineering skills in 'The Bridge Builders', and the French-speaking 'Herbert Spencerian' Hurree Babu in Kim. Kipling is at pains to emphasize the international composition of the 'Aerial Board of Control' who run the Planet in 2065, but its representatives are all white men apart from one Japanese, and not even the rebellious 'Serviles' (=democrats) seem to think of women as possible leaders or administrators.

The exhilaration at the terrifying natural forces which Kipling's machine-minders skilfully control, and the enormous power which their machines command, leads to an anxious insistence on the need for an idealized heroic masculinity and on ever tighter social control of those outside the male outsiders' charmed circle that led Virginia Woolf to her mocking description of 'Men who are alone with their Work'.[9] A psychoanalytic account of Kipling on communications technology would surely read it as an aridly successful subduing of the libidinal energies of the self into a fantasy of asexual energy controlled by figures of idealized heroic masculinity who repress dangerous feeling through self-punishing dedication and subjection to 'the judgment of your peers' (*W*, 324). The only imaginable threat comes not from inner weakness or cowardice, still less from sexuality because that has been written out of the picture, but from the unruly Power that the technologists need to exploit and subdue. Hence the emotional aridity of Kipling's stories about ships and railways and air travel.

MACHINES AND GHOSTS

So far, it would seem, so depressing. If Kipling's fascination with communications were solely a matter of idealized white administrators making a recalcitrant world safe by controlling and guarding their lines of communication, there would be little to say about his stories of technology except to lament their emotional aridity outside their few moments of lyricism about half-tamed energy. But what makes Kipling's fictions of communication emotionally interesting is his awareness that the 'Power' of steam or electricity or radio connects with something beyond human understanding.

Nor is Kipling's response to the spread of mass communications that made him an international best-seller a simple matter of thematic emphasis. This preoccupation inspired three stories collected in *Traffics and Discoveries*, about the ways in which these technologies impinge on and transform ordinary lives: the moving cinematograph in 'Mrs Bathurst', the most puzzling and intricately written of Kipling's stories, which holds the image of a feared and desired woman in endless repetition, the motor car in 'They', which enables the narrator to cross the boundaries of English counties as the ghostly children traverse the boundaries of mortal life, and the radio waves in 'Wireless', which allow far-off voices from Poole to be heard in a chemist's shop in a coastal town one freezing night in January, where the consumptive shop assistant is briefly possessed by the spirit of a poet he has never heard of. These technologies of communication thus put the narrator in touch with numinous powers, which in each story are associated with the figure of a woman who without being exactly to blame for the terror or power or grief invoked, is somehow implicated in it. There is a clear parallel between this

133

conjunction of technology, an unexplained numinousness associated with women, and the ambivalent 'modernism' of Kipling's writing.

The effect is similar to his poems whose traditionalism and conservative pieties are contradicted by their ironies and their participation in parody and pastiche, linking them both with the modernist T.S. Eliot and with Ezra Pound for whom, not unlike the Futurists, 'the language of engineers – materials, speed, precision – helped define modernity as part of a stress on Aristotelian *techne*.'[10] Not that Kipling himself is a modernist of Pound's stamp: when he wrote of his own *techne* he resorted to imagery of the Arts and Crafts movement like sable-hair brushes and Indian ink to delete superfluous words, or else enamel-work and inlay as metaphors for narrative construction (*SM*, 207–8), and lamented his own inability ever to build a 'three – decker' novel, an 'East Indiaman worthy to lie alongside *The Cloister and the Hearth*' (*SM*, 228). Yet even though he defines writing in terms of old-fashioned craft, Kipling is subtly aware in a very modern way of his own belatedness. Those 'East Indiaman' sailing ships were already obsolete when he was born, as he very well knew.

Kipling's conservative pieties are likewise much less secure than they look, as indeed his endless need to repeat them as loudly as possible betrays. He insists on the value of Duty and Honour because he fears that civilized life would collapse without them, while knowing that these values are guaranteed by no theological or philosophical principle but are simply the necessary fictions by which men have to live – as C.S. Lewis realized when he saw at the centre of Kipling's work ethic 'a terrible vagueness, a frivolity or scepticism.[11] Like T.S. Eliot for whom 'Human kind / Cannot bear very much reality',[12] Kipling prayed to the God in whom he may or may not have believed for deliverance from seeing 'the wheel and drift of Things...Lest we should hear too clear, too clear / And unto madness see!' (*W*, 614). This scepticism is closely connected with Kipling's brilliance as a writer of short stories and relative failure as a novelist, at least outside the picaresque *Kim*. The absence of a totalizing explanatory vision produces a multitude of intensely seen provisional truths and miniaturized local effects, usually from the point of view of a narrating 'I' who is himself in some way limited, so that each collection of his short stories offers a series of brilliant fragments. That scepticism also, Louis Menand argues, makes Kipling paradoxically a fellow of Wilde and Nietzsche, not because he agreed with their opinions (which he very obviously didn't) but because he shared their modernist mind-set:

> a view that elected not to make an issue of truth claims; that held fundamentally sceptical views on the autonomy and integrity of the subject and the possibility of originality; that accepted a generally materialistic and deterministic account of phenomena; that understood meaning to be a function of relation and value to be a function of interest.

Hence, says Menand, the fascination with the ghost story displayed by modernist writers preoccupied by the invocation of a particular effect, for 'the ghost is a melodramatic allusion to the interiority of experience.... the inner flashings forth in image and sensation of the data transmitted by the neural machinery'.[13]

Hence also the peculiar power of 'Mrs Bathurst', Kipling's most modernist ghost story. Like *Heart of Darkness* this combines a mysterious death in the African forest and an elaborate narrative frame: Kipling's usual anonymous narrator hears it in fragments from his uncomprehending and unreliable companions, – so it becomes as Menand says *'a story about the telling of a story'*[14] – or rather, about the impossibility of either telling it completely or interpreting it. The men speak of Vickery, a sailor known as 'Click' because of his ill-fitting false teeth, who had some sort of relationship with one Mrs Bathurst. She is described as a sort of innocent *femme fatale* and owner of a superior bar in Auckland patronized by sailors, famous for her generosity and courage – 'she never scrupled to feed a lame duck or to set 'er foot on a scorpion' (*TD*, 351) and still more for her 'blindish' way of looking which is, apparently, devastatingly attractive – perhaps because of its vulnerability (like the blind woman in 'They' who laments that 'we blindies' suffer because 'everything outside hits straight at our souls' unlike the sighted who 'have such good defences in your eyes – looking out': *TD*, 315–16). That Vickery had a relationship with her is learned by Pyecroft, one of the sailors, whom the visibly agonized man had asked to accompany him, first to one of the early documentary films which happens to show Mrs Bathurst, and then to a joyless drinking spree for the rest of the evening, repeating this programme on five more evenings: 'five minutes o' the pictures, and perhaps forty-five seconds o' Mrs B', followed by drinking to oblivion. He learns that Vickery believes 'she's looking for me' and that 'I am *not* a murderer because my lawful wife died in childbed six weeks after I came out' (doubly baffling, because if the child whose birth killed his wife was his, then he clearly did 'murder' her in the sense of causing her death, however 'innocently'). Vickery has then gone 'up-country' and not returned. Hooper takes up the tale, describing two unexplained tramps found by the railway 'beyond Bulawayo', one standing and the other 'squattin' down lookin' up at him', both struck by lightning and burned to charcoal; the standing tramp had tattoo-marks (confirmed by Pyecroft as Vickery's), and false teeth – 'I saw 'em shinin' against the black' (*TD*, 364). Those false teeth ought to be proof positive of his death, but even that remains uncertain:

> 'We buried 'em in the teak and I kept... But he was a friend of you gentlemen, you see.'
> Mr Hooper brought his hand away from his waistcoat-pocket – empty.'
>
> (*TD*, 361)

The riddles of 'Mrs Bathurst' are many. What was Vickery so guilt-stricken about? Was Mrs Bathurst really looking for him in London, or was that only his fantasy? Why did he need to see her image again and again? What, if anything, had she to do with his death? Was she a good woman as Pritchard insists, or an avenging fury? Why is the story called 'Mrs Bathurst' when the tragedy seems to be Vickery's?

There is no really satisfactory way of answering all these questions. Readings that make partial sense of the story are certainly possible: perhaps Vickery had contracted a bigamous marriage with her – which explains his guilt but not his death by lightning nor the presence of the other 'tramp'; or perhaps the love between Vickery and the devastatingly attractive 'Mrs Bathurst' is a literally all-consuming *coup de foudre* (lightning-flash), as witnessed by their two lightning-charred corpses –

which explains his death but neither the guilt he feels, nor how she got from London to Bulawayo, nor why she should be 'squatting to look up at him' instead of embracing. Explanations must, anyway, in a sense miss the point of 'Mrs Bathurst', which lies precisely in its undecidability, leaving the reader with a sense of the mysteriously devastating power of *eros* that has somehow burnt Vickery and his companion to charcoal as black as Africans (who are otherwise oddly invisible in this story set in South Africa). The evocation of Mrs Bathurst as at once a 'real' person and a mythical agent of magic is caught especially well in her brief appearance in the documentary film, described by Pyecroft:

> 'I'd never seen it before. You 'eard a little dynamo like buzzin', but the pictures were the real thing – alive and movin'.'
>
> 'I've seen 'em,' said Hooper. 'Of course they are taken from the very thing itself – you see.'
>
> 'Then the Western Mail came in to Paddin'ton on the big magic lantern screen. First we saw the platform empty an' the porters standin' by. Then the engine come in, head on, an' the women in the front row jumped: she headed so straight. Then the doors opened an' the passengers came out and the porters got the luggage – just like life. Only – only when anyone came too far towards us that was watchin', they walked right out o' the picture, so to speak. I was 'ighly interested, I can tell you. So were all of us. I watched an old man with a rug 'oo'd dropped a book an' was trying' to pick it up, when quite slowly, from be'ind two porters – carryin' a little reticule an' lookin' from side to side – comes our Mrs. Bathurst. There was no mistakin' the walk in a hundred thousand. She come forward – right forward – she looked out straight at us with that blindish look which Pritch alluded to. She walked on an' on till she melted out of the picture – like – like a shadow jumpin' over a candle, an' as she went I 'eard Dawson in the tickey seats be'ind sing out, 'Christ, there's Mrs. B.!' (*TD*, 355–6).

The key difference between this and the explanatory accounts of radio or gas-power in other Kipling stories is the emphasis not on technique but experience – not what makes the film work but on how it feels to watch a medium which seems to be both real, 'taken from the very thing itself' and magical, 'like a shadow jumping over a candle'. This experience of presence-in-absence – Mrs Bathurst seen 'live' on Paddington Station, half a world away from the watchers – makes the filmed image into a ghost whose unseeing 'blindish' gaze approaches her guilty lover and disappears when she comes close. The effect of her seen and lost image is like the false teeth that Hooper *doesn't* hold up at the end of the story, making them more powerfully present to the reader's mind than any description could do. Now you see her, now you don't.

'Seeing things' is the theme of the poignant ghost story 'They' in the same collection. Here the narrator – a much less knowing character than Kipling's usual 'I' – drives across southern England in late spring, revelling in its peace and serenity, to find himself in an enchantingly beautiful house and garden where children flit about, laughing and playing but never coming close. He is welcomed as a friend by the owner of the house, a blind woman who loves the children she can never see. He returns in high summer and again in autumn, always glimpsing the children but never managing to reach them, until on his last visit after a game of hide-and-seek through the old house, one of them approaches him as he sits by the fire:

> The little brushing kiss fell in the centre of my palm – as a gift on which the fingers were, once, expected to close: as the all-faithful half-reproachful signal of a waiting child not used to neglect even when grown-ups were busiest – a fragment of the mute code devised very long ago.
> Then I knew.

(TD, 332)

What he now understands, the reader will have guessed long before. The children are dead, called to the lovely house by the blind, childless woman's yearning for them. But once he has understood this, he knows that, unlike her, he has to leave, even though the prospect is like death: 'For you it is right....I am grateful to you beyond words. For me it would be wrong', (*TD*, 334). He must go, it seems, because unlike this crippled yet psychically gifted woman who has 'neither borne nor lost' a child (*TD*, 333), he has the life 'on the other side of the county' (*TD*, 309) which he never describes but to which he must return, and if he stayed with the ghosts, he would never leave.

There is no obvious connexion in this story between the ghosts and the technology by which the narrator meets them, as there is, however obscurely, between Mrs Bathurst's apparition at the Cape Town cinema and Vickery's death in the African forest. True, during the second visit the motor car seems to represent the beneficent forces of progress: the narrator drives round the country to summon medical help for a desperately sick child in the local village, through a 'long afternoon crowded with mad episodes that rose and dissolved like the dust of our wheels; cross-sections of remote and incomprehensible lives through which we raced at right angles' (TD, 322). But next time he comes, we learn that the child died anyway. Otherwise, the car seems to be a plot device that effortlessly takes him sixty miles from home to the haunted house, almost as if it knew the way, across 'villages where bees, the only things awake, boomed in eighty-foot lindens that overhung Norman churches [and] miraculous brooks diving under stone bridges built for heavier traffic than would ever vex them again' (TD, 303). It sounds as if the narrator and his car were part of this quiet ancient world, but the truth is that he is already 'racing at right angles' through 'remote and incomprehensible lives'. (And twenty-first century readers of the story can hardly forget that the motor car which was a rich man's privilege in 'They', would even in Kipling's own lifetime have spoiled these peaceful villages.) The motor car seems to promise the ability to traverse the land as one wishes, not bound to the predicted railway but going anywhere one wants; but the promise is finally empty.

The ghostly voices in 'Wireless' are different from these apparitions of feared or longed-for presences, in that they complicate Kipling's intuition of the impossibility of fully making sense of human experience with a modernist sense of literary belatedness. While young Mr Cashell is concentrating on his Morse messages from Poole, a stranger kind of transmission is taking place in the shop via Mr Shaynor, the assistant who is minding the shop all night. He is a conscientious, rather pathetic young man with a nasty cough for which he smokes 'asthma cigarettes', and sufficiently in love to be persuaded by a coarsely sexy girl to walk with her to 'St Agnes' church in a freezing January wind. Coughing blood afterwards, which he explains as a 'rasped throat from cigarettes' (TD, 220), he accepts a strong drink from the narrator and falls into a trance, staring at the poster of a girl advertising toothpaste in the coloured electric light from the shop window and muttering 'And threw warm gules on Madeline's young breast'. More lines from *The Eve of St Agnes* follow, and the young shop assistant seems to become Keats as he, struggling to turn his cheap and ordinary yearnings into poetry, only produces doggerel parodies of the great romance like 'The hare, in spite of fur, was very cold' (*TD*, 229). The parallels with Keats' life are obvious: Shaynor is a chemist's assistant, as Keats trained as an apothecary, like him will die of tuberculosis, and like the Keats of post-Romantic mythology pining for the unworthy *femme fatale* Fanny Brawne, is hopelessly in love with the blowsy 'Fanny Brand' (*TD*, 226). He is thus unconsciously 'living' the myth of Keats as the young doomed poet whose imminent early death made his mastery of romance, 'the pure Magic...the clear Vision' (*TD*, 235) the more complete and poignant.

Yet Shaynor is ignorant of Keats, unconscious of being possessed by him, and when he wakes up is untouched by the whole experience; he is only a caricature of his great original. The more he resembles Keats and the closer he comes to writing Keats' own lines, the more diminished he is by the comparison. When the excited narrator says, watching him at work, that 'my every sense hung on the dry, bony hand all brown-fingered with chemicals and cigarette smoke', he is evidently recalling Keats' late poem about 'this living hand, now warm and capable' that when dead would 'haunt thy days and chill thy dreaming nights',[15] a threat which Shaynor is incapable of making. The point of the transcendent Romantic poetry that he gropes towards seems to be precisely that the poor uneducated modern fool cannot reach it. This reaching out to an ungraspable past romance is implied in Kipling's wonderful description, at once highly up-to-date and Keatsian, of the lit-up chemist's shop on a winter's night:

> Across the street blank shutters flung back the gaslight in cold smears; the dried pavement seemed to rough up in goose-flesh under the scouring of the savage wind.... Within, the flavours of cardamoms and chloric-ether disputed those of the pastilles and a score of drugs and perfumes and soap scents. Our electric lights, set low down in the windows before the tun-bellied Rosamund jars, flung inward three monstrous daubs of red, blue and green, that broke into kaleidoscopic lights on the facetted knobs of the drug-drawers, the cut-glass scent flagons, and the bulbs of the sparklet

bottles. They flushed the white-tiled floor in gorgeous patches; splashed along the nickel-silver counter-rails, and turned the polished mahogany counter-panels to the likeness of intricate grained marbles – slabs of porphyry and malachite (TD, 222).

This crudely mixed assault on the senses of sight and smell represents a deliberate reminiscence of colour and sensuousness of 'The Eve of St Agnes'. But just as Shaynor isn't so much a reincarnation of the great Romantic poet as a grotesque imitation of him, so the shop's interior, all cut-glass bottles and electric lights, represents a vulgarly commercial twentieth-century parody of the richness and exoticism of a Keatsian setting. The effect anticipates the famous passage from 'A Game of Chess' in The Waste Land where, in a deliberately mocking pastiche of Shakespearean splendour, the poet describes a claustrophobically rich room over-full of disturbingly abundant scents and colours where 'in vials of ivory and coloured glass / Unstoppered, lurked her strange synthetic perfumes... troubled, confused/ And drowned the sense in odours' (like Kipling's mixed smells of chloric-ether, drug and soap scents), while the eye is teased by 'green and orange' light,[16] just as Kipling's 'daubs' of electric light behind the glass jars 'flush' the white floor and turn the polished wooden counter to 'porphyry and malachite'.

These close parallels and the very similar active verbs governed by inanimate objects (Kipling's lights that 'flung'... 'splashed'...and turned wood to 'intricate grained marble' and Eliot's scents that 'drowned the sense...ascended...flung their smoke') suggest to me that Eliot was probably drawing on Kipling's description (especially as the memory in 'Burnt Norton' of the hidden children in 'They', also from Traffics and Discoveries, indicates that he had read this book with attention[17]). But the critical point here is not so much whether or not Eliot was really echoing Kipling, as the way both texts – Eliot's high modernist 'Waste Land' and Kipling's apparently middlebrow story – juxtapose a great poetic original with an ultra-modern interior to show up the shortcomings of the contemporary world. Eliot's lady is a poor parody of Cleopatra, just as Mr Shaynor is a poor imitation of Keats – making the past magnificence invoked in the descriptions seem impossibly distant, to be apprehended only as parody or fragment. So in

Kipling's story, the brilliance and richness of Keats' imagination exist in the present only at second-hand, as parody and burlesque – or else as broken voices on the ether.

The role of the narrator is important, as in all these stories. In 'Mrs. Bathurst' he is as uncomprehending as the men he listens to; in 'They' he must not realize the significance of what he sees until the very end because knowledge brings exile; and in 'Wireless' he does realize what is happening but is powerless to control it. It is the narrator, not the oblivious Shaynor, who recognizes the scribbled bits of Keats' poetry and who grasps the correspondence of the hare hanging outside a game-shop, its 'belly-fur...blown apart in ridges and streaks as the wind caught it, showing bluish skin underneath' (*TD*, 217), with Shaynor's 'The hare, in spite of fur, was very cold' (*TD*, 229). But all he can do is listen to the power that almost speaks through Shaynor like a faulty radio that only gets 'a word here and there. Just enough to tantalise' (*TD*, 239). Like Charlie in 'The Finest Story in the World', the bank clerk and aspiring author of Swinburnian doggerel who unknowingly describes experiences from his past lives as a Greek galley slave and a Viking raider with a freshness and authority of which his waking self is incapable, Shaynor seems to offer the narrator access to a realm of power and imagination, yet frustrates him by being impossible to control or direct. (Both the bank clerk and the shop assistant are comparatively uneducated subordinates used to receiving orders, presumably to emphasize their ignorance compared with the narrator's knowledge, and to contrast their subjection and narrow options in the present with the vitality and romance of their 'unconscious' lives in another dimension). But the twist here is that, though the interest of Shaynor's mutterings depends on the narrator's knowledge of their origin in Keats' *œuvre*, that knowledge actually limits him: he cannot know what the 'brown-fingered hand' feels as it writes, only what he already knows – that is, the poems of which the hand is transcribing its garbled versions. It is a reality that, for Kipling as for other modernists, can only be evoked, never grasped.

8

Kipling in the Great War: Mourning and Modernity

> If any question why we died,
> Tell them, because our fathers lied.
>
> (*W*, 390)

> Loss is the great theme of this war: not victory, not defeat, but
> simply *loss*.
>
> Samuel Hynes[1]

MOURNING AND TRADITION

World War 1 – or the 'Great War' as its survivors called it –
represents a widely accepted, though not uncontested, 'break'
with tradition that marks the beginning of 'modern memory',
characterized by irony, discontinuity and a sense of the
evacuation of traditional patriotic values and rhetoric. The
literary historians Paul Fussell and Samuel Hynes[2] have traced
the way that traditional patriotic and pious language and
imagery give way, even among writers not usually thought to be
modernist, to a new, bleakly fragmentary response to a war
whose devastation defeated traditional forms of representation.
Jay Winter, conversely, has argued for the conservative
continuity of English and European cultural responses of
mourning, arguing that after the Great War, 'most men and
women were still able to reach back into their 'traditional'
cultural heritage to express amazement and anger, bewilder-
ment and compassion, in the face of war and the losses it
brought in its wake.'[3]

Characteristically enough, Kipling's contribution to the literature of mourning corresponds to both these models without quite
fitting either. His principal public tributes to the dead, including
his contribution to the Imperial War Graves Commission which he
joined in 1917, are traditional and formal in nature: the solemn
inscriptions he proposed for the war cemeteries; the lyrics of grief,
the hymns of hate and the elegiac sequence 'Epitaphs of the War'
– and in prose, the splendid though largely unread *History of the
Irish Guards in the Great War* which relates the experiences of the
officers and men in minute detail. In contrast to these formal
public commemorations, the short stories in which Kipling
explored the experience of bereavement, especially the two which
focus on women, 'Mary Postgate' *(D of C)* and 'The Gardener'
(DC), have the pared-down irony and ambiguity of modernism,
and moreover implicitly question Kipling's own insistence on the
virtues of iron discipline, practicality and terse self-control,
representing the women who live by these values as more or
less unconscious victims of repression and denial.

Kipling's own experience of the war was as a civilian, a public
man of letters, a patriot prepared for 'iron sacrifice' *(W,* 330) but
bitter against the politicians who, by failing to prepare for war,
had betrayed the young men who fought, and of course as a
grief-stricken bereaved father.[4] He helped his son to find a
commission in the Irish Guards (by pulling strings with Lord
Roberts the Colonel-in-Chief), and in 1915, shortly after his
eighteenth birthday, John Kipling went with his regiment's
Second Battalion to the Western Front, and promptly went
'missing believed killed' during the Battle of Loos in a skirmish
at which the Guards, as Kipling tersely wrote, 'lost seven of their
officers in forty minutes' *(HIG* 2, 24). The boy's body was never
found during Kipling's lifetime; a corpse identified by elimina-
tion as John Kipling was discovered in 1992 but some doubt of
the identification still remains.[5] This experience of shattering
loss which devastated Kipling physically as well as emotionally
(after his son's death he was in constant pain from a long-
undiagnosed duodenal ulcer)[6] increased his fury against the
German people, whom he referred to as 'Huns' and regarded as
monsters. In a 1915 recruiting speech he said that 'there are only
two divisions in the world now, human beings and Germans'[7]
and later in the same year he wrote that

wherever the German man or woman gets a suitable culture to thrive in he or she means death and loss to civilised people, precisely as germs of any disease ... mean death or loss to mankind – as far as we are concerned the German is typhoid or plague – Pestio Teutonicus if you like.[8]

The other side of Kipling's unforgiving rage is his own experience of consuming grief for his lost son, which, typically, he hardly ever spoke of apart from one brief outburst to a childless friend – ' Down on your knees, Julia, and thank God that you haven't a son'.[9] This grief is allied to a more generalized sorrow for the lost and damaged men of the Army, whom he commemorated both in his own writings and in his work for the Imperial War Commission, to which he contributed inscriptions including the motto for the altar-like 'Stone' of the war cemeteries; as Hynes relates, 'Lutyens asked Kipling to suggest what that inscription should be, and Kipling suggested "Their Name Liveth For Evermore", taken from the familiar passage in Ecclesiasticus 44 beginning "Let us now praise famous men"'. The immediately preceding verses run 'And some there be, which have no memorial; who are perished as though they had never been; and are become as though they had never been born; and their children after them.' (Like John Kipling – and others – whose bodies were never found.)

Very much to Kipling's credit, he was instrumental in the War Commission's decision (which met considerable opposition at the time), to make no distinction between graves of officers and men or between races and creeds, arguing strenuously for the principle of 'equality of treatment', and insisting that 'the wealthy should not be allowed to "proclaim their grief above other peoples' grief" simply because they had larger bank accounts. ... the movement for special graves was unacceptable because it was a "demand for privilege in the face of death'.[10] As he wrote in 'Equality of Sacrifice' the first of the 'Epitaphs of the War',

A.'I was a "have"'.B. 'I was a "have-not"'.
(Together): 'What hast thou given which I gave not?' (*W*, 390)

This is not one of Kipling's most elegant epitaphs, both the dramatization of 'A' and 'B' and the eye-rhyme 'have-not / gave not' reading somewhat awkwardly; but it is among his most emphatic.

Of his public commemorations of the dead, Kipling's *History of the Irish Guards in the Great War* is and will probably remain the least known. Its permeation by Kipling's anti-German attitudes and his belief that the war represented the defence of civilization against barbarism, meant that his book was never going to form part of the influential post-war 'literature of disillusion' represented by Graves' *Goodbye to All That* or Remarque's *All Quiet on the Western Front*. And his relentless insistence on the bravery and fighting spirit of the troops may grate on modern readers, as it clearly did on the ex-soldier Edmund Blunden who complained that Kipling did not fully appreciate 'the pandemonium and nerve-strain of war'.[11] Yet no discussion of his contribution to the literature of mourning ought to ignore this work, the most thorough and successful attempt by any English civilian writer to recreate the experience of fighting men. Kipling began writing it in 1917, having been asked by the Colonel to write it as 'a memento of your son',[12] but in fact John Kipling appears only on one page of Volume 2 that records how at 'Chalk Pit Wood' he joined an advance under fire, during which '2nd Lieutenant W. Cuthbert was shot ... and 2nd Lieutenant J. Kipling was wounded and missing' (*IG* 2, 20). Kipling's attempt to recreate the experience of the fighting men of the regiment deliberately precluded any analytic overview of the war: as he wrote in his Introduction, 'The point of view is the Battalions' ... [and] a battalion's field is bounded by its own vision ... From first to last, the Irish Guards, like the rest of our armies, knew little of what was going on round them.' (*IG* 1, 23). Relying on the 'Regimental Diary', on available letters and documents and on his own interviews with survivors, Kipling chronicled the movements and activities of both battalions from 1914 to 1919 in scrupulous detail, describing not only the great battles in which the Guards served but their movements in and out of the 'Line', sporting events, military awards for individuals' regimental dinners, occasions when hot baths were available, 'load[ing] his records with detail and seeming triviality, since in a life where Death ruled every hour, nothing was trivial' (*IG* 1, 28). Such 'trivialities', which also include the daily and weekly losses of men even when nothing much is going on (three officers and forty-seven men killed and wounded on a routine twelve-days 'tour' of the trenches [*IG* 1, 144], is a typical sample), alternate with intensely felt and detailed descriptions, for instance that of the fortifications which the English troops were set to attack at the Battle of the Somme, 1916:

Here the enemy had sat for two years, looking down upon France and daily strengthening himself. His trebled and quadrupled lines of defence, worked for him by his prisoners, ran below and along the flanks and on the tops of ranges of five-hundred-foot downs. Some of these were studded with close woods, deadlier even than the fortified villages between them; some cut with narrowing valleys that drew machine-gun fire as chimneys draw draughts; some opening into broad, seemingly smooth slopes, whose every haunch and hollow covered sunk forts, carefully placed minefields, machine-gun pits, gigantic quarries, enlarged in the chalk, connecting with catacomb-like dug-outs and subterranean work at all depths, in which brigades could lie till the fitting moment. Belt upon belt of fifty-yard deep wire protected these points, either directly or at such angles as should herd and hold up attacking infantry to the fire of veiled guns. Nothing in the entire system had been neglected or unforeseen, except knowledge of the nature of the men who, in due time, should wear their red way through every yard of it.

(*IG* 1, 145)

Kipling's account of the preparations made by a fiendish, apparently all-powerful enemy reads almost like an anticipation of the descriptions of Mordor massing its forces of enslaved evil against the remnants of the free peoples in Tolkien's *The Lord of the Rings*. As Paul Fussell[13] points out, the assonance, alliteration, and deliberately shocking colour-adjective of the culminating phrase 'wear their red way' are highly rhetorical. So, as he might have added, are the repetitions: 'trebled and quadrupled lines of defence,' 'belt upon belt of wire', the nightmarish adjectives – 'gigantic quarries', 'catacomb-like dug-outs', and most of all those 'broad smooth slopes whose every haunch and hollow' conceals a deadly threat, whose body-language turns the landscape into a treacherous veiled *femme fatale*. This ominous calm leads to a vivid account of the chaos experienced by the attacking troops, in which nothing is clear but fragmentary, appalling details:

It was a still day, and the reeking, chemical-tainted fog of the high explosives would not clear. Orders would be given and taken by men suddenly appearing and as suddenly vanishing through smoke or across fallen earth, till both would be cut off in the middle by rifle bullet, or beaten down by the stamp and vomit of a shell. There was, too, always a crowd of men seated or in fantastic attitudes, silent, with set absorbed faces, busily absorbed in trying to tie up, stanch or plug their own wounds – to save their own single lives with their own hands. When orders came to these they would shake their heads impatiently and go on with their urgent, horrible business. Others, beyond hope but not beyond consciousness, lamented themselves to death. The Diary covers these experiences of the three hours between 8 a.m. and 11 a.m. with the words, 'In the meantime, despite rather heavy shelling, a certain amount of consolidation was done on the trench, while the work of reorganisation continued.' (*IG* 1, 163).

For once, Kipling's habitual mode of understatement is treated with irony; this passage is almost as sarcastic about the ludicrous distance between the euphemistic language of an official report and the horrific chaos experienced by men on the ground as the memoirs of soldier-writers Sassoon and Graves. Especially telling are the conjunction of the figurative 'stamp and vomit' of an exploding shell with the literal 'fantastic attitudes' of injured men, suggesting how the battlefield becomes a confused nightmare turned real, and the strangely formal phrase 'lamented themselves to death' for the wails and screams of dying men.

Yet to read the *History* at length is to be struck by the continual oscillation between these great set-piece descriptions of battles as experienced by men on the ground, and the matter-of-fact, week-by-week record of death 'each day with its almost unnoticed casualty that in the long run makes up the bulk of the bills of war, and brings home the fact that the life-blood of the Battalion is dripping away' (*IG* 1, 149). Thus we learn that before the battle of Neuve Chapelle in March 1915 'the month's losses had been 4 officers and 34 men killed, 5 officers and 85 men wounded or 128 in all' (*IG* 1, 84). In the run-up to the Battle of the Somme 'bombing-practice led to the usual amount of accidents, and on the 2nd March (1916) Lt. Keenan was wounded in the hand by a premature burst; four men were also wounded and one of them died' (*IG* 2, 69). After a ' tour' of the trenches near Boesinghe 'they were relieved with only two casualties. The total losses of the tour had been – one officer missing (Lt. Manning), one (2nd Lt Gibson) wounded; one man wounded and missing; eighty-nine missing; fifty-nine wounded and seventeen killed.'(IG 2, 149). The effect of reading these endless dry summaries of the killed and wounded is *not* the intensification of feeling by understatement on which Kipling's rhetoric so often relies, but – very interestingly – the reverse. The seemingly endless chronicle of losses becomes so familiar that the reader, shockingly, finds herself getting used to the chronicle of death and even a little bored by it, at least until the next shattering battle. This aspect of the narrative corresponds to the anti-rhetorical language of war defined by literary historians as specifically modernist: 'plain, descriptive, emptied of value statements... a rhetoric of pure description, without metaphors and without values, naming no values, not even implying any'.[14] And by this constant alternation between unemotional factuality and horror, Kipling's narrative succeeds in communicating something of the way in which British soldiers in the Great War got used (as the absence of large-scale mutinies indicates they must have done) to taking death and loss for granted alongside sport, billets, rations and the dreary and dangerous work of 'fatigues', as simply part of ordinary existence.

Kipling's short stories of the loss, damage and bereavement inflicted by the Great War on civilians and soldiers are written in a very different and far less 'literary' register, dealing with the lives, deaths, memories and dilemmas of very ordinary, often unreflecting people. These stories divide sharply along gender lines: on the one hand, the fairly numerous stories of damaged men attempting more or less successfully to deal with the effects of war, often through shared memories and mutual help; on the other, the much darker ghost stories of women enduring loss and guilt, notably 'Mary Postgate' (1915, D of C 1917) and 'The Gardener' (DC, 1926), discussed below. The keynote of the stories about soldiers and war veterans is male *camaraderie*. Many are set in the imaginary London Masonic Lodge 'Faith and Works 5837' whose guiding spirit is Brother Burges, a well-to-do tobacconist and bereaved father who first appears in the wartime story 'In the Interests of the Brethren' (DC), running the Lodge as a drop-in centre for serving soldiers on leave, offering food, tobacco and the comforting companionship of fellow Masons as well as the therapy of Masonic ceremonies:

'"All Ritual is fortifying. Ritual's a natural necessity for mankind"' (*DC*, 61). The benevolent Mr Burges and his colleagues find solace in helping other men both during and after the War, through the shared open secret of Masonic knowledge and ceremony; the community of 'Faith and Works' can thus be seen as a fictional equivalent to what Jay Winters describes as the actual 'progression of mutual help ... [through] which many groups and individuals sought to provide knowledge, then consolation, then commemoration'.[15]

Some stories deal with 'shell-shocked' veterans and sufferers from what would now be called 'post-traumatic stress disorder', almost always emphasizing the companionship of brother Masons and the therapeutic effects of acknowledging memories, however terrible. As the wise Dr Keede advises, 'Suppose we face Bogey instead of giving him best every time' ('A Madonna of the Trenches', *DC*); Kipling's hysterical victims can always be cured if they can bring themselves to face the origin of their traumas. Some wartime memories are even benign, as in 'The Janeites' (*DC*) where the reader is taken *via* Kipling's usual narrating 'I', first into the warmth and intimacy of the Lodge where damaged men are helped by being given small jobs to do, and then *via* the reminiscences of Humberstall, victim of an exploding ammunition-dump at 'Eatables'[=Étaples] and subsequently mess-waiter to his beloved artillery regiment 'The 'Eavies', into an inner circle of officers and rankers united by their love of Jane Austen's novels. Humberstall himself joins this 'secret society' after being inspired to name the company's guns after Mr Collins, General Tilney and Lady Catherine 'De Bugg', 'an upstandin' 'ard-mouthed Duchess or Baronet's wife 'oo didn't give a curse for anyone 'oo wouldn't do what she told 'em to' (*DC*, 159), though the officers think the company's chattering 'Navy twelve-inch ought to have been christened Miss Bates' (*DC*, 165). The story's charm lies in Humberstall's unschooled but genuine pleasure in these characters, in the close Inner Ring of soldiers who are also Austen fans, and of course in the comic contrast between the novels' protected feminine society and that of the hard-pressed soldiers whose world the reader is privileged to enter.[16]

GRIEVING AND MODERNITY

Kipling's stories of women and the war are far darker, especially 'Mary Postgate' which interrogates several aspects of war's violence: the death of innocent civilians, German guilt, the fury of the bereaved woman who finds a horrific satisfaction (of which Kipling may or may not approve) in punishing it, and the uncertainty of information in wartime that leaves people – including the reader – not knowing what or whom to believe. Mary, a lady's companion described as 'thoroughly conscientious, tidy, companionable and ladylike' *(D of C*, 420), helps bring up her employer's nephew the 'unlovely orphan' Wyndham Fowler, checking his laundry and submitting devotedly to his casual insults. When war comes, he joins the Air Force and has his brief moment of glory 'swell[ing] and exalt[ing] himself before his womenfolk' and scolding Mary for her ignorance: '"You *must* have had a brain some time in your past. What did you do with it?"' (*D of C*, 422). When he is killed on a trial flight, Mary whose training is 'not to let her mind dwell on things' (*D of C*, 420), responds to Wynn's death by saying, apparently without irony: '"It's a great pity he didn't die in action after he had killed somebody"' (*D of C*, 426). Having decided to burn Wynn's possessions Mary, while walking to the village to get paraffin (it is a drizzling English autumn day and the books won't catch fire without it), thinks she hears a plane in the clouds overhead, and a little later what sounds like an explosion as a house collapses, killing almost immediately a little girl – 'for an instant, before she could shut her eyes, Mary saw the ripped and shredded body' (*D of C*, 433). The doctor overtakes the silent, furious Mary on the way home and warns her not to spread alarm and despondency by telling people that it was a bomb, assuring her that the roof had collapsed from dry rot; she doesn't believe him and he may not believe himself (the uncertainty of wartime life in which rumour and fantasy are indistinguishable from fact is central to the story). Lighting the grim bonfire in the 'dank little shrubbery', she becomes aware of a groaning wounded pilot who asks for help in broken English; 'there was no doubt of his nationality' (*D of C*, 436). Instead of bringing help, Mary arms herself with the pistol she bought 'after reading certain Belgian reports' and as the fire of Wynn's

151

books and oddments blazes and then burns low in the rain, she watches the man's death agony with a 'secret thrill' which is unmistakably sexual:

> She leaned upon the poker and waited, while an increasing rapture laid hold of her. She ceased to think. She gave herself up to feel. Her long pleasure was broken by a sound that she had waited for in agony several times in her life. She listened, smiling ... the end came very distinctly in a lull between two rain-gusts. Mary Postgate drew her breath short between her teeth and shivered from head to foot. 'That's all right,' said she contentedly, and went up to the house, where she scandalised the whole routine by taking a luxurious hot bath before tea, and came down looking, as Miss Fowler said when she saw her lying all relaxed on the other sofa, 'quite handsome!'
>
> (*D of C*, 440–1)

Without being at all 'difficult' like 'Mrs Bathurst' with its baffling interrelations of deaths and narrators, 'Mary Postgate' is full of uncertainties for the reader. For Mary things are simple: the wrecked pilot is a 'bloody pagan' (*D of C*, 438) who not only personifies the Germany which committed atrocities against Belgians, described in 'certain newspaper reports' and by starting the War caused the death of her beloved Wynn, but has bombed little Edna Gerritt to pieces. Presumably the 'newspaper reports' referred to the 1915 Bryce Report of the German army's atrocities when they invaded Belgium, a mixture of hearsay horrors[17] and real atrocities, for massacres of Belgian civilians by German soldiers certainly did take place.[18]

Mary's ecstasy of rage untainted by guilt may well be approved of by her creator. Her feeling that the German airman is not human but a disgusting 'thing' parallels Kipling's own public speeches in 1915, the year 'Mary Postgate' was written, equating Germans with 'typhoid or plague'. And the placing of the story between the sinister 'Swept and Garnished' in which a German *hausfrau* is haunted by the ghosts of murdered Belgian children and the furious poem 'The Beginnings' whose repeated refrain 'When the English began to hate' (*W*, 673) ends the book (*D of C*, 442), indicates that Mary's response to this German pilot's death is very possibly intended to be exemplary – or at least, as William Dillingham has argued, as a catharsis by which she is 'purged of the repressions that have smothered her identity'.[19]

On the other hand there are numerous indications, both in the ambiguous events of the story and in its deadpan omniscient narration, that Mary's exultation is as horrible and pitiful as the 'disgusting' dying enemy himself. The narrator repeatedly emphasizes Mary's suppression of her own feelings, her unquestioning and unselfconscious acceptance of 'the teaching that had made her what she was, "one mustn't let one's mind dwell on these things"' (*D of C*, 434). And her ecstasy represents the return of repressed hatred as well as frustrated love. The broken man whose hair is 'pale as a baby's, and so closely cropped that she could see the disgusting pinky skin beneath'(*D of C*, 436) eerily recalls Wynn the 'unlovely orphan' who endlessly abused and insulted her before he fell to his death. Her funeral bonfire of his pathetic schoolboy belongings, listed by Kipling in poignant detail from the 'thumbed and used Hentys, Marryats...and catalogues of Olympia Exhibitions' to 'fret-saw outfits and jigsaw-puzzles', (*D of C*, 431) is both an act of piety 'as she lit the match that would burn her heart to ashes' (*D of C*, 435) and an unconscious revenge; as John Bayley puts it, 'she both possesses and exorcizes Wynn himself through his *alter ego*, the German airman'.[20] (More recent critics go further still, one calling Mary's 'rapture' at the dying German's agony an 'obscene pleasure' and another rather crassly describing her as 'giv[ing] herself an orgasm by leaning on a poker while he dies'.[21]) When the pilot at last dies, she repeats her reaction after learning at Wynn's funeral that he had fallen 4000 feet: 'Then *that's* all right' (*D of C*, 427, 441).

Mary thinks Edna has been killed by a bomb, but this is left unproven, and doubt is cast by the doctor who tells her not to spread this story around as it could be bad for civilian morale – though his denial sounds much like Mary telling herself 'not to let her mind dwell on things'. She is sure the airman is German, but no evidence is given for this except his shaved head and foreignly accented broken English and French '"Laty! Laty! ...Tout cassée [All broken]"'(436–8). He may not even exist. His appearance at the very moment when Mary so ambivalently burns all that is left of the beloved and hated Wynn is to say the least of it a remarkable coincidence; and furthermore, no one but Mary sees him.

Both the absence of independent witness and the pared-down, overtly unemotional style of the story makes it impossible, just as in Henry James' ghost story *The Turn of the Screw*, to know whether the heroine is experiencing reality or fantasy. If the dying pilot is Mary's hallucination, then her sexual pleasure in his death agony makes her a pathological 'case', as Trudi Tate reads her – a neurotic 'Female of the Species more deadly than the Male' (*W*, 367), led by anti-German propaganda and her own Id to a 'patriotism...displaced into a form of perverse sexuality – dangerous, disgusting, yet compelling'.[22] The problem with this reading is not that it ascribes to Kipling a creative detachment about German atrocities in Belgium (treated by Trudi Tate, wrongly, as propagandist fantasy), which the evidence of his speeches and letter in 1915 contradicts, for this objection can be simply answered by D.H.Lawrence's famous 'Never trust the teller. Trust the tale'.[23] Yet the tale itself is not detached but ambivalent. Despite the narrator's insistence that Mary is the product of a repressive training and the ambiguous status of its key events, it is told so much from her point of view that it becomes impossible for the reader *not* to identify with her, however appalling her response. The point is made forcefully by Kipling's most alert and subtle reader, Randall Jarrell:

> This truthfully cruel, human-all-too-human wish fantasy is as satisfying to one part of our nature as it is terrible to another. What happens is implausible but intensely actual: the German pilot isn't really there, of course, except in our desire, but his psychological reality is absolute, down to the last groan of the head that 'moved ceaselessly from side to side'...we are forced to believe in him just as Freud was forced to believe in his first patients' fantasies of seduction.[24]

The key words here are 'fantasy' and '*our* desire' (my italics). Mary's blind pleasure when she sees her wish come true (or experiences her hallucination, if you read her so) is the exact reverse of Gwendolen's horrified self-realization 'I saw my wish outside me' when the tyrannical husband whom she murderously hated drowns in front of her eyes in George Eliot's *Daniel Deronda*;[25] unlike Gwendolen, Mary does not arrive at self-knowledge. And because the story is narrated almost wholly through Mary's eyes (apart from that final chilling moment when her employer sees her after her bath 'all relaxed...and quite handsome' (*D of C*, 441) the reader, merely by responding to the scene, cannot help sharing her experience of 'rapture'. The story thus both gives revenge fantasy an unforgettable outing *and* shows it to be pathological.

'The Gardener', also the last tale in its collection, is differently ambiguous. The opening tells us that 'All the village knew' how Helen Turrell brought up the son of her dissolute brother – hinting though not saying (a) that the elaborate story of Michael's adoption by his intrepid aunt is an ingenious cover-up, and (b) that the village people probably guess this but collude with Helen in keeping everything respectable, for 'Helen was as open as the day' (*DC*, 400) – or possibly as secret as the night. Unlike Mary Postgate caring for the ungrateful Wynn, Helen's loving relationship with Michael has no ambivalence apart from the unspoken secret of his birth, which means there can never be complete truth between them. When Michael is buried by a shell 'so neatly that none but an expert would have known that anything unpleasant had happened' (*DC*, 205) – just like the secret of his birth – Helen is devastated. When his body is identified after the war and she journeys to his grave, she meets the ghoulish Mrs Scarsworth who visits graves for other people with a camera: ' "My system is to save them up and arrange them, you know. And when I've got enough commissions for one area to make it worthwhile, I pop over and execute them. It *does* comfort people" ' (*DC*, 410). But these photographic 'commissions' are only an excuse for the guilty secret she confesses to the reluctant Helen about a dead soldier who ' "was everything to me that he oughtn't to have been – the one real thing – the only thing that's happened to me in all my life; and I've had to pretend he wasn't" ' (*DC*, 411–2). Helen's maternally compassionate response meets a sharp rejection: ' "Is *that* how you take it?" ' (*DC*, 412) – perhaps because the other woman, sensing Helen's own secret, is offended at being 'forgiven' by a fellow-sinner; or perhaps because she wanted not pity but the witness which Helen at last receives. For in this vast cemetery Michael's grave is invisible in 'a sea of merciless black crosses, bearing little strips of stamped tin ... a waist-high wilderness as of weeds stricken dead'. A young man appears and offers help; she asks for ' "Michael Turrell – my nephew" ' ... slowly and word for word, as she had many thousands of times in her life' (*DC*, 413); and the man looking at her with 'infinite compassion' offers to take her ' "where your son lies" '. After visiting Michael's grave she does not see the strange young man again and 'went away, supposing him to be the gardener' (*DC*, 414).

The charge of sentimentality has been laid against this story[26] whose final words, as Kipling's original readers would instantly have recognized, are a biblical quotation: Mary Magdalene, weeping because the body of Jesus is not in its tomb, unknowingly meets the risen Christ 'supposing him to be the gardener' (John 20: 15). But here the divinity is known only to the reader; unlike her gospel counterpart, Helen does not recognize the risen Christ, and we cannot know what release she experienced, if any. The gospel parallel also raises the question: If Helen was a sinner, what was there to forgive in her life? True, the fact that Mary Magdalene was famously a sexual sinner indicates that Michael really *is* Helen's illegitimate son. Yet his off-stage conception is treated as error rather than sin; what is truly destructive is the respectable conspiracy of silence which Helen herself enforced and in which the narrative's own ambiguous understatements collude, at least until its final words. As with 'Mary Postgate', the drily matter-of-fact narrative participates in the pathology which the story reveals in its protagonist, so that despite their overt realism, both stories exhibit an acute modern self-irony and ambiguity.

The poetic sequence 'Epitaphs of the War', begun in 1917, the last of Kipling's works of mourning discussed here, is more closely akin to the solemn inscriptions Kipling chose for the war dead than to his historical and fictional narratives of loss. It consists of thirty-four short poems 'spoken' by the widest possible variety of the dead: soldiers, non-combatants, airmen, nurses, politicians and others. It is not perfect; some of the poems are awkward, a few wordy despite their epigrammatic form, and those commemorating dead children and bereaved parents sometimes verge on sentimentality, like 'A Son' who inadvertently killed his mother: 'She / Blessing her slayer, died of grief for me' (*W*, 387). As with *Barrack Room Ballads*, its plurality of speakers carries the limitation that, while displaying great sympathy and respect for men of different ranks and creeds, Kipling tends to represent them as types rather than individuals (though this 'typing' is probably inherent in the elegiac genre anyway). Kipling's most sympathetic critic J.M.S. Tompkins, wrote of these 'Epitaphs' that 'They suggest in turn a line cut on a headstone, or pencilled in a pocket-book, or scratched by the dead man's mates on a broken oar, up-ended in the sand...The deaths commemorated are at once very near, and seen in the long perspective of sacrifice'.[27] That long perspective is itself partly the effect of the poems' classical locutions; Kipling called them 'naked cribs [= plagiarisms] of the *Greek Anthology*',[28] which is illuminating but misleading. Although there is a connection with the *Anthology* poems, which I explore below, these poems, far from copying the Greeks, draw largely on the traditions of Latin verse and English epigram. Their formalized, archaic diction means that the speakers of the *Epitaphs* are not killed but 'slain', and address others as 'thou' and 'ye', not 'you': the register of heroic war rhetoric brilliantly mocked by Fussell ('nothing = *naught*, nothing but = *naught, save*, to win = *to conquer*', etc., etc).[29] Yet in the best Epitaphs these archaisms make for fine poems, as in 'A Drifter off Tarentum':

> He from the wind-bitten North with ship and companions descended,
> Searching for eggs of death spawned by invisible hulls.
> Many he found and drew forth. Of a sudden the fishery ended
> In flame and a clamorous breath known to the eye-pecking gulls.

(W, 391)

Combining the hexameter and pentameter of classical elegiac couplets with English rhyme, and evoking the sinuosities of Latin syntax in the delayed verb 'descended' and the inversion of 'many he found', this taut quatrain has the compressed energy of a classic Latin epigram. The archaic language with its compound adjectives 'wind-bitten' and 'eye-pecking', and the ingenious allegory whereby underwater mines laid by submarines become legendary 'eggs of death spawned by invisible hulls', assimilate the steamships and exploding mines of modern industrialized warfare into classical elegy, so that the dead men become at once ancient warriors and modern heroes. There is a similarly terse conjunction of imagery, compared by Harry Ricketts with the Pound of *Des Imagistes*,[30] in 'The Beginner': 'On the first hour of my first day / In

157

the front trench I fell./ (Children in boxes at a play/ Stand up to watch it well)' (*W*, 389).

The 'long perspective of sacrifice', naturalized by this traditional approach clearly takes for granted both the justice of the Allied cause and its harsh necessity. Not all Kipling's speakers died heroic deaths: 'The Coward' confesses that 'because I could not look on death...Men led me to him, blindfold and alone'; another is shot for sleeping on sentry duty, and a draft dodger 'bombed in London' is surprised to meet his death 'in the air!' (*W*, 387, 389). But none of them expresses any resentment at his fate, nor are any of them blamed. Most striking in its sympathy with an unlikely object is 'The Refined Man':

I was of delicate mind. I stepped aside for my needs,
Disdaining the common office. I was seen from afar and killed.
How is this matter for mirth ? Let each man be judged by his deeds.
I have paid my price to live with myself on the terms that I willed.

(*W*, 389)

The discreet formality of the phrase 'my needs' and the archaic word 'office' for 'privy' may initially obscure this compressed narrative: a soldier preferring not to urinate in company is picked off by a sniper. This might almost be a joke if it weren't for that sternly measured last line, italicized in the original, which reminds readers that it's not their business to judge what others think important, that different people have their own kinds of pride, and that no death is ludicrous to its victim. Again, the poem's strength lies in its surprisingly complex conjunction of emotional and intellectual oppositions emphasized by the terse form which, as with the semi-mythical imagery of 'A Drifter off Tarentum', or the ironic pathos of 'The Beginner', is invested with heroic seriousness by the formalized archaic language.

The tradition of classical elegy can be felt most strongly, although no one to my knowledge has yet commented on this, in the best-known couplet of the sequence, 'Common Form' quoted at the head of this chapter:

If any question why we died,
Tell them, because our fathers lied.

(*W*, 390)

This echoes, aurally and thematically, J.W. Mackail's translation of Simonides' epigram commemorating the last stand of 300 Spartan soldiers at Thermopylae in 480 B.C., who were ordered to fight the Persian invaders to the death, and did so:

> Go tell the Spartans, thou that passest by,
> That here obedient to their laws we lie.[31]

In both poems the dead men ask their unknown living readers to 'tell' their message to their survivors. But the Spartans' acceptance of the 'laws' by and for which they died turns in Kipling's poem both to accusation, pointed up by its cynically colloquial title ('common form' meaning roughly 'the usual story') and to ambiguity. As Jay Winter has pointed out, the last line can be read in at least two ways: 'The phrase "because our fathers lied" can be seen as an answer to the question in the first line of the couplet. But it is also possible that Kipling is suggesting that the answer to the question "why did they die?" lay in the mind of the reader. Only he or she can do better than the lies told by the fathers.'[32] It is noticeable that the clinching rhyme-sound is almost identical in both couplets, the change of meaning in 'lie/lied' from 'lie dead' to ' 'uttered untruths' altering the message from a heroic statement to an ironic accusation: a movement articulated not only in semantic change but in the shift from present to past tense. Simonides / Mackail's 'we lie' confers on its fictional dead speakers a perpetual present that is renewed whenever the words are read, whereas Kipling's 'lied' implies both that such heroic confidence belongs only to the distant past, *and* that the 'lies' practised by the fathers have included feeding the young with classical pieties about the virtue of obedience and the immortality of heroic memory. Without being either formally modernist or explicitly inter-textual, Kipling's epigram implies both that its original cannot now be believed in, and more subtly, that its own tradition of poems formally commemorating heroes has already receded into the past.

9

Epilogue: The Final Years

George Orwell's 1941 statement 'Kipling spent the later part of his life in sulking', tells less about Kipling than about his own talent for plain-man epigrams, proving how right at the time was the description of the writer of 'The Wish House' and 'Dayspring Mishandled' as the 'Kipling that nobody read'.[1] Kipling's work from 1919 to 1936 displays extraordinary energy and variety, especially coming from an ageing man who was often in severe pain from a duodenal ulcer (undiagnosed and therefore untreated until 1932). True, Orwell's slightly patronizing summary of the elderly Kipling's politics ('Somehow history had not gone according to plan. After the greatest victory she had ever known, Britain was a lesser world power than before, and Kipling was quite acute enough to see this'[2]) is more or less right. Kipling certainly deplored the Versailles Settlement as much too soft on Germany and was furious about the establishment of the Irish Free State in 1921, the post-war activities of nationalists in India (he was one of General Dyer's supporters after the 1919 Amritsar massacre), the increasing political ascendancy of the USA and what he regarded as the Socialism of post-war England (*i.e.* the mild Labour reformism of Ramsay MacDonald and Baldwin's Conservative-dominated 'National Government'). But he took little part in public life after the war except in his work for the War Graves Commission and, more indirectly, through his friendship with King George V for whom he wrote the first radio Christmas message for the Empire,[3] broadcast on Christmas Day 1932. On the other hand, unlike the dominant Tory 'appeasers' of the 1930s, who regarded Nazi Germany as a bulwark against international Bolshevism, Kipling detested Hitler whose rise to power inspired his prescient political poem 'The Storm Cone' about the English ship of state threatened by a long and deadly tempest ('The storm is near, not past;/ And worse than present jeopardy / May our forlorn to-morrow be': W, 834). The same reason moved him to remove from his book covers his old trademark the Hindu good-luck swastika as now 'defiled beyond redemption'.[4] As David Gilmour has rightly argued, Kipling had much in common with Winston Churchill[5] and his loathing for Nazi Germany was both a patriotic English response to the resurgent power of the 'Hun' and an intuition of evil. He knew too much about lawlessness and cruelty not to hate and fear Hitler and everything he represented.

Given this dramatic historical context, it is striking how little Kipling's political views seem to impinge on his later works. In addition to the two-volume 1923 *History of the Irish Guards* (discussed in Chapter Eight), which anyway focuses on the soldiers' experience of war rather than the reasons for fighting it, he published two post-War collections of stories, *Debits and Credits* (1926) which includes three of his best tales, 'The Wish House', 'The Eye of Allah' and 'The Gardener'. *Limits and Renewals* (1932) is not quite so vintage but contains the classic 'Dayspring Mishandled' as well as 'The Church that was at Antioch' and 'The Manner of Men' which successfully revisit the terrain of Ancient Rome explored earlier in the 'Puck' books. The subject matter of these stories includes ghosts, passionate sexual love, Freemasonry, a Jane Austen fan club, shell-shock, mourning, cancer, bull-fighting, medieval medicine, a failed literary hoax, motor cars, films, psychosomatic illness and the missionary journeys of St Paul (the list is not exhaustive). He also published the last of his children's books *Land and Sea Tales for Scouts and Guides* (1923), an uneven collection which nevertheless, as Hugh Brogan has shown in *Mowgli's Sons*,[6] includes much excellent previously uncollected material together with the splendid new story 'His Gift' about the fat lazy boy who turns out to be a brilliant cook. He also published the direly sentimental *Thy Servant A Dog* (1930), narrated in the embarrassing baby-talk of the terrier 'Boots' ('I wented back to Walk, because I were hungry again. Ben said me lots about his bone. I said back. I danced' *TSD*, 46) which promptly sold 100,000 copies to the dog-loving British public.[7] Finally, in a very different key, he composed his spare, reticent, moving memoir *Something of Myself* (1937, published posthumously).

Many of these late stories are highly 'literary' like 'The Propagation of Knowledge' where schoolboys debate the authorship of Shakespeare's plays, or 'Dayspring Mishandled' in which a character invents a new addition to the 'Canterbury Tales', complete with the following Chaucerian lyric 'Gertrude's Prayer'. ('His Gift' is likewise followed by the charming uncollected 'Prologue to the Master-Cook's Tale' about the pleasures of French cookery – 'tripes of Caen, or Burdeaux snailes swote / And Sainte Menhoulde wher cooken piggés-foote', *LST*, 100). Some allusions are relatively obscure, like the nearly-damned lovers in 'Unconvenanted Mercies' quoting Christina Rossetti's 'I charge you at the Judgement – make it plain'[8] (*LR*, 395–7), or the shell-shocked Wollin in 'Fairy-Kist' hearing voices in his head from a Victorian children's book by Mrs Ewing (*LR*, 176–8). Characters in other stories respond to literature naïvely but perceptively, like Beetle discovering the 'incommunicable splendour' of Tom-a-Bedlam's 'With a heart of furious fancies' [*sic*], *DC*, 277) or the gunner Humberstall in 'The Janeites', finding like a humanist critic that Austen's ' "characters was no *use*! They was only just like people you run across any day" '. There are also some enjoyably light-hearted literary allusions. These appear most elaborately in the verse translations of imaginary Horace Odes printed with several late stories and the 'Orientalist' pastiche fable 'The Enemies to Each Other',[9] where an almighty marital row is described in the euphemistic style ('When the steeds of recrimination had ceased to career across the plains of memory and the bird of argument had taken refuge in the rocks of silence...', *DC*, 19) which Indians in *Kim* use[10] when they want to be particularly indirect; most simply in the response of an irreverent Beetle asked to paraphrase Oswald's speech in *King Lear*: ' "Give it up! He's drunk" ' (*DC*, 291).

Other late Kipling stories not so obviously concerned with literature have also been construed as literary fables. The artist-bull Apis in 'The Bull That Thought' (*DC*) is usually considered a semi-autobiographical allegory of art and the artist,[11] and more recently 'His Gift' (*LST*) has been read in the same way, the fat boy's discovery of his vocation as cook being taken as a

162

figure for Kipling finding his own genius as a writer.[12] These self-reflexive allegorical readings seem to me unsatisfactory, in that they turn what would otherwise be stories of action into narcissistic infinite regression. Kipling doesn't shine as a practitioner of 'Art for Art's sake', his late allusive method working best in relation to sharply realized human dramas: the forged Chaucer fragment enabling different kinds of treachery in 'Dayspring Mishandled'(discussed below), the buried biblical quotation about Mary Magdalene opening up the single moment of release in 'The Gardener', or Abbot Stephen in 'The Eye of Allah' destroying the microscope which could help his Infirmarian diagnose and treat his Lady Anne's 'eating malady', because he foresees that Mother Church would burn them all for witchcraft if they were found using it.

For all their much greater literary and narrative elaboration, these late stories have much in common with the early, powerful 'Indian' tales. The 'knowing' attitude of the young colonial narrator recurs stylistically in the highly self-conscious allusions and thematically in the recurring narrative motif of secrets revealed, while the younger Kipling's at once crude and subtle insistence on the limits of rationality reappears in a preoccupation with the inexplicable (which, as in the ghost stories discussed in Chapter Seven, is associated with female sexuality). This is especially noticeable in the two late gems 'The Wish House' (*DC*) and 'Dayspring Mishandled' (*LR*), stories in which intensely enduring sexual passions transform or destroy the lives of those who experience them.

In the first story, set in a post-war Sussex of football matches, charabancs shaking cottages as they go by and wireless aerials in back gardens, the Sussex-born retired London cook Grace Ashcroft gradually unfolds to an old friend how in middle-age, at home on a hop-picking holiday, she fell in love with the much younger Harry Mockler, who briefly became her lover, and what came of it. Harry follows her to London ('" 'E was me master, an' – O God help us! – we'd laugh over it walking after dark in them paved streets, an' me corns fair wrenchin' in me boots! I'd never been like that before. Ner he! Ner he!"' *DC*, 123), but inevitably he leaves her after a few months. The real hidden drama of her life then begins when a little girl who has fallen 'crazy-fond' of her (' "you know how liddle maids first feel

163

it sometimes"', 124) puts her in touch with an empty house inhabited only by a 'Token – a wraith of the dead or, worse still, of the living' (126) which can grant the wish to bear another person's suffering. Visiting her relatives at home and seeing a 's'runken an' wizen' Harry deadly sick from a poisoned foot and not expected to live (126), she returns to a hot London dusk with 'dried 'orse-dung blowin' from side to side and lyin' level with the kerb' (127) to make her wish at the haunted house. She is promptly rewarded by news of Harry's recovery together with a wound on her shin that turns into 'a nasty little weepin' boil..., that wouldn't heal no shape' (133). She gradually realizes that this lingering cancerous sore is a bodily link with her lover (as she still thinks of him) that enables her to enter his existence in the closest possible way, her own pain growing and fading, according as the absent Harry is ill or well:

> 'He'd inflame up – for a warnin' – an' I'd suffer it. When I couldn't no more – an' I 'ad to keep on goin' with my Lunnon work – I'd lay me leg high on a cheer till it eased. Not too quick. I knowed by the feel of it, those times, dat 'Arry was in need... Year in, year out, I worked it dat way, Liz, an' 'e got 'is good from me 'thout knowin' – for years an' years' (135).

Cancer has, paradoxically, given meaning and value to her life; through her pain, this jilted middle-aged widow still feels she owns Harry despite his indifference. '"I've got ye now, my man,"' she tells him silently (134) – age and illness clearly not having turned this passionately possessive woman into a selfless guardian angel. Harry, only son of a widowed mother and now a jobbing driver working all over England 'for one o' them big tractorisin' firms', has not married and she insists that he never will. '"I reckon my pains 'ull be counted against that"', she asserts fiercely (136). We cannot know whether she is right, any more than whether the Token is 'real' or only a hallucination bred of desire (significantly, the little girl describes a 'gigglin', like' behind the haunted door, whereas Grace hears 'a heavy woman in slippers' [127, 131], as if each were meeting a projection of herself). The story ends with an unanswered question.

'It *do* count, don't it – de pain?' The lips that still kept trace of their
original moulding hardly more than breathed the words.
Mrs Fettley kissed them and moved towards the door (138).

'Dayspring Mishandled' is as different as a story could be
while also dealing with enduring passion and the desire to
control another person's life. Whereas Grace Ashcroft and her
friend Liz Fettley are working women who take their holidays
hop-picking and enjoy a 'cold boiled pig's tail to help down the
muffins' at teatime (*DC*, 117), the main characters here are
scholars and gentlemen. Alured Castorley the literary hack
turned Chaucer expert is a repellent opportunist who estab-
lishes his reputation 'by his careful speech, his cultivated
bearing and the whispered words of his friends...fawning,
snubbing, lecturing, organising and lying as unrestingly as a
politician' (*LR*, 7–9) – although he does have a genuine
enthusiasm for the medieval poet whom he insists on calling
'Dan Chaucer'. His would-be nemesis James Manallace earns his
living by writing competently formulaic historical novels,
making enough to pay for the care of his great love, a beautiful
woman who 'suffered and died because she loved one
unworthy' (4) after rejecting the young Castorley to marry a
man who left her to die slowly of paralysis. 'Only her eyes could
move, and those always looked for the husband who had left
her. She died thus in Manallace's arms.. in the first year of the
War' (7). Later, when the two men are colleagues in the wartime
'Office of Co-Ordinated Supervisals', Castorley says something
so unspeakably awful about the dead woman that it provokes
Manallace to his 'real life-work and interests'. While the ever
more intolerable Castorley achieves eminence as 'the Supreme
Pontiff on Chaucer' (8), Manallace, while playing hanger-on to
the great man, takes up a series of apparently pointless hobbies
– boiling oak-galls and wine into ink, using a hand-mill to grind
flour, and messing about with medieval parchment and amateur
efforts at illuminated capital letters. And then Castorley makes
his great discovery: a fifteenth-century parchment by a known
Dutch scribe, stuffed in an old Bible and containing the precious
fragment of a lost Canterbury Tale, evidently vintage Chaucer:
'"The freshness, the fun, the humanity, the fragrance of it all
cries – no, shouts – itself as Dan's work. Why, 'Daiespringe
mishandled' alone stamps it from Dan's mint. Plangent as doom,

my dear boy – plangent as doom!"' (13–14). Of course he speaks more truly than he knows, for the narrator recalls these lines being recited by a drunken Manallace twenty years earlier, as Manallace himself confirms. Having used Castorley's own boastfully declaimed knowledge of medieval scribal techniques, he is waiting for his victim to be awarded his coveted Knighthood, unsure whether to surprise the man by publishing the story in the 'baser Press' or to tell him privately 'that he must now back the forgery as long as he lived, under threat of Manallace betraying it if he flinched'. At the narrator's protest 'If you tell this you'll kill him', he answers 'I intend that' (20).

But this is not quite what happens. Manallace, who was always too passively clever to make a likely assassin, rapidly realizes that his beautiful plot has only formed one strand in the stickier and more deadly web woven by Castorley's wife, a ladylike Englishwoman as frighteningly vicious as Lady Macbeth or Goneril. This 'unappetising ash-coloured woman' (10), bored with her husband and intelligent enough to sense that there is something wrong with his find, is unlike Manallace quite prepared to commit murder, slowly and respectably. She undermines Castorley's already poor health (he is suffering from what turns out to be terminal cancer) by driving him to overwork on the 'Chaucer' fragment while hinting doubts about its real status, meanwhile conducting a secret affair with her husband's doctor Gleagg during what she calls the 'sacred hours' when he and Manallace are working on the 'Chaucer' text – which, since it includes a not-too-difficult acrostic of Manallace's own name, is an obvious time bomb. The forger who gleefully planned his moment of revelation now tries desperately to find ways of putting off the moment when the book can appear, going abroad to make himself unavailable (uselessly, because this only makes Castorley more ill and anxious), comforting the distressed man on his death-bed – '"You've nothing to worry about. It's *your* find – *your* credit – *your* glory – and all the rest of it"', (31) –, and afterwards is forced by loyalty to insist on posthumous publication. At Castorley's cremation, as 'the coffin crawled sideways through the noiselessly-closing door-flaps, I saw Lady Castorley's eyes turn towards Gleeag' (*LR*, 32).

These stories of ordinary people leading their secret lives of passion, shame and betrayal, imply, subliminally but powerfully, a baffled awe at the alarming energies of female sexuality. Their theme of secrecy repeats a common enough trope in Kipling's late work, but with the difference that, unlike the relatively straightforward tales of 'repressed' memory like 'A Madonna of the Trenches' or 'Fairy-Kist', they subtly avoid closure. For although Grace Ashcroft in 'The Wish House' makes a series of ever more intimate revelations, first her secret love for Harry, then her decision to suffer his pain, and finally the cancerous sore itself, displayed when the nurse undoes the bandages, the final disclosure remains enigmatic, not just because Kipling describes the wound so obliquely ('Mrs. Fettley looked, and shivered' [138] – very telling since we know she is virtually blind) but because we can't know what her passionately embraced suffering means or if it really 'counts' for anything. And while in 'Dayspring Mishandled', the 'secret' of the practical joke is disclosed half-way through, followed by the joker's ever more frantic attempts to protect his victim, it is the briefly appearing women named only as ''Dal's mother' or 'Castorley's wife' who are the real hidden power-houses. Castorley's boasted scholarship and even the revengeful Manallace's chivalrous devotion to the memory of a wronged woman, look like weakness compared with the total attachment of ''Dal's mother' (who apparently never thanks him or even notices his devotion) to her faithless cad of a husband, and the unswerving hatred and lust which draw Castorley's ladylike viper of a wife to betray the husband whom she so badly wants dead. It is a strangely fitting finale from the writer whose first book *Plain Tales from the Hills* opened with the tale of 'Lispeth' the jilted Kashmiri girl whose passion and honesty lead her to reject the respectable, deceitful English.

Notes

PROLOGUE

1. David Gilmour, *The Long Recessional; The Imperial Life of Rudyard Kipling* (2002), 276.
2. George Orwell, 'Rudyard Kipling' 1941, reprinted in A. Rutherford (ed.) *Kipling's Mind and Art* (1964) 70; Randall Jarrell *Kipling, Auden & Co,* (1980), 335.
3. The four later 'Stalky' stories are 'Regulus' (*D of C 1917*), 'Stalky' (*LST* 1923), 'The United Idolaters' and 'The Propagation of Knowledge' (*DC* 1926).
4. Jarrell, 338, 341, 343.
5. Kipling in H. Orel (ed.) *Kipling: Interviews and Recollections* (vol II), 1983, 256–7.
6. Dixon Scott 1912, in Roger Lancelyn Green (ed.) *Kipling: The Critical Heritage,* (1971), 313.
7. M. Oliphant, 1891, Robert Buchanan, 1899, in Lancelyn Green (1971), 137, 247–8.
8. Zohreh Sullivan *Narratives of Empire: The Fictions of Rudyard Kipling* (1993), 9.
9. T.S. Eliot 'Preludes' IV, *Collected Poems 1909–1962,* (1963), 24.
10. Orwell, *The Road to Wigan Pier* (1937), 215, 153, and in Rutherford (1964), 80.
11. Helen Gardner, *The Composition of Four Quartets* (1978), 83.
12. John Willett, *The Theatre of Bertholt Brecht,* (1977), 89–90.
13. *Kipling Journal,* vol. 76, no. 302, June 2002, 8–9.
14. In 2003, the right-wing organisations www.heritage.org, *www.southernparty.org* and *www.americanpatrol.org* all cited the line 'The Gods of the Copybook Headings with terror and slaughter return!' from 'The Gods of the Copybook Headings', Kipling *W,* 795, on their websites.
15. Patricia Cockburn, *The Years of 'The Week',* 1968, 247, quoting from 'A General Summary', W, 4; Moshe Lewin, *The Making of the Soviet System* (1985), 53 slightly misquoting (presumably from memory, no reference

being given) from 'The Masque of Plenty', *W*, 39.

16. Anecdotal information from my Russian-speaking sister Catherine Grace. Kipling's popularity in Russia confirmed by Boris Kagarlitsky (personal communication).
17. Noel Annan, 'Kipling's Place in the History of Ideas' in Rutherford (1964), 97–125.
18. Jarrell (1980), 355.
19. John Keats, letter to Richard Woodhouse, 27 October, 1818.
20. Annan in Rutherford (1964), 99.

CHAPTER 1 KIPLING IN INDIA: KNOWING THE UNKNOWABLE

1. Crockett, Whibley, Oliphant in Lancelyn Greene (1971), 180, 60, 137; also cited in Bart Moore-Gilbert's *Kipling and 'Orientalism'* (1986), 19.
2. Sullivan (1993), 67.
3. Craig Raine, 'Kipling: Controversial Questions' in *Kipling Journal* vol. 76, no 303, 14.
4. R.G. Collingwood, *The Principles of Art*, 1938, 68. For a longer analysis of this passage, see my essay 'Latin, arithmetic and mastery' in *Modernism and Empire*, 2000 (eds. H. Booth and N. Rigby).
5. Thomas Richards, *The Imperial Archive: Knowledge and the Fantasy of Empire* (1993), 18.
6. Hummil's nightmare repeats an image from Kipling's early semi-jocular poem 'La Nuit Blanche' in *Department Ditties* (1885) about nightmares that include 'a Face ... blind and weeping / And It couldn't wipe Its eyes': *W*, 28.
7. Sullivan (1993), 76.
8. According to the *Encyclopaedia Britannica*, the work of detailed survey began in 1791. The detailed large-scale mapping of Ireland was carried out from 1824 to 1842; that of England and Wales was begun in 1840, and the Ordnance Survey map of the whole United Kingdom was undertaken in 1854. *Encyclopaedia Britannica*, vol. 17, LORD to MEC, (11th edition, Cambridge, 1910): entry under 'Maps', 649–50.
9. Sullivan (1993), 20.
10. Harry Ricketts, *The Unforgiving Minute: a Life of Rudyard Kipling* (1999), 106
11. Julia Kristeva, *Powers of Horror: an essay on Abjection*, tr. Leon Roudiez (1982), 2–4.

CHAPTER 2   IMAGINING A LANGUAGE: KIPLING'S VERNACULARS

1. *Shorter Oxford English Dictionary*, revised ed. C.T. Onions, p2348.
2. Ricketts, *The Unforgiving Minute*, 12.
3. Wittgenstein, Aphorism 19 of *Philosophical Investigations*.
4. Peter Finley Dunne (1867–1936) was a Chicago journalist who commented on current affairs through the imaginary Boston Irishman 'Mr Dooley', quoted here by Claud Cockburn in *I, Claud* (1962), 200.
5. Tony Crowley 'For and against Bakhtin', *Language in History*. (1996), 41, 48.
6. Crowley, (1996), 175–6.
7. Robert Buchanan in Lancelyn Green (1971), 241.
8. Isobel Armstrong, *Victorian Poetry: Poetry, Poetics and Politics* (1993), 481.
9. Dixon Scott, 'The Meekness of Rudyard Kipling', 1912, in Green (1971), 315.
10. William Wordsworth, Preface to the *Lyrical Ballads* (1802).
11. Robert Buchanan in Lancelyn Green (1971), 241.
12. Brecht, 'Soldiers' Song, *Dreigroschen Opera* (1924). English translation from the website *http://webgiant.sdf1.org/carnivale/kanonen-song.html*.

CHAPTER 3   THE DAY'S WORK

1. C.S. Lewis *They Asked For a Paper* (1961), 75.
2. Randall Jarrell (1963), 363.
3. C.S. Lewis (1961), 79. The Kipling quote is from 'A Walking Delegate', *DW*, 76.
4. C.S. Lewis (1961), 81.
5. George Orwell in Rutherford, 75.
6. Bertolt Brecht 'Questions from a worker who reads', *Poems 1913–1956*, edited and translated by John Willett and Ralph Manheim, (1976), 252.
7. Mark Kinkead-Weekes, Rutherford (1964), 211.
8. Wordsworth, *The Prelude* (1805 version), book V, 471–3.
9. C.S. Lewis (1961), 84.
10. Shakespeare, *The Tempest*, Act IV Scene 1, lines 152–4.
11. Zohreh Sullivan (1993), 126. See also Ann Parry's excellent essay 'Imperialism in "The Bridge Builders": Metaphor or Reality?', *Kipling Journal* 60: 237, March 1986, 12–22.
12. Morag Shiach, *Modernism, Labour and Selfhood in British Literature and Culture* (2004), 6, 16.

CHAPTER 4 BEING A MAN

1. Edward Said, *Orientalism* (2002), 227.
2. Virginia Woolf *A Room of One's Own* (1968), 101.
3. Woolf (1968), 101.
4. Gilmour (2002), 11.
5. Gilmour (2002), 59.
6. Tennyson 'Sir Galahad' *Collected Poems* (ed.) C. Ricks (1968), 610.
7. Sullivan (1993), 136–8.
8. C.S. Lewis (1961), 82.
9. In the 'Stalky' story 'The Moral Reformers', M'Turk observes that 'Bullies like bullyin'. They mean it. They think it up in lessons' (*S & C*, 137). But unlike the bullying of the 'fag' Clewer in this story, the hazing of new recruits in 'His Private Honour' is not represented as either vicious or punishable.
10. Max Beerbohm 'P.C.X 36', *A Christmas Garland* (1912), 11.
11. Craig Raine (ed.), *Rudyard Kipling: Selected Poetry* (1992), xi.
12. Daniel Karlin, introduction to Penguin Classic *Jungle Books* (1989), 23.

CHAPTER 5 *KIM*

1. Harry Ricketts in conversation, September 2001, responding to my question why his biography *The Unforgiving Minute* didn't say more about *Kim*.
2. For comparisons with Dickens, see Angus Wilson (1977), 129, comparing Kim and the lama with Mr Pickwick and Sam Weller of *Pickwick Papers*, and Kim with Oliver and the Artful Dodger in *Oliver Twist*; with Chaucer, see Edward W. Said, *Culture and Imperialism* (1992), 167. The comparisons of Hurree Babu with Shakespeare's Falstaff and the Sahiba with Cleopatra are my own.
3. Angus Wilson (1977), 130.
4. Thomas Richards (1993), 17–18.
5. Edmund Wilson in Rutherford (1964), 30.
6. Edward W. Said, *Culture and Imperialism*, (1992), 177–8.
7. The old soldier's allusion to Queen Victoria's 1887 Jubilee, 'When the Kaiser-I-Hind had accomplished fifty years of her reign' as a recent event (*K*, 75), places the narrative in the late 1880s or early 1890s.
8. Said (1992), 176.
9. Said (1992), 163.
10. Angus Wilson (1992), 132; also Kipling (*SM*, 140).
11. Abdul R. JanMohamed 'The Economy of Manichean Allegory: The Function of Difference in Colonialist Literature,' Henry L. Gates ed.

Race, Writing and 'Difference', (Chicago, 1986) 97.

12. Said (1992), 166.
13. Zohreh Sullivan (1993), 151.
14. Joseph Bristow *Empire Boys: Adventures in a Man's World* (1991), 211.
15. 'At the end of every Psalm throughout the Year...shall be repeated: 'Glory be to the Father, and to the Son: and to the Holy Ghost, As it was in the beginning, is now and ever shall be: world without end, Amen', *Book of Common Prayer* (1880), 6.
16. Bristow *Empire Boys*, 209.
17. Shakespeare, *Henry IV Pt II*, Act I, scene 2, line 11.
18. Mark Kinkead-Weekes, 'Vision in Kipling's Longer Fictions' in Rutherford (1964); Clara Claiborne Parks, 'The River and the Road: Fashions in Forgiveness', *The American Scholar* vol. 66 no.1, Winter 1997, reprinted in *Kipling Journal* (32:511, Sept 2004, 32–50).
19. Colonel Creighton's presence in *Kim* is analyzed at great (and to my mind disproportionate) length by Edward Said, Thomas Richards and Zohreh Sullivan – an over-emphasis which indicates the pitfalls of heavily thematic readings of *Kim*.
20. Ricketts (1999), 125, 158.
21. See Enobarbus's speech in Shakespeare's *Antony and Cleopatra* Act III, scene 2, line 27: 'The barge she sat in, like a burnished throne / Glowed on the water'.
22. Said (1992), 167.
23. Richards (1993), 29.
24. Kinkead-Weekes in Rutherford (1964), 221.

CHAPTER 6   KIPLING'S POETRY: VICTORIAN TO MODERNIST

1. This underlines the Statesman's dishonesty by alluding to the parable of the unjust steward: 'I cannot dig; to beg I am ashamed', Luke: 16, 3.
2. Dan Jacobson, 'Explicit England', *TLS* March 11, 2005, 13. I am grateful to Tim Cawkwell for drawing this to my attention.
3. Orwell, 'Rudyard Kipling' (1941), in Rutherford, 80. The 'Munich period' means the weeks leading up to the Munich Agreement between Chamberlain and Hitler in October 1938, which allowed Germany to invade Czechoslovakia unopposed. 'Dane-Geld' is one of the songs written for C.R.L. Fletcher's *History of England* (1911), with the refrain 'Once you start paying the Dane-Geld / You never get rid of the Dane': *W*, 712.
4. See the websites 'Is it nothing to you? Lest we forget', (The Royal Canadian Legion website), 'Lest We Forget: World War II (World War

II website)' and 'Lest We Forget: The Triumph Over Slavery' (The Schomburg Centre for Research in Black Culture); 'Lest We Forget' (Guardian Unlimited).

5. Craig Raine, introduction to *Rudyard Kipling: Selected Poetry* (1992), xi.
6. Tennyson 'Britons, Guard Your Own' in C. Ricks (ed.) (1969), 997.
7. For discussion of T.S.Eliot's engagement with Kipling, see chapters 1 and 8 . For Brecht's admiration, see chapters 1 and 3. Ezra Pound knew early Kipling well enough to quote a line from his poem 'La Nuit Blanche' when annotating Eliot's early draft of *The Waste Land*: see Valerie Eliot, (ed.), *The Waste Land* 1971, 11.
8. Edward Mendelson (ed.) *The English Auden* (1976), 242, 48, 289.
9. Donald Davie, *Under Briggflatts: A History of Poetry in Great Britain 1960–1988*, 1989, 215–16 and Harry Ricketts, preface to *Rudyard Kipling: The Long Trail: Selected Poems* (2004), xv.
10. James Fenton, 'The Ballad of the Imam and the Shah', *Out of Danger*, (Penguin, 1994).
11. W.H. Auden 'A Poet of the Encirclement', *Forewords and Afterwords* (1973), 356.
12. This alludes to the Bunyan's 1671 allegory *The Holy War*.
13. The final injunction to *'hold your head up high . . . Because he was the son you bore'* indicates that the anxious questioner must be the dead boy's mother.
14. Orwell, in Rutherford, 81, Raine, xi.
15. Cyril Connolly, *Enemies of Promise* (1938), 215–17; Edmund Wilson 'The Kipling That Nobody Read', Rutherford (1964), 17; George Orwell 'The Road to Wigan Pier', 1937, 215.
16. Orwell in Rutherford (1964), 'Rudyard Kipling', 81.
17. Craig Raine, preface to *Rudyard Kipling* (1992), xvi–xxiii; Harry Ricketts, (2004), xiii–xv.
18. Gilmour (2002), 275–6.
19. Bernard Knox, *Essays Ancient and Modern* (NY 1989), 200; Mendelson (1976), 245.
20. The 'lines' are 'marriage-lines', *i.e.* a marriage certificate.
21. The refrain consists of two accentual trimeters and an accentual hexameter, scanned as follows:
    ˉ ˘/ˉ ˘ ˘ /ˉ ˘ ˘ (trochee, dactyl, amphibrach)
    ˉ ˘/ˉ ˘ ˘ /ˉ ˘ (trochee, dactyl, iamb)
    ˉ ˘/ˉ ˘ ˘/ˉ ˘ ˘ /ˉ ˘˘˘ /ˉ ˘ ˘ /ˉ ˘ ˉ / (trochee, dactyl, dactyl, irregular dactyl, dactyl, amphimacer).
22. Tennyson, 'Claribel' (Ricks, 1969), 161 ; Byron, 'The Destruction of Sennacherib', Thomas Hardy 'The Darkling Thrush', both in A. Quiller-Couch, (ed.) *The Oxford Book of English Verse* (1900).
23. Martin Scofield, *T.S. Eliot: the poems* (1988), 189.
24. T.S. Eliot, (1966), 9; Ezra Pound 'Sestina: Altaforte', *Selected Poems 1909–*

1959, 1975, 20.

25. Walter Savage Landor, 'Rose Aylmer' in Quiller-Couch, 680.
26. Roland Barthes 'The Death of the Author' in Barthes, *Image–Music–Text*, 1977, 146.
27. Kipling, letter to Horder, quoted in Gilmour (2002), 121.
28. Rowan Williams, Address to Kipling Society, January 26, 2006, reproduced in *Kipling Journal* 34:519, June 2006, 8.
29. Sara Suleri *The Rhetoric of English India* (1992), 22.

CHAPTER 7   COMMUNICATIONS, MODERNITY AND POWER

1. F.T. Marinetti, 1909, in U. Apollonio 'Futurist Manifestoes' (1973), 3.
2. Apollonio, 3.
3. Harry Ricketts (1999), 249.
4. Lockwood Kipling, letter to Edith Plowden quoted by Harry Ricketts (1999), 164–5.
5. Zohreh Sullivan (1993), 41, presumably alluding to Kipling's 1889 cruise from India to England via the USA, his tour of New Zealand and Australia after his semi-breakdown in London in 1890, his honeymoon journey through Japan to the USA in 1891, and his winter trips to South Africa between 1898 and 1908.
6. W.H. Auden (1973), 354.
7. For Kipling's conversation with Marconi in 1899, see page 33 of John H. McGivering's essay 'Wireless', *Kipling Journal* 68:271, 24–38, citing 'A Chat with Kipling' by Cyril Clemens (1941), collected in H. Orel (ed.) *Kipling: Interviews and Recollections* (MacMillan, 1983).
8. Tim Armstrong, *Modernism, Technology and the Body* (1998), 78.
9. Virginia Woolf (1968), 101.
10. Armstrong (1998), 63.
11. Lewis (1961), 81.
12. T.S. Eliot (1966), 190 ('Burnt Norton').
13. Louis Menand in Maria DiBattista and Lucy MacDiarmid, *High and Low Moderns: Literature and Culture 1889–1939* (New York 1996), 151.
14. Menand, 163.
15. Keats 'This living hand' 1819.
16. T.S. Eliot 'The Waste Land', *Collected Poems 1909–1962*, (1966), 66.
17. See Chapter 1 n. 11.

CHAPTER 8   KIPLING IN THE GREAT WAR: MOURNING AND MODERNITY

1. Samuel Hynes *A War Imagined: The First World War and English Culture* (1991), 52.
2. Paul Fussell *The Great War and Modern Memory* (1975).
3. Jay Winter *Sites of Memory, Sites of Mourning: The Great War in European cultural history* (1995), 8–9.
4. Ricketts, Lycett and Gilmour are all good on Kipling's response as a writer to the Great War. See also Hugh Brogan's excellent, measured account of Kipling's war poetry in 'The Great War and Rudyard Kipling', *Kipling Journal* 72:286, June 1998, 18–34.
5. Ricketts (1999), 328, Gilmour (2002), 257.
6. Ricketts (1999), 342.
7. Kipling in the *Morning Post*, 22 June 1915, cited by Frank Field, *British and French Writing of the First World War* (1993), 260.
8. Kipling, letter to *Daily Express*, quoted in Angus Wilson (1977), 299–300.
9. Wilson (1977), 304.
10. Gilmour (2002), 279.
11. Edmund Blunden, reviewing *History of the Irish Guards*, cited in Gilmour (2002), 268.
12. Gilmour (2002), 334.
13. Paul Fussell *The Great War and Modern Memory* (1975), 172.
14. Hynes (1991), 112, 192.
15. Winters (1995), 29.
16. Kipling seems to have been right about the appeal of these novels to soldiers in danger. My father Hugh Montefiore who served in Burma during World War II used to read Jane Austen when time permitted during the Battle of Kohima (April–June 1944).
17. Trudi Tate *Modernism, History and the First World War* (1998), 38; Hynes, 121.
18. Brogan (1998), 33, citing Barbara Tuchman *The Guns of August* (New York, 1963).
19. William B. Dillingham (2002), 39.
20. John Bayley *The Uses of Division* (1976), 66.
21. Gilmour (2002), 260.
22. Trudi Tate *Modernism, History and the First World War* (1998), 39.
23. D.H. Lawrence *Studies in Classic American Literature* (1924), 8.
24. Randall Jarrell (1982), 364.
25. George Eliot *Daniel Deronda* (1971), 760–1.
26. Frank Field (1993), 171.
27. J.M.S. Tompkins, *The Art of Rudyard Kipling*, (1968), 189–90.
28. Kipling, quoted in Fussell, 181 *The Greek Anthology* is a famous

collection of Ancient Greek lyrics and epigrams, of which J.W.Mackail, the husband of Kipling's cousin Margaret Burne-Jones, published a well-known translation (1911).

29. Fussell (1975), 22.
30. Ricketts (1999), 337; Tate (1998), 40.
31. Simonides tr. Mackail, *Concise Oxford Dictionary of Quotations* (1968).
32. Winters (1993), 220.

CHAPTER 9   EPILOGUE: THE FINAL YEARS

1. George Orwell and Edmund Wilson in Rutherford (1964), 72, 17.
2. Orwell in Rutherford, 72.
3. Gilmour, 308.
4. Letter from Kipling, 1935, quoted in Gilmour (2002), 304. Ganesh, whose elephant head continued to appear on Kipling's books, was the Hindu god of good luck whose symbol was the right-pointing swastika.
5. Gilmour, 311.
6. Hugh Brogan, *Mowgli's Sons: Kipling and Baden-Powell's Scouts* (1987), 53–61.
7. Gilmour, 284.
8. Kipling's lovers are quoting the penultimate line of sonnet XI in Christina Rossetti's sonnet sequence 'Monna Innominata': 'I charge you at the Judgement make it plain / My love for you was life and not a breath' (*Complete Poems of Christina Rossetti* ed. R.W. Crump. (Louisiana State University, vol II, 1986, 92).
9. 'The Enemies to Each Other' is dedicated 'with apologies to Mirza Mirkhond' (1433–98) a Persian historian of Herat in Afghanistan. 'The story's language, with its elaborate metaphors and explanatory brackets, parodies the over-literal translation of Mirkhond's Rauzat-us-Safa by E. Rehatsek [Bombay: Oriental Translation Fund, Royal Asiatic Society, 1891, 4 vols.], of which there is a set in Kipling's study' (entry for *DC* in the online *New Reader's Guide*).
10. Mahbub Ali after foiling spies feels that he 'had muddied the wells of inquiry with the stick of precaution' (*Kim*, 32). Later on Kim plays truant and, hoping Mahbub will pacify his irate patron, pleads via a Indian letter-writer 'Let the Hand of Friendship turn aside the Whip of Calamity' (182).
11. See the readings of 'The Bull That Thought' by Bonamy Dobrée, C. A. Bodeson and Elliott Gilbert.
12. See W. Dillingham's essay 'Kipling's Calling', *Kipling Journal* 313, March 2005, 34–56.

Select Bibliography

WORKS BY RUDYARD KIPLING

Place of publication is London unless otherwise stated.

COLLECTED EDITIONS

The Sussex edition of the Complete Writings in Prose and Verse of Rudyard Kipling (35 vols) (Macmillan 1937-9). 2nd edition by Doubleday, New York 1941. Beautifully produced definitive edition of all Kipling's writings, available in some libraries.

Pocket Edition (Macmillan 1932) The blue-covered cheap edition that stayed in print until the 1960s (books from it often appear in second-hand bookshops). Includes all of Kipling's novels, short story collections and children's books, and selections from his verse, travel writing and speeches.

Definitive Edition of Rudyard Kipling's Verse (Hodder and Stoughton, 1940). Omits the early privately printed work and some uncollected verse but not yet superseded.

The Poetical Works of Rudyard Kipling, based on the *Definitive Edition* (Wordsworth Classics, 1994).

Letters of Rudyard Kipling edited by Thomas Pinney (5 vols) (University of Iowa Press, Iowa, U.S.A, 1990–2005) The definitive edition.

Writings on Writing, eds. Sandra Kemp and Lisa Lewis (Cambridge University Press, 1996).

SEPARATE EDITIONS

Schoolboy Lyrics (Lahore: Privately printed, 1881).

Echoes, by Rudyard Kipling and Alice Kipling (Lahore: Privately printed, 1884).

Departmental Ditties and Other Verses (Lahore: Privately printed, 1886; enlarged edition, Calcutta: Thacker, Spink/London & Bombay: Thacker, 1890).

Plain Tales from the Hills (Calcutta: Thacker, Spink/London: Thacker, 1888; New York: Lovell, 1890; London & New York: Macmillan, 1890). Reprinted with an introduction by David Trotter (Harmondsworth: Penguin, 1994).

Soldiers Three, includes *The Story of the Gadsbys* and *In Black & White* (Macmillan 1888). Reprinted with an introduction by Robert Hampson, (Harmondsworth: Penguin, 1993).

Wee Willie Winkie and Other Stories including *Under the Deodars* and *The Phantom Rickshaw*: Macmillan, 1888). Reprinted with an introduction by Hugh Haughton (Harmondsworth: Penguin, 1988).

Life's Handicap (Macmillan 1891). Reprinted with an introduction by P. N. Furbank (Harmondsworth: Penguin, 1988).

The Light That Failed (Macmillan, 1891).

The Naulahka (with Wolcott Balestier) Macmillan, 1892.

Many Inventions (Macmillan, 1892).

The Jungle Book, The Second Jungle Book (Macmillan 1894 and 1895, the latter illustrated by Lockwood Kipling). Reprinted together with the *Jungle Book* as *The Jungle Books* with introduction and notes by Daniel Karlin (Harmondsworth: Penguin, 1990).

Captains Courageous (Macmillan, 1896, illustrated by I.W. Taber). Reprinted with an introduction by John Seelye (London: Penguin, 2005).

The Day's Work (Macmillan, 1898), reprinted with an introduction by Constantine Phipps (Harmondsworth: Penguin, 1988).

Stalky & Co. (Macmillan, 1899). Reprinted by Wordsworth Classics (London, 1994).

From Sea to Sea (Macmillan, 1899) Collected travel writings including the early Indian *Letters of Marque*, first published in Allahabad, 1888.

Kim (Macmillan, 1901) Reprinted with introduction and notes by Edward Said (Harmondsworth: Penguin, 1990). Later reprinted with introduction and notes by Zohreh T. Sullivan (New York: W.W. Norton Critical Editions, 2002).

Just-So Stories for Little Children (Macmillan, 1902, illustrated by the author. Reprinted by Penguin, 1990).

Traffics and Discoveries (Macmillan 1904). Reprinted with introduction and notes by Hermione Lee (Harmondsworth: Penguin, 1990).

Puck of Pook's Hill (Macmillan 1906, illustrated by H.A. Millar). Reprinted with an introduction by Sarah Wintle (Harmondsworth: Penguin, 1990).

Actions and Reactions (Macmillan, 1909).

Rewards and Fairies (Macmillan, 1910, illustrated by H.A. Millar).
Reprinted with an introduction by Roger Lewis (Harmondsworth:
Penguin, 1990).

A History of England (with C.L.R. Fletcher; Oxford: Clarendon Press,
1911).

A Diversity of Creatures (Macmillan 1917). Reprinted with an introduction by Paul Driver (Harmondsworth: Penguin, 1990).

The Irish Guards in the Great War (2 volumes, Macmillan, 1923). Reprinted
with an introduction by Harry Webb (Staplehurst: Spellmount,
1997).

Land and Sea Tales for Scouts and Guides (Macmillan, 1923).

Debits and Credits (Macmillan, 1926). Reprinted with an introduction by
Sandra Kemp (Harmondsworth: Penguin, 1990).

Limits and Renewals (Macmillan, 1932).

'Proofs of Holy Writ' (*Strand* Magazine 1934); reprinted in Sussex
edition and in *Writings on Writing* (eds. Kemp and Lewis,
Cambridge University Press, 1996).

Something of Myself for my Friends Known and Unknown (Macmillan 1937).
Reprinted by Penguin (Harmondsworth, 1981) and by Cambridge
University Press with introduction and notes by Thomas Pinney
(Cambridge, 1990).

SELECTIONS AND ANTHOLOGIES

T.S. Eliot (ed. & intro) *A Choice of Kipling's Verse* (Faber, 1941) Classic
selection, but includes neither the early *Departmental Ditties* nor the
late parodies.

Raine, Craig (ed. & intro) *Rudyard Kipling: Selected Poetry* (Penguin, 1990)
Excellent choice of poems with an introduction which is particularly good on Kipling's auditory effects and his modernist qualities.

Ricketts, Harry *The Long Trail: Selected Poetry of Rudyard Kipling*
(Manchester, Carcanet, 2004). A fine selection emphasizing parody
and pastiche, made and introduced by Kipling's most sensitive
literary biographer.

Rutherford, Andrew (ed.) *Short stories* (2 vols) *A Sahibs' War and other
Stories* and *Friendly Brook and other stories* (Harmondsworth,
Penguin, 1971). Good selections from the early and late stories.

BIBLIOGRAPHY AND REFERENCE

Green, Roger Lancelyn (ed.) *Kipling: The Critical Heritage* (Routledge,
1971). An anthology of reviews and criticism up until 1937,

including key early reviews by Robert Buchanan, Margaret Oliphant and Dixon Scott. Indispensable for research on Kipling's reception.

Harbord, Reginald *Reader's Guide to the Works of Rudyard Kipling* (8 vols, 1955–1965) Currently being updated as the *New Reader's Guide* (general editor John Radcliffe), available online through the Kipling Society's home page.

Martindell, E.W. *A Bibliography of the Works of Rudyard Kipling* (John Lane, 1923).

Page, Norman *A Kipling Companion* (Macmillan 1984). A useful guide.

Radcliffe, John (general editor) *New Reader's Guide to the Works of Rudyard Kipling* A comprehensive guide updating Reginald Harbord's work. Easily available online through the home page of the Kipling Society.

Young, W. Arthur *A Dictionary of the Characters and Scenes in the Stories and Poems of Rudyard Kipling, 1886–1911* (Routledge 1911). Updated by John McGivering as *A Kipling Dictionary* (Macmillan 1967).

BIOGRAPHY

Carrington, Charles *The Life of Rudyard Kipling* (Macmillan, 1955). Authorised biography with material from Kipling's daughter Elsie Bambridge.

Gilmour, David *The Long Recessional: The Imperial Life of Rudyard Kipling* (John Murray, 2002). Detailed and excellent on Kipling's historic and political context.

Lycett, Andrew *Rudyard Kipling* (Weidenfeld and Nicolson, 1999), Highly detailed and very readable.

Mallett, Philip *Rudyard Kipling: A Literary Life* (Palgrave Macmillan, 2003) A good short literary-critical biography.

Orel, Harold (ed.) *Kipling: Interviews and Recollections*, 2 volumes (Macmillan, 1983).

Ricketts, Harry *The Unforgiving Minute: A Life of Rudyard Kipling* (Chatto and Windus, 1999). Detailed and with excellent critical readings of Kipling's work.

Wilson, Angus *The Strange Ride of Rudyard Kipling* (Secker and Warburg, 1977) Very well written and sympathetic; contains some very intelligent critical readings.

CRITICISM

(Apart from fairly recent studies of Kipling, gender and the numinous

[Kemp 1988, Crook 1990] and Kipling's Indian fictions [Sullivan 1993], the relatively few full-length critical studies of Kipling mostly date from the 1960s or even earlier. Furthermore, many influential accounts of Kipling often appeared in essay form. Consequently, much of the Kipling criticism listed here consists of short pieces written for magazines or as contributions to books.)

Annan, Noel 'Kipling's Place in the History of Ideas' (1959, reprinted in Andrew Rutherford's *Kipling's Mind and Art* (1964, see below) An elegant pioneering analysis of the early Kipling as an 'anthropological' writer.

Auden, W.H. 'A Poet of the Encirclement', *Forewords and Afterwords* (Faber, 1973) An illuminating account of the relationship between the Law and the daemonic in Kipling's poetry.

Bayley, John 'The Puzzles of Kipling', *The Uses of Division* (Chatto and Windus, 1976). Essay on the contradictions of Kipling, containing a good reading of 'Mary Postgate'.

Bodelson, C.A. *Aspects of Kipling's Art* (Manchester University Press, 1964). Analysis of Kipling as a literary writer.

Bristow, Joseph *Empire Boys: Adventures in a Man's World* (Harper Collins, 1991). Well known account of masculinities in imperialist literature for boys, including an influential if slightly crude account of *Kim*.

Brogan, Hugh (i) *Mowgli's Sons: Kipling and Baden-Powell's Scouts* (Jonathan Cape, 1987). A lively, elegant and detailed history of Kipling's creative relationship with the Scout movement.

—— (ii) 'The Great War and Rudyard Kipling' (*Kipling Journal* 72: 286, June 1998). A historian's measured and perceptive defence of Kipling's war poetry.

Claiborne, Clara 'The River and the Road: Fashions in Forgiveness', *American Scholar* vol. 66 no.1, reprinted in *Kipling Journal* 309, June 2003. Sympathetic study of *Kim*, comparing the hero to Twain's Huckleberry Finn.

Crook, Nora *Kipling's Myths of Love and Death* (Macmillan 1990). Fine close readings emphasising gender and intertextuality of tales including 'Mrs Bathurst', 'A Madonna of the Trenches' and 'The Wish House',

Dillingham, William, B. (i) 'Grief, Anger and Identity: Kipling's "Mary Postgate"', *Kipling Journal* 76:301, March 2002.

—— (ii) 'Kipling's Calling: *Kipling Journal* 313, March 2005, 24–56. Close reading of the late Scout story 'His Gift' as an autobiographical fiction of creative self-discovery

Dobrée, Bonamy *Rudyard Kipling, Realist and Fabulist* (1955, revised edition 1967). Well-written but old-fashioned account of Kipling as a literary artist.

Eliot, T.S. 'The Poetry of Rudyard Kipling', *A Choice of Kipling's Verse* (Faber, 1941, reprinted 1971). Admiringly cagey account of Kipling's poetry.

Gilbert, Elliott *The Good Kipling* (Ohio, USA: Ohio University Press 1971, Manchester University Press, 1972). Close readings of selected stories, with a strong emphasis on the artistic achievements of Kipling's late work. Reads Kipling as a humanist artist rather than a political writer.

JanMohamed, Abdul R. 'The Economy of Manichean Allegory: The Function of Difference in Colonial Literature', Henry L. Gates (ed.) *Race, Writing and 'Difference'*, (Chicago: Chicago University Press, 1990): a critical but sympathetic reading of *Kim*.

Jarrell, Randall 'On Preparing To Read Kipling' (1961) in *Kipling, Auden & Co.: Essays and Reviews 1935–1965* (Manchester: Carcanet, 1980). Kipling never had a better reader than Jarrell, whose short, brilliant, subtly post-Freudian analysis of Kipling's qualities arguably remains the finest single account of this writer. The book also contains two more excellent studies of Kipling's short stories.

Kemp, Sandra *Kipling's Hidden Narratives* (Oxford: Blackwell, 1988) Close readings of selected Kipling stories, focusing on themes of gender and the numinous.

Keating, Peter *Kipling as Poet* (Secker and Warburg, 1994). Reads Kipling as a poet of the people.

Kinkead-Weekes, Mark 'Vision in Kipling's Novels' (Rutherford, 1964). A fine analysis of the theme of sight in several fictions including *Kim*.

Lewis, C. S. 'The Inner Ring', *They Asked for a Paper* (Geoffrey Bles, 1961). A shrewd essay on the psychology of Kipling's work ethic.

Mason, Philip *Kipling: The Glass, the Shadow and the Fire* (Macmillan, 1964) Literary study of Kipling, emphasizing the late stories.

Montefiore, Janet 'Latin, arithmetic and pedagogy': useful essay on public school syllabuses, empire and modernity in *Kim* and 'Regulus' in Howard Booth and Nigel Rigby (eds.) *Modernism and Empire* (Manchester: Manchester University Press, 2000).

Moore-Gilbert, Bart *Kipling and Orientalism*, (Croom Helm, 1986): very intelligently contextualizes Kipling's 'Indian' writings within the political-literary history of 19th century English-ruled India.

Nagai, Kaori *Empire of Analogies: Kipling, India and Ireland*. Informed and subtle account of the relationship between 'imperialist' and 'nationalist' analogies in the work of Kipling and of Indian and/ or Irish writers (Dublin, Eire; Cork University Press, 2006).

Orwell, George 'Rudyard Kipling' (1941), reprinted in Orwell's *Collected Essays Letters and Journalism*, vol. 2 'In Front of your Nose' (Secker and Warburg, 1968); also in Andrew Rutherford's *Kipling's Mind and*

Art (1964, see separate entry below). Classic polemical account of Kipling as a populist 'good bad poet'.

Raine, Craig 'Kipling's Poetry' (introduction to *Rudyard Kipling: Selected Poetry* (Penguin, 1990). Reads Kipling as a proto-modernist: excellent on the poetry's underestimated auditory subtleties.

Richards, Thomas *The Imperial Archive: Knowledge and the Fantasy of Empire* (Verso, 1993). Highly informed, elegantly Foucauldian analysis of imperialist assumptions in the work of Kipling and others.

Rutherford, Andrew *Kipling's Mind and Art* (Edinburgh: Oliver & Boyd, 1964). The classic collection of short writings on Kipling. Includes key contributions by Noel Annan, George Orwell and Edmund Wilson as well as contributions by leading Kipling critics.

Said, Edward *Culture and Imperialism* (Chatto and Windus, 1992) Contains Said's critical but sympathetic reading of *Kim*, reprinted and revised from his 1989 Penguin classic introduction.

Sandison, Alan *The Wheel of Empire: a study of the imperial idea in some late nineteenth-century writers* (Macmillan, 1967). An intelligent conservative's analysis of Kipling's imperialism.

Stewart, J.I.M. *Rudyard Kipling* (Victor Gollancz, 1966). Sympathetic survey of Kipling's writings, reprinted from Stewart's *Eight Modern Writers* (Oxford, Clarendon Press, 1963).

Suleri, Sara *The Rhetoric of British India* (Chicago: Chicago University Press, 1992). Post-colonial critic's study of Kipling, Forster and other 'Anglo-Indian' writers, with a subtle account of Kipling's contradictory colonial writings.

Sullivan, Zohreh, T. *Narratives of Empire: the fictions of Rudyard Kipling* (Cambridge University Press, 1993). Important, theoretically informed post-colonial account of Kipling's writing which takes a Lacanian approach to *Kim* and the early 'Indian' stories.

Trilling, Lionel 'Kipling' (1943, reprinted in Rutherford, 1964). An intelligent liberal's highly critical brief account.

Tompkins, J.M.S. *The Art of Rudyard Kipling* (Methuen, 1959, revised 1965). The most comprehensive and sympathetic of all the book-length studies of Kipling. Focuses on key themes of revenge, horror, laughter, healing, ignoring all issues of gender or politics; this is an old-fashioned, thorough appreciation of Kipling as a literary writer.

Wilson, Edmund 'The Kipling That Nobody Read' (194). Reprinted in Wilson's *The Wound and the Bow* (London, 1951; Methuen, 1966) and in Rutherford (1964). The first important revaluation of Kipling by a major critic.

OTHER WORKS MENTIONED IN THE TEXT

Armstrong, Isobel *Victorian Poetry: Poetry, Poetics and Politics* (Routledge, 1996).

Armstrong, Tim *Modernism, Technology and the Body: a cultural study* (Cambridge, 1998). Subtle, theoretically informed account of the representation of technology in modernist writing.

Cockburn, Claud *I, Claud* (Harmondsworth: Penguin, 1966).

Crowley, Tony *Language in History: Theories and Texts* (Routledge 1996).

DiBattista, Maria and Lucy MacDiarmid (eds.) *High and Low Moderns: Literature and Culture* (New York: Columbia University Press, 1996). Emphasizes the relation between 'high' and 'popular' modernisms, and includes Louis Menand's excellent analysis of 'Mrs Bathurst' as a sceptical modernist text.

Fussell, Paul *The Great War and Modern Memory* (Oxford University Press, 1975). Classic account of the literature of the First World War, especially poetry.

Hynes, Samuel *War Imagined: the First World War and English Culture* (London: Bodley Head, 1990) Intelligent, sympathetic and comprehensive study of the response to World War by British writers including Kipling.

Said, Edward *Orientalism* (1978, reprinted by Penguin 2005) The classic study of imperialist discourse in European writers, including Kipling.

Shiach, Morag *Modernism, Labour and Selfhood in British Literature and Culture, 1890-1930* (Cambridge University Press, 2004). Important study of the representation of labour and gender in British literature.

Tate, Trudi *Modernism, History and the Great War* (Manchester University Press, 1998). Key study of gender and modernity in Great War literature; includes an intelligent reading of 'Mary Postgate'.

Trotter, David *The English Novel in History, 1885–1920* (Routledge, 1993) Admirable contextualizing of British fiction which includes a persuasive reading of 'Mary Postgate'.

Winter, Jay *Sites of Memory, Sites of Mourning: the Great War in European Cultural History* (Cambridge University Press, 1995) Classic study of the literature of mourning, including Kipling's work.

Index

Printed in the United Kingdom
by Lightning Source UK Ltd.
122679UK00001B/199-264/A